The Life of JONATHAN BALDWIN TURNER

A Centennial Edition

Published as part of the University of Illinois observance
of the National Centennial of the Land-Grant Colleges
and State Universities, 1862–1962

The Life of

JONATHAN BALDWIN TURNER

by Mary Turner Carriel

University of Illinois Press, Urbana, 1961

The dedication of this volume is to
THE GRANDCHILDREN AND WORKING PEOPLE
whom my father loved

Introduction

It was fortunate for the State of Illinois and for the land-grant state university movement, which was to result in the creation of and support for a system of state universities across the country, that Jonathan Baldwin Turner decided in 1833 to become a teacher at Illinois College, Jacksonville, instead of returning from Yale to farm his family homestead in Massachusetts.

Illinois College had been founded not long before (1827) under Presbyterian auspices, and its development was encouraged by Eastern church leaders. It was the President of Yale University, Jeremiah Day, who personally encouraged Jonathan Baldwin Turner to go to Illinois, promising to award him the diploma even though Turner should leave before graduation.

Turner's enlistment in Illinois education and the reasons for it had the quality of a volunteer for missionary duty. Indeed, it was the impulse to advance " home missions " in the West and to seek the development of the religious frontier through educational service that led to the formation of the " Yale Band," a group of seven Yale students, including Jonathan's older brother, Asa Turner, Jr. They organized in 1829 " The Illinois Association " for the " promotion of the interests of learning and religion by the preaching of the Gospel and the establishment of a seminary of learning in such a part of the United States as may be designated by the Association." [1]

In the decision " to go West," which affected his life and the lives of many others who followed in the wake of his achievements, Turner revealed the quality which was to mark all of his endeavors—missionary dedication. All of his life he was an evangelist of ideas in three areas which consumed his interest—religion, politics, and education.

In all three, Turner's views were unorthodox and he was the subject of severe criticism and some abuse. In the church (he combined preaching with his teaching), he attacked some of the conventional views of his denomination; in politics, his was one of the first voices in Illinois against slavery; and he fought for education for those who normally did not get it, the sons and daughters of " the working classes," and he wanted a kind of education suited to their aptitudes, interests, and careers.

In each of these areas of public debate Turner brought vigor, eloquence, and imagination. In all, he was so much the center of public turmoil that finally he gave up his professorship at Illinois College in 1848, and turned to his first love, agriculture. Here, too, his unorthodox and imaginative analysis of the problems to be solved led him into achievement in horticulture. His experimentation with and promotion of the use of the Osage Orange made it possible to fence the prairie. Other agricultural products also blossomed under his touch.

Of the social causes which had Turner's attention, and among all the ideas which attracted his mind and held his heart as well, education was first. While he taught a wide range of subjects at Illinois College, he was concerned with the advancement of education at the lower levels. Both during and after his tenure at Illnois College he traveled throughout the state and sometimes beyond its borders to lecture on his ideas about broadening the opportunities for education, both in content and in opening the way for the

---

[1] Rammelkamp, C. H., *Illinois College, A Centennial History* (New Haven, Conn.: Yale University Press, 1928), p. 23.

people to attend better schools. Like Horace Mann, he used every occasion he could find—teachers' meetings, sermons, county fairs—to awaken the people to a greater interest in their schools and in how to advance their welfare. President Edmund James of the University of Illinois described him: "A prophet of democracy in this western country, he early came to recognize the necessity for a scientific education of the practical man, if he was ever to take the place which belonged to him by virtue of the importance of his occupation . . . if he was ever to rule in reality, as he seemed to rule in form, under our so-called free institutions." [2]

This long involvement in thinking, talking, and planning about education finally led Turner into concrete proposals for the creation of an industrial university. His theories took specific form. His speech before the Illinois Teachers Institute at its annual meeting in Griggsville, Illinois, on May 13, 1850, entitled "A Plan for a State University for the Industrial Classes" is a blueprint for what followed in the organization of public higher education in the United States.

There is debate as to the extent of influence of Jonathan Baldwin Turner upon Justin Morrill, who sponsored the legislation which popularly carries Morrill's name, legislation which gave national impetus to the ideas of the early leaders in the land-grant movement. Whether Turner was actually first with the ideas and whether he personally influenced Morrill has not been firmly established, although many have claimed for Turner the original definition of the idea and its transmission to Morrill. President James contributed to the heat of the argument by developing the thesis in 1912 that " the real credit for originating the plan incorporated in the Land-Grant Act, belongs to an Illinois farmer and professor, Jonathan B. Turner." [3]

While documentation on the James claim is debatable, it

[2] James, Edmund Janes, " Jonathan Baldwin Turner," *The Alumni Quarterly*, Vol. VI, No. 3 (Urbana: University of Illinois, July, 1912), pp. 188-191.
[3] *Ibid.*, p. 188.

is agreed that Turner along with Morrill and Clemson must
be given credit for early leadership in the movement which
developed nationally; it is also agreed that without Turner's
strong advocacy in the Middle West, including the organization of his ideas in the content of the movement, the legislative outcome might have been different. Also, without
Turner's work, President Lincoln might have viewed the
subject differently, for Lincoln knew Turner and had followed the Illinois discussions of the land-grant movement.

Turner's work did not stop with the enactment of the
land-grant legislation. After 1862 he worked with equal
energy for the establishment of his industrial university in
Illinois. The plans for the university did not always follow
the lines which he suggested and for a period in the site
quarrel, he actually was estranged from the sponsors of the
early institution. He was present, however, at the laying of
the cornerstone of the new University Hall at the Illinois
Industrial University in 1871, and for the rest of his life he
remained a friendly interpreter of the progress of the institution that was to become one of the large, distinguished
prototypes in the fulfillment of his vision.

In a sense, then, Jonathan Baldwin Turner is not only a
forebear of the land-grant movement but also of the University of Illinois. Many persons may be identified in the
period 1850-67 as contributing to the founding of the
University of Illinois but certainly none had a more prominent part nor greater influence than had Jonathan Baldwin
Turner.

It is exceedingly fitting, then, that in this year of the
Centennial observance of the signing of the Land-Grant Act
by a President of the United States from Illinois, a fulfillment of a movement to which an Illinois pioneer gave
leadership, the letters, papers, and biographical information
about Jonathan Baldwin Turner should be issued under the
aegis of the University of Illinois Press.

This book is a reissue of the account by Mary Turner
Carriel, the daughter of Jonathan Baldwin Turner, who was
also the second woman to be elected to the Board of Trustees

of the University of Illinois. The book was printed privately in 1911.

Mary Turner Carriel, of course, looks at her father's life with the affectionate regard and admiration of a daughter. Some of her editorial judgments will have to be appraised accordingly. However, Turner is allowed to speak at length in his own words and the biographical account is confined pretty largely to connecting the speeches, letters, and essays.

Turner often employed the purple passages, the sonorous periods, and the grand manner which characterized mid–nineteenth-century oratory. At the same time, the force, imagination, wisdom, and insight of the man comes through, often with real eloquence. Many of the paragraphs are as commanding in verbal effect today as they must have been when they were first presented. Turner had a classical education, and taught at Illinois College nearly every subject in the humanities, specializing in rhetoric, Latin, and Greek. It is therefore not surprising that in diction, style, and allusion Turner reflects the academic manner and tradition of his day. However, his great personal sincerity and his profound conviction about the importance of his cause, burnished in the public forum as preacher, editor, and lecturer, gave his expression uncommon force and directness.

Jonathan Baldwin Turner is someone to know. The example of his life as a John the Baptist of a great national educational movement may well inspire us in the tasks which confront our own generation. " Professor Turner through a long life, in season and out of season, at home and abroad, in his study and in the field, in rain or shine, in storm and stress, battled for these ideals as valiantly as ever a knight of King Arthur's circle battled for his ideals. Opposed, misunderstood, maligned, he kept withal a sweetness of temper, and a certain mildness of manner, in spite of his seeming brusqueness, which testified to the depths of good sound common sense and the sound and hearty good will for his fellow man, which were found in his nature." [4]

---

[4] *Ibid.*, p. 191.

Jonathan Baldwin Turner is someone to know for his ideas. His philosophy still has validity. Certainly, his creed as expressed at Monmouth in 1866 may well guide us today:

The sun never shone on such a nation, and such a power, as this would soon be, with such facilities of public advancement and improvement put into full and vigorous operation. Set all the millions of eyes in this great Republic to watching, and intelligently observing and thinking, and there is no secret of nature or art we cannot find out; no disease of man or beast we cannot understand; no evil we cannot remedy; no obstacle we cannot surmount; nothing that lies in the power of man to do or to understand, that cannot be understood and done.[5]

DAVID D. HENRY

URBANA, ILLINOIS
May, 1961

---

[5] Turner, Jonathan Baldwin, Address, County Fair, Monmouth, Illinois, Oct. 4, 1866, quoted in Vol. 1, *Report*, Illinois Industrial University Board of Trustees, Introduction, VII (Springfield, 1868).

Contents

Preface

This book is, of course, a labor of love; and yet, the needs of the student of history have been kept chiefly in mind in making it. For this reason, original documents have been freely used in it. For the most part, these are printed in full, as also are extracts from letters, speeeches, and addresses.

The volume has been delayed year by year by sickness, and by the final giving up, by the Turner household, of the house where it was established in 1837.

At first the plan was to record in a general way the life of a man who lived, in thought and action, fifty years before his time, and therefore was honored by only the few who could appreciate the vigor and unselfishness of the motives that ruled his life.

But as the years passed, and inquiries began to come from different people, seeking proof of this or that historical point in the life of various interests,—especially in reference to the beginning of the Land-Grant Industrial University Movement,—it became evident that a biography of deeper importance than one of grateful remembrance for friends and relatives must be prepared.

Legal proof for statements must be found, records searched, and the whole history of the University Movement written with the greatest care.

Feeling incompetent to do this, I placed the whole subject,

with all my collection of material, in the hands of the most
competent to treat it; but professional duties interfered, and
the documents were returned. The work was finally revised,
and is printed with confidence in the accuracy and legal proof
of all its statements.

The delay has been all the more regretted because of the
death, before its publication, of Bronson Murray, the one
true friend who, through all the years of doubt and labor,
stood shoulder to shoulder with Professor Turner, and by
word and pen, by generous gift of money and true sympathy,
had been a constant inspiration to him and the University
Movement. Mr. Murray died January 5, 1911, in New York
City, in the ninety-fifth year of his age. On the 20th of
December, 1910, I called upon him; he seeemd so well then
that I little thought that I was seeing him for the last time.
Although confined to his bed, frail in body, and blind, he
yet kept his wonderfully vigorous mind, and was interested
in all questions of the day. He said to me then:

" Another fact you must put in your book. In February,
1854, the first anti-Nebraska meeting in Illinois was held in
Springfield, Illinois. I was appointed chairman of the Committee on Resolutions; I was not then accustomed to writing
on political subjects, so I requested your father to write them
for me, as he had been in the habit of doing in our University
work, preparing even those articles signed by my own name,
as President of the Industrial League.

" I can see the little room now, and the few men gathered
there." He hesitated a minute or two, smiled as if the vision
were pleasing, then added: " For it was a momentous occasion, as we all well knew. Those resolutions were afterward
used in preparing the questions for the Lincoln and Douglas
debates of 1858.

" We tried to induce Mr. Lincoln to attend that meeting,
but he would not, saying he was not yet ready to identify
himself with it. He was accused many times of having been
present, and once by Douglas in those famous debates; but
Mr. Lincoln always denied being there, and he spoke truly,
for he was not.

" A second meeting * was held in Ottawa, La Salle County, at that time my home, when I was again appointed on the Committee of Resolutions, and where similar resolutions were adopted.

" Put that in your book, for it is not well known. Editors and publishers were not ambitious for such items at that time."

Perhaps it was best that the name Industrial University, at first selected for the Land-Grant University, given to each State and Territory by the generous appropriations of Congress, should be changed to the " State University." It certainly was not wise to transfer the word " Industrial " to our reformatories, in such a way that every boy and girl who, through unfortunate heredity or environment, is compelled to go there, is branded through life with a term originally of the most honorable significance, but now perverted by usage to a lifelong badge of shame.

Dr. S. A. Forbes, while Dean of the College of Science of the University of Illinois, in a public address used the following words:

" That reaching upward of the masses for more power and light, spreading eastward, gave us later the long line of land-grant colleges, and gives us now the State experimental stations also, as a sort of second growth from the seed first sown, through recognized acceptance of the natural sciences as a necessary part of the course of study in a true people's school.

" That this fruitful movement arose earlier and went further here than elsewhere, I attribute to the fact that it had here in Professor J. B. Turner an able and devoted leader, who, himself an educated man, had those great human qualities which no learning can overlay, and which gave him access to all classes and power with all."

The " Industrial University Plan " of my father, so far-reaching, so far-seeing, and whose value has been so clearly

---

* See " History of La Salle County," pages 262-267, published in 1886 by the Inter-State Publishing Company, Chicago.

proved by the decades that have passed, may well deserve the name of prophecy.

I am grateful for the assistance of many friends in the preparation of this work; and in particular I wish to acknowledge the kindness of the Illinois State Historical Society, to which I owe the loan of the cuts of my father and of Gov. Richard Yates, which appear in this volume.

MARY TURNER CARRIEL

JACKSONVILLE, ILLINOIS
February 1, 1911

CHAPTER I

Genealogy and Early Life

Jonathan Baldwin Turner was born on a farm two miles south of Templeton, Worcester County, Massachusetts, December 7, 1805. He was a son of Captain Asa and Abigail (Baldwin) Turner, being the third son and sixth child in a family of four sons and five daughters. He was a grandson of Edward Turner, a lieutenant in the Continental Army, and, on the maternal side, of Jonathan Baldwin.

The Baldwin family were descendants of the Baldwins of Buckingham, England; in that neighborhood the name was to be met with before the Conquest. Jonathan Baldwin was the first justice of the peace in his township, and the first Representative elected from that township to the Colonial Legislature in 1774. He owned a large saw and grist mill, the vicinity taking its name from it and being known as Baldwin's Mill. It grew into the town now called Baldwinsville. Jonathan Baldwin's third child, Abigail (known as " Nabby "), married Asa Turner of Templeton, and became the mother of Jonathan Baldwin Turner.

The Turner family was of French or Norman origin, " Le Sire de Tourneur " having gone to England with William the Conqueror in 1066. His descendant, John Turner, came to America in the *Speedwell* in 1635. The name of Edward Turner, grandfather of Jonathan, appears, with the rank of sergeant, on the Lexington Alarm Roll, in Captain Joel

Fletcher's company of Minute-men, Colonel Ephraim Doolittle's regiment, which marched from Templeton on the
alarm of April 19, 1775. Later his name appears again, with
the rank of lieutenant, on the Continental pay account, in
Colonel Putnam's regiment.

At the battle of Bunker Hill, when the fire of the English
was concentrated on the narrow causeway over which the
American soldiers had to retreat after their ammunition gave
out, it was Colonel Putnam's regiment that made a heroic
defense and prevented a disastrous rout. Lieutenant Turner
sprang upon an embankment and bravely encouraged the
soldiers to maintain an orderly retreat. After this battle his
company was ordered to Saratoga, and witnessed the sur-
render of General Burgoyne. Later the company was sent
to Half Moon, near Albany, New York, for vaccination, and
from the effects of this Lieutenant Turner died, December
26, 1777, at thirty-three years of age, leaving a widow and
seven children—six boys and one girl. The names of the
children were: Adam, Lewis, Asa (father of Jonathan), Ellis,
Ebenezer, Polly, and Amasa.

His widow cared for the seven little ones in the cabin in
the forest after their father's death, as she had done when he
had been called away from home as a soldier. She fed them
on vegetables and wild berries in the summer, and on dried-
pea soup in the winter; she protected them from cold and
sickness, from the wild beasts of the forest and the wilder
Indians. And yet, through a long life, she was never heard
to complain, or to intimate that her life had not been comfortable and happy. Intrepid and fearless, she proved herself
a Spartan mother.

Asa Turner was his mother's helper in the field and home.
One day she told the boy to catch and harness the horse—a
vicious animal. He demurred and pleaded with tears, but in
vain. He must obey. The horse, which appeared to be quietly
feeding, never lifted his head until the boy attempted to put
on the bridle; then he gave a sudden snap and bit a piece of
flesh out of the boy's leg just below the knee. Antiseptics
were not then known, and although Asa Turner lived to be

eighty-eight years old, the wound never healed. Perhaps for this reason, his mother always made her home with him.

One day, shortly after he had brought his timid young bride home, his mother heard a commotion in the kitchen. She went to investigate, and found three or four Indians, who, thinking no one but the young wife was at home, were demanding that she cook a dinner for them. The mother seized a long-handled fire-shovel and started after them, and the Indians fled.

This sturdy woman was never known to be sick, and always stood ready to help neighbors and friends. She expired (rather than died) at the age of ninety-eight years, at the home of her son Asa, the little cabin by that time having given place to a large New England farmhouse.

After the Revolutionary War there were great hardships and much suffering, especially in western and central Massachusetts. People began to complain of the large salary paid to the Governor, the aristocratic bearing of members of the Legislature, and the refusal to issue paper money to meet the necessities of the time. In what is known as " Shays' Rebellion " (1786-87), under the leadership of Daniel Shays, in September, 1786, a regiment of angry citizens took possession of several towns, including Worcester, Massachusetts, and prevented the session of the Supreme Court at Springfield in that State. A few months later they attempted to seize the arsenal at Springfield, but were defeated by a force of the State militia. Asa Turner was a captain in this rebellion, thus revealing a characteristic tinge in the blood of his line, which manifested itself in resistance to laws they believed to be unjust, no matter now unpopular their opinions might be in the minds of persons of influence and authority.

CHAPTER II

Life at Yale College

Into this farm home upon the hills, with its beautiful view across the valley to Gardner and South Gardner, and its grand old pine trees,—with its fields rich only in rock and stone and the sturdy industry of its owner, to whom the one word " shiftless " expressed all the crimes of the social ages, where four miles of stone wall were built, and trees were felled early and late in the never-ending task of clearing the land,—ambition for a different life entered.

Asa was the brother next older than Jonathan. He was the favorite school-teacher in the neighborhood, being noted for the rapid progress of his pupils and for his good discipline. Sometimes he obtained this by giving the little ones a ride on his foot while he heard the older classes recite. During a revival in the town in which he was teaching, Asa became interested in religion. When he returned home he tried to interest his father and brothers and sisters, and finally he gained his father's permission to begin each day with family prayers—a custom which the father kept up after Asa went away to college; for the boy's next request was that he be allowed to attend Yale College and afterward the Yale Theological Seminary, to prepare for his life work as a missionary, to which he had consecrated himself. His record later as a missionary and leader in education in the West, first at Quincy, Illinois, and, after 1848, at Denmark, Iowa, has been most interestingly told in his biography by George F. Magoun, President of Grinnell College, Iowa. The following incident illustrates his character.

A few years before his death, at the age of eighty-six years, the Rev. Asa Turner's niece was traveling on the Upper Mississipi River, on her way to Minneapolis, with her babies and their nurse. One of the passengers on the boat, an old gentleman, on hearing that she was a niece of " Father Turner " of Iowa, told her this story:

When I was a young man on my first trip away from home, I happened to reach Burlington, Iowa, then a little village with one poor excuse for a tavern, one stormy Saturday night in midwinter. Weary, lonely, and homesick, I was sitting in the office, parlor, bar-room,—all in one,—playing cards, a thing I had never done before, to while away the miserable hours before bed-time. A man came in, engaged a room to stay all night, and immediately went to it. We noticed that he was different from the other guests. About nine o'clock he returned, with a Bible in his hand, and said: " Gentlemen, it is my custom to have family prayers at night before retiring. I am away from home, and lonely, detained unexpectedly over Sunday by the bad roads. If you do not object, I would like to have prayers with you."

A chorus of answers came, most of them assenting—" Tune up, old man," " Go ahead," " I'll bet on you," etc. He seated himself in an arm-chair in the middle of the room, opened his Bible and began to read. The singing and ribald jest, the clinking of glasses at the bar, and the betting at the card-tables continued without interruption. After reading a chapter, the man knelt and prayed, and such a prayer I never heard. It seemed as if the roof would rise from over our heads, and that each individual soul was being carried to the throne of grace. The voices were hushed, the glasses ceased to clink, the cards lay upon the tables, and every eye was turned to the kneeling figure. After the " Amen " he rose and said, " I thank you, gentlemen; good night," and disappeared. Not a word was said; but soon one, and then another, quietly departed. For the first time in the history of that bar-room, it was closed before midnight on a Saturday night. Probably many there were, as I was, young men away from Christian homes, in danger of forgetting. That prayer took us home.

It was the wish of the family that Jonathan should remain on the home place. To encourage him to do this, his father gave him, when he was twenty-one years old, a deed to all the property. In 1827 Asa, who had graduated from Yale College and had just entered the Theological Seminary of Yale, walked all the way home and back, two hundred and forty miles,—starting out with only sixty cents,—in order to persuade his father to let Jonathan attend Yale College. The mother added her persuasive voice, and the father's consent changed the whole course of Jonathan's life. At the age of twenty-two he entered college.

Jonathan was a strong and vigorous youth. His feats of strength and endurance were the pride of the family, as well as of his class, afterward, at Yale. The money he had earned by teaching in the winter seasons ever since he was fifteen years of age, and by working for neighbors when his labor was not needed at home, had always been turned into the family treasury. But his brother Asa—who had received from his father ten dollars in money and a " God bless you " when he carried Asa to college in a one-horse buggy—had found no difficulty in earning his way, and now Jonathan followed his example, working in gardens and sawing wood.

Ex-President Dwight's sons, Sereno and Henry, had recently returned from Europe, full of the German gymnasium idea (the Germans use the word to describe a preparatory school, not an athletic hall). Through their influence, the first gymnasium school in America was organized, in connection with Yale College. Jonathan was appointed an instructor in primary studies and in athletics. The New Haven Harbor was the boys' swimming-pool, and their favorite lesson a swim far out into its waters. For two years Jonathan remained in this work, at the same time continuing his preparatory course for entering Yale College. The stone building purchased by subscribers for use as a gymnasium was a mile from the college and near the center of the town, and commanded a fine view of the harbor, the Sound, and Long Island. We read in the Yale catalogues of that day, in reference to the location of New Haven: " The town is very accessible, being within eight hours' travel from New York, and within twenty-four from Boston, Albany, and Philadelphia, and it has a direct and easy communication with every part of the United States." The pupils, the greater number of whom were between six and fourteen years of age, were allowed to remain at the gymnasium all the year round. Jonathan had under his care and training about eighty boys, most of whom were from the South.

During his senior year in the Preparatory Department, in 1829, a temperance wave swept over the land, and awakened great interest among the students and instructors of Yale. At that time liquor was used almost universally. President Dwight had managed a " grocery " (saloon), for the benefit of the students, in the college building itself. Many "drunks" had been traceable to that source, and it became so notorious that the trustees tried to abolish it, but were unable to do so while President Dwight remained. With the advent of President Day, however, the students' " grocery " disappeared.

The Turner family home in Templeton had always been a social center, especially for the ministers and deacons who enjoyed Captain Turner's conversation, but who enjoyed more the " flip " which he used to make before the great fireplace and served to his guests. Jonathan's part in the entertainment had been, at the close of these social evenings, to steer the guests through the gate to the middle of the road, from where they were expected to navigate safely to their own firesides. That the minister was one of the most frequent guests on these occasions did not lessen the respect and reverence which the presence and preaching of New England clergymen always inspired.

During his preparatory course Jonathan lived in the same house with two notable instructors of foreign birth, having a room directly over a suite occupied by them, and he formed an intimate acquaintance and lasting friendship with these neighbors. One was Charles A. Colomb, A.M., who had been for many years aide-de-camp to Napoleon Bonaparte, and had participated in two hundred engagements with him. After Napoleon's downfall he had been banished because of

his devotion to his chief, whom he idolized as something
more than human. Of large stature and great physical strength,
Colomb was a perfect specimen of the chivalrous gentleman,
and nothing aroused his resentment so much as any allusion
to the faults and failings of the man whom he adored. The
other neighbor was the instructor in Spanish, Joseph A.
Pizarro, A.M., who was also a man with a history. He, too,
had been a soldier for many years, and had been exiled from
his native land because of his devotion to a lost cause. At
the battle of Corunna he and the French teacher had fought
on opposite sides; but, like true soldiers, they became warm
friends and close companions in the land of their exile. Both
of them crippled and somewhat broken in health, they were
yet able to continue their teaching of French and Spanish
in the Dwight Gymnasium. Both came from families of
wealth, and their relatives and friends in France and Spain
often sent them gifts—pipes of wine and brandy, fruits and
vegetables of all kinds, clothing—in fact, anything that could
be safely shipped across the Atlantic.

Jonathan went on errands for these men, and helped them
in many ways, and he was often invited to share their foreign
dainties. The question of danger from the use of liquor had
never occurred to him. When the temperance wave reached
Yale, however, he became convinced that its advocates were
right, and that he ought to make a decision one way or the
other. The great struggle was to tell his two old friends that
he thought it dangerous, or even unwise, to follow their example, and thus refuse to join them in their social glass; for
it had been his greatest delight to listen to their stories, as
they fought over again, as friends, the battles in which, as
enemies, they had confronted each other.

One Saturday Jonathan went out into the woods, climbed
a high knoll overlooking the Sound, and wrestled all day
with the problem. At night, drenched by a cold, drizzling
rain, hungry and weary, he returned to his room. At the
usual hour he went down to wait upon his friends; but, when

they offered him a glass of liquor, he thanked them and said he would not take any. They at once understood, and never afterward offered him wine or liquor of any kind; but, by their gentle manner and kindness even greater than before, they showed that they knew of his struggle, and appreciated and approved of his decision.

When he had completed his preparatory course, Jonathan entered the Classical Department of Yale College. He ranked well in his studies, and took a number of prizes in English composition and Greek. At one time, having received word that his mother was very ill, he walked one hundred and twenty miles to his home to see her, and, when she grew better, returned in the same way.

Yale College, always a stronghold of classical culture, was especially so at that time. President Barnard, of Columbia College, in his annual report of 1872, speaking, from personal knowledge, of the conditions that existed at Yale College between 1820 and 1830, says:

" The amount of classical reading in those days was vastly greater than it is at present. In them was accomplished all of the two large volumes of Dalzel's ' Græca Majora,' embracing Xenophon's ' Anabasis ' and ' Memorabilia,' with liberal extracts from Herodotus, Thucydides, Lucian, and Socrates; Plato, Aristotle, and Longinus, and the poets, Sophocles and Euripides. To these were added several books of Homer's ' Iliad ' and the oration of Demosthenes ' On the Crown.' In Latin, the reading embraced eight books of Livy's History, the entire volume of the poetical works of Horace, including the ' Odes,' ' Satires,' ' Epistles,' and ' The Art of Poetry '; Cicero's ' De Officilis,' ' De Senectute,' ' De Amicitia,' ' De Oratore,' and ' De Republica '; and, finally, Tacitus' ' Historiæ,' ' Agricola,' and ' De Moribus Germanorum.' Besides these, the whole of Adam's ' Roman Antiquities ' was read from cover to cover."

An extract from one of Jonathan's letters to his sister Dulcina illustrates the spirit of the student while attending Yale College:

NEW HAVEN, April 10, 1831

Dear Sister:

I received a letter from Asa, and one from Edward [his youngest brother] to-day. Asa is as well as usual, thinks much of his wife, says she is quite a worker, makes all his butter, etc., etc.* Pray go and see Mother, and tell me the particulars about her. Give my love to her, and tell her if I come home it will be on her account, as nothing else would induce me to meet the expense until fall. If she says come, I will come. Tell her to be plain and her son Jonathan will obey with the greatest pleasure. She must let me know soon. I can spend the vacation free from expense. The cost of going to Templeton will be twelve dollars, as I am unable to walk. Also, if I come this spring, they must not expect me again in the fall. You must pardon my poor writing. I have lost much sleep of late; have been up with the sick all night, and my nerves are weak. Much love to all, especially to you and our dear Mother and Father.

JONATHAN B. TURNER

After the summer vacation of 1832, Jonathan returned to Yale to enter upon his senior year, riding in a stage-coach all the way from his home to New Haven. He was sitting on the back seat of the coach, half asleep, when four fun-loving girls got in at Springfield, Massachusetts, to ride to Somers, Connecticut. One of these, who seeemed to be the leader in fun and frolic, thinking he was asleep, began to imitate him and make him a subject of entertainment for her companions. He watched her out of the corner of his eye, and, when the stage stopped at the hotel in Somers, he went in, after the girls had left, and inquired who she might be. A few days after his return to Yale he wrote to her. Her friends were not so romantic as was he, and demanded to know who and what he was. In answer to one of these inquiries by letter, the following was received by a friend of her family:

---

* Asa's wife, who came from a wealthy family of Hartford, Connecticut, had gone as a young bride to the wilds of Illinois, and was now wife of a home missionary, on the munificent salary of two hundred and fifty dollars a year.

YALE COLLEGE, November 16, 1832

Dear Sir:

I have but little acquaintance with Jonathan B. Turner. I find, however, by inquiring of President Day, that he sustains in all respects a desirable character—as a Christian, exemplary and pious; as a scholar, among the first in his class.

There are probably very few young men in whom there is more reason to confide or to hope for in the future life.

Yours respectfully,

N. W. TAYLOR

As a result of this correspondence, the young lady, who was Miss Rhodolphia S. Kibbe, a few years later accompanied the subject of this biography to the Far West as his bride.

CHAPTER III

A Call to the West; Letters to His Sweetheart

One night in February, 1827, a band of Yale students, standing on the campus of their alma mater, beneath the beautiful elm trees, with only the stars above them as their witnesses, pledged themselves to go to Illinois as missionaries. Illinois in those days was less known and less accessible than the foreign fields of Asia, to which a neighbor's son and playmate of the Turner brothers, the Rev. William Goodell, had recently gone. The seven who formed this association, pledged to promote "religion and learning" in the West, were: Theron Baldwin, John F. Brooks, Elisha Jenny, Mason Grosvenor, William Kirby, Julian M. Sturtevant, and Asa Turner. Later these seven, with three others, became the first trustees of Illinois College, at Jacksonville, Illinois, which was organized through their efforts. This and two other colleges were the first incorporated institutions west of the Alleghanies.

In the winter of 1832-33, Jonathan's senior year as a student at Yale, Dr. Edward Beecher, President of Illinois College, wrote to Jeremiah Day, President of Yale College, asking that he send him a teacher whom he could recommend as a future professor. President Day spoke to Jonathan, offering to excuse him from all examinations and his commencement oration, and to send him his diploma when his classmates received theirs at the end of the term. So the course of Jonathan's career was again changed, and the rest of his life was devoted to the "Great Northwest." His duties at Illinois College began in the spring of 1833. On the journey West he wrote several letters to Miss Rhodolphia Kibbe in Connecticut, the first from New York.

WASHINGTON HOTEL, NEW YORK
April 10, 1833

Dear Rhodolphia:

. . . Called on my brother and sister. Next morning I took stage for Yale, and Tuesday last, as I unclasped the warm hand of my friend Sykes on board of the *Superior,* I broke the last tie that bound me to New England.

BALTIMORE, MARYLAND

Dear Rhodolphia:

You see by the last date my march is still onward. I left New York at six o'clock yesterday (Friday) morning, and, by the aid of coaches, steamboats, railroads, locomotives, etc., arrived at Philadelphia last evening. Left at six this morning, and by the same magic power of steam I am here at Baltimore at five o'clock this evening, two hundred miles distant. Our company from New York has consisted of about two hundred persons. All rode to-day by land in one chain of cars drawn by a single engine at the rate of one mile in three minutes, averaging through the day fifteen miles per hour. Our ride down the Delaware and Chesapeake was delightful—trees in abundance and all in full bloom. I believe a trip to Baltimore would thoroughly cure you of your predilection for the banks of the Connecticut. Our watchword is still "Onward," and we move again on Monday at six A.M. for Fredericksburg, Va., by steam (railroad), and if we fly as we have done yesterday and to-day we shall get through in two or three weeks from date. My brother's youngest child, however, is dangerously ill, and we may be detained here; but we shall start as soon as possible, for these hotels, especially in a land of slaves (and they are for the first time about me), do not tally so well with purses "lean and lank" like Pharaoh's kine—at least, if we pay, as at our last quarters, one dollar per meal and one dollar for single bed, etc. But never mind, I am rich yet, and if I am

not, the Lord feeds the poor. Some wiseacre may doubt, however, whether he feeds the prodigal—and I am not quite so sure
of it. I have scarce walked a mile since I left New Haven but
that I have met a coachman, a servant, a shoe-black, or a slave,
with his hat in hand, bowing and scraping for " fees," " fees,"
" fees "; and one must fee the poor devils for their obsequious-
ness, if for nothing else.

Dear Rhodolphia:

I would like to place you on board of one of these floating
volcanoes of the nineteenth century [the steamboat] and glide
you over the silent waters of the Ohio—the " Beautiful River,"
say the French, and say truly: so full of little islands covered
with luxuriant foliage, and so circuitous is it in its course, that
you can seldom see more than five or ten miles either way. Not
unfrequently you ride for hours through an unbroken forest.
Then we came to Cincinnati, the far-famed emporium of the
great valley, an anomaly in nature, a city of six thousand inhabitants surrounded on all sides by a dense and apparently unbroken
forest. Here I called on Dr. Lyman Beecher, and left Miss Patton;
the Doctor's son, my old and well-tried friend George, gave me
a most hearty reception. In the morning we mounted a couple
of fine steeds and galloped into the country, passing the site of
Lane Seminary, a most delightful and romantic spot indeed. The
banks of the Ohio are much the same below Cincinnati as above,
except not so many villages; they are not generally so beautiful
as those of the Mississippi, whose waters are more turbid and
rapid, but intersected more frequently with beautiful islands and
presenting a still greater diversity of scenery on the banks. I
might write a sheet or two of little incidents and the numerous
inconveniences, bad food, dirty sheets, etc., inseparable from so
long a tarry in the public vehicle. Once we ran our boat upon
a rock, and once upon a sandbar, and were obliged to throw out
about one hundred tons of freight to lighten her each time, and
then were detained a day or two to refit, and now we reach
Jacksonville.

Jonathan Turner arrived at Illinois College May 8, 1833,
and a few days later he wrote the following letter to Miss
Kibbe:

ILLINOIS COLLEGE, May 14, 1833

Dear Rhodolphia:

I am sitting in my domicile in the east side of a spacious brick edifice and daily surrounded by all the conveniences and luxuries, too, of the sumptuous East.

[The rosy hue here pictured of the new Western surroundings, it was no doubt hoped, would reach to the New England home and touch the sweetheart's mother with its glow; for a young man in the wilds of Illinois presented an entirely different aspect from that of a young man winning high honors at Yale, and expected to fill some position of honor nearer home.]

For a general description of the society here I will refer you to the papers which I shall, from time to time, send you, with your permission, barely observing that you cannot find a village east of the Hudson, of the same number of inhabitants, possessing so many men of literary eminence and moral worth, nor a community of greater refinement in taste and manners. . . . I arrived here on the 8th of May (Saturday), and found the institution in a flourishing condition. The faculty consists at present of five members: President Beecher, Messrs. Sturtevant, Post, Colton, and myself. The two former and their ladies are exceedingly agreeable.

I have become strongly attached to President Beecher. He is about two years older than myself. Our spare hour for exercise is usually spent in talking, walking, or swinging.* He is surely a most lovable man. Mr. Sturtevant is equally worthy, and perhaps more so, but not quite so much like myself in his taste and feelings. Their ladies, I would again say, are lovely women; all seem to exert themselves to make me contented and happy. I hear recitations at present from three to five hours per day in Latin and Greek, and study from three to ten hours. We have about three hundred acres of superior soil, sixty or seventy acres of which the boys and our farmer have planted with corn this spring. It looks beautifully now, as it is about knee-high. Often you will see one hundred acres in one field. Apple trees were in full bloom as we passed along April 20th.

Hundreds of people pass through here from the East and from Europe every year, and all say it is indeed the most delightful

---

* Swings were the only apparatus for athletic contests in those days, and the grove west of the college their only gymnasium.

spot on earth, especially the sight from the college buildings. But I must forbear, and refer you to Mr. William Peters' letters in the New York *Observer*, I think, in February or March last. I will only add, when you hear " a different story," you must remember Illinois is a great State, as large almost as all New England. Of course, some parts of it are most wretchedly poor, unhealthful, and unpleasant, especially the southern forests on the banks of the Mississippi. . . .

By the way, I have passed through and alongside of sixteen or seventeen different States of the Union, and I know of no one equal to old New England, except it be those which abound in prairies. I would not clear a farm in Ohio, Indiana, or Kentucky, if you would give me twice its value. You think it a great distance here, I suppose, but it is only a mere step. It is nothing to come over here or to return, and had I a little more cash and time, I assure you it would delight my heart to ride over and take tea with you some afternoon. My secretary, books, clothes, etc., I shipped via New Orleans; they have not yet come, and may not; but I obtained an insurance upon them of about three hundred dollars, so that I shall not incur much loss if they are not delivered. My health is at present very fine, and I am able to devote myself with more than usual energy to the duties of my profession and studies.

I have written as fast as I could since ten o'clock, and since I must rise to hear a Latin recitation at five, I must bid you good night—or, rather, good morning. The young ladies who came out with us are delighted with their situation here. Miss Crocker has opened a female seminary and Miss Blood an infant school. Both are experienced and approved teachers, as well as amiable and interesting girls. And now I can only commend you and yours to Him who careth for you. May He guide you and me in all our ways, and, however unworthy, may we at last be received into His beloved presence, where is fullness of joy for evermore. This is the daily prayer of your absent friend, who still rejoices that he is not forgotten by you.

J. B. TURNER

CHAPTER IV

Cholera and Indians

Jacksonville, the little village of a thousand people, was one mile east of Illinois College. In its center was a park, around which ran a wide street. A street ran north, south, east, and west from the center of each side, and two narrower streets at right angles to each other from each corner of the square.

The original settlers had hoped to locate the town on the beautiful mound to the west, but the owners of the land would neither give nor sell; so the land sloping down for miles on that side gave the village the appearance of nestling in a hollow.

Morgan Street ran west from the southwest corner of the square, and was the aristocratic street of the village; here were built all the better houses, and later the Episcopal church and the "Female Academy" were located there.

The only avenue was College Avenue, one block south of Morgan Street and parallel to it, leading straight to the college grounds. Little houses, most of them built of logs, were scattered sparsely about the village. There were no sidewalks, only a footpath over the prairie, which was grassy and beautiful in the summer, but for part of the year deep with mud, especially the ravine between the college and the village, which was sometimes almost impassable to a man on foot, even when he wore hip-boots.

But these discomforts were more than compensated for by

the extensive view. There were no trees to obstruct this, except two or three on College Avenue and two more to the southeast.

The land from College Hill sloped far away north, south, and east over the prairie, with its tall, waving grass and beautiful flowers in summer, and its equally beautiful mantle of snow in winter, to the distant timber which followed the windings of the Mauvaisterre Creek. A few years later the Academy girls, promenading on their new front porch, could see Governor Duncan's mansion in Duncan Park, and, on the opposite side of the street, the little schoolhouse he built for the College Hill children.

A little more than two months after Professor Turner's arrival in Jacksonville, that place and a number of other Illinois towns were swept by a cholera epidemic, which resulted in much suffering and many deaths among the pioneer population. The appalling conditions produced by this visitation are graphically described in the following letters, which impart knowledge of a calamity of which few people of the present day have had any conception.

ILLINOIS COLLEGE, July 15, 1833

Dear Rhodolphia:

. . . As to the Indians, I fear them about as much (though not quite as much) as I should the mosquitos in Broadway, New York City. There are men and arms enough in Jacksonville to shoot every Indian west of the Alleghanies. They dare not come within a hundred miles of us without an olive branch in their hands and peace in their hearts. As to the cholera, this is a more insidious and dangerous foe. It has almost depopulated some villages on the Mississippi River, as you have probably learned. In Quincy, a village of about seven hundred people, where my brother Asa is stationed, twenty-two have died, fourteen of them in about four days. It cuts down, almost instantly, the most robust and temperate as well as the feeble. Of course, there can be no security, only to meet and trust God forever. It is no longer confined to the intemperate; it sweeps all indiscriminately to the tomb by the hundred. Carrollton, a village of seven hundred inhabitants about sixty miles south of here, has already been reduced, by flight and death, to about seventy or eighty souls. It has been even more terrible than it was in New York last season. We hope it will not sweep over Jacksonville; there has been but one death since last Saturday. We expect it will prevail extensively in the city, but do not expect it will rage on College Hill, at least not violently, owing to its peculiar elevated, airy, and healthful situation. . . .

JACKSONVILLE, August 28, 1833

Dear Rhodolphia:

Soon after I wrote you, the cholera, that awful scourge of humanity, commenced its ravages in this place. It had been for a long time skirmishing on our borders. One sixth of the entire population in Carrollton (next county south) had died, one fifth of the population in Palmyra, one fifteenth of that in Quincy, etc.

At last, although from our healthy location we hoped to escape, it came down upon us like a thunder-clap. Mrs. Ellis, wife of the Presbyterian minister, Rev. John M. Ellis, a lady of rare accomplishment, was taken sick one afternoon, and died before six o'clock. She had two little children; one was taken at one o'clock that same night, and died before morning; the other, and a niece, Miss Conn, a beautiful young girl of eighteen, died soon after. Mr. Ellis was away at the time, and when he returned he stopped at the church to attend prayer meeting before going to his home. As he entered the door he heard a friend praying for their " stricken pastor so suddenly bereft of all his family." He fell to the floor as if he had been struck by a butcher's ax. Immediately after this, forty-seven families, and as many single persons as could leave, fled.

Shops are closed, streets deserted, and " every human face divine " overcast with gloom or bedewed with grief. This increased our grief much. It was impossible to procure help, even to cook, much less to nurse. The people in the village were so frightened that the students were obliged to take the whole care of the Ellis family, with the help of a poor old aunt who could scarce crawl from watching and sorrow. Not a single person could be found to enter the house, even to put the last one who died, the niece, into her coffin. One truly noble-minded student on the Hill, Mr. George T. Purkitt, in spite of etiquette and town gab, went through the whole ordeal alone with the old aunt. What else could they do? Though many of the students were made sick, and one most excellent young man, Nelson of the freshman class, died, the rest have all recovered.

From this time the daily yea, the hourly report, was " He is sick," " He is dead," " He is buried." To meet a man at night and attend his funeral in the morning has ceased to alarm, much less to surprise. Some die in three hours, seldom do they live twelve, and very rarely twenty-four. As I have walked through the streets in the evening, I have seen through the windows and doors the sick and the dying, sometimes four or five in the same room in a log hut, some on the bed, others on the floor, and perhaps one or two sorrow-smitten beings crawling from bed to bed to give a cup of water or to brush away the flies. On every face was written " Woe," and on every door-post " Death," and on not a few " Utter desolation." Notwithstanding our village was reduced by flight and otherwise to about six or seven hundred, as was supposed, they have been dying off through the whole month of August at the rate of one, two, three, four, five, and even six a day. Soon the disease began to spread into the country, where, from the thinness of the population, distance from medical aid, want of conveniences and often the bare necessities of life, it was still more distressing. For some weeks not a soul was seen approaching from the country, except here and there a man on a horse upon the full run for " The doctor! The doctor! For Heaven's sake, sir, can't you tell me where is the doctor? My father is dying, my wife is dead, and my children are dying. The doctor! The doctor! " All this came to be answered at last by a stupid stare, or a shake of the head, or perchance, " They are all sick." For, at one time, out of eight or ten doctors not one could be had. Only one, however, died—Dr. Allen, my much-beloved friend and room-mate at the gymnasium in New Haven, who came out here to see the country with his lady, whom he married two years since.

A week or two since I took a bronco and rode out to Naples, twenty miles west, to take a little rest and fresh air. Nothing could exceed the beauty of the prairies; they are in many places covered with tall prairie-grass, variegated with flowers of every size, shape, odor, and hue, from one to six feet high. It looks like enchanted ground. But what a contrast within doors! Cholera, cholera—death, death. In a settlement on the way, called Bethel, I saw a man shoeing a horse, when I rode out in the evening. Next morning, when I returned, they had dug his grave and were placing him in it. I called at the tavern. The landlord was dead, the family sick. I had lost my way, and called to inquire; but found some sick, some dead. The poor people here think the disease is contagious, and dare not go into an infected house. They are often struck down at once, like an ox under a butcher's ax. A man and his wife sank upon the floor of their log hut, unable to reach the bed, or to give each other a drop of water; the man was found dead. A woman, whose husband had died, was found lying dead on her bed, where she had been two days, and her two little sons were trying to dig a hole in front of the house to put her in. Instances have occurred of whole families leaving the house and suffering their diseased friend to die alone.

There are many heartrending tales of this sort in circulation. But in the midst of judgments the Lord has remembered mercy to us on College Hill. We sent off all the students we could at first; the rest began to sicken. All our female domestics except one, an excellent old maid, fled. Of course, we gentlemen professors, as we are sometimes called, gave up Latin and Greek, and turned cooks, bottle-washers, etc. The college was a perfect hospital for more than two weeks. We required ten watchers every night, though there was not twice that number of well persons on the Hill. I was up about every other night for some weeks. . . . One night a student who had been watching was taken violently sick and sent immediately for the doctor. They were all sick. One, however, sent back some medicine and requested me to administer it. I was up with him alone in the fifth story all night; I thought he would die. His hands shriveled, his eyes sunk, and his limbs became cold in less than an hour. I thought he was gone. " I will either kill or cure him at once," I said, and I doubled and shortly after quadrupled the ordinary dose. I gave him about one hundred and fifty drops of laudanum, two tablespoonfuls of strongest tincture of red pepper in pure alcohol, and two glasses of brandy. This threw him into a perspiration, and, by repeating it once an hour, broke up the disease. Calomel has been tried here, but usually proves fatal. If the disease comes in your region, take laudanum and pepper; drink it by the spoonful. It is astonishing how much the disease requires. When this has been administered at once, the patients have more generally recovered; but an hour's delay would in most cases be fatal. Here in the West, however, the disease is different; especially in one respect, there are no premonitory symptoms, often; also, the most temperate as well as the drunken and worthless are stricken.

I have sent you no papers and letters lately, for the former were so full of cholera and nothing else that I did not wish to alarm you until it was all over and I could tell the whole story; the papers, by the way, do not tell more than half of it. Doubtless more than one tenth of the present population have died since I came here; that is, more than one hundred persons. But this does not prove the place unhealthful—not at all; for what place or people are healthy or safe, when God sees fit to scourge them with the cholera? But my trust is in Him. I have gone along, perfectly cheerful and content; my trust, I hope, is in Him alone, not regarding the disease so much as to change or restrict my diet in the least. The woods have been full of blackberries, which the people were forbidden by ordinance to eat. I had to have something, as there were not enough well people to cook for the living, so used to go at night, when I could, and eat all I wished. I am sure they helped me; and now the woods are full of plums of all kinds. Twelve persons gathered twelve bushels in about three hours the other day; also the fields are full of melons as large as pumpkins, which none dare eat except Post and myself, hence we live well. One o'clock in the evening, and my horse, saddle, bridle, and pistols are all ready for the morning. No letters in the office to-night. Sorry, sorry indeed!

Yours truly,

J. B. TURNER

The summer vacation was almost spent, and there had been no relief from care and intense anxiety. Seeking a change from a life so trying, three of the Illinois College professors planned a horseback trip to Chicago.

ILLINOIS COLLEGE, September 28, 1833

Dear Rhodolphia:

On August 28 Professors T. M. Post, Erastus Colton, and I decided to make an exploring tour on horseback, and see if we could not find some relief from the terrible experiences of the cholera epidemic through which we have just passed. We rode to Quincy to visit my brother Asa, who is pastor of the Congregational church he has organized, hoping also to find some one going to Chicago who would guide us there. At Quincy we heard that a party was going from Galesburg, and so we pushed on to that place, where we found a band of Pottawatomie Indians, who were going to attend the giving up of their land at Chicago to the government. They, through an interpreter, allowed us to go with them. We started in true Indian style, the young chief and braves first, older men next, followed by the squaws and their pappooses with their ponies and camping outfit, and we last of all. In single file we rode through the tall prairie-grass, in many places higher than our heads while we were on horseback, through the theater of the last season's Indian war to Lake Michigan. We were not altogether comfortable with our strange traveling companions, for the Indians were not well pleased with the idea of giving up their land at Chicago. But they treated us well, and the novelty of the proceedings made it interesting. Suddenly, when about fifty miles from Chicago, the young chief in front snatched up his gun, cocked it, and said something over his shoulder to the one immediately behind him, and so went the word down the whole line, the excitement growing as the guns clicked, clicked. We were alarmed, as we had seen nothing and could see nothing to cause the sudden excitement. Professor Colton was sure they intended to murder us, and wanted us to put spurs to our horses and at least make an attempt to escape; they had gotten us far out on the prairie and intended to wreak their vengeance on us, the only whites within reach. But Professor Post and I persuaded him that would be foolish; we could not possibly escape in a race, for their horses were tougher and fresher than ours. We had better watch and try some other way, if they really intended to kill us. By this time the squaws and children were equally excited, all jabbering at once. Not a thing could we understand, and not a word from us could they understand. Soon, however, we noticed they were not looking at us, but far away to the south. By rising in my stirrups and looking in the same direction, I saw a deer bounding over the high grass. The chief left the line and started after him.

When we reached Chicago I told the Indian agent there of the incident, and said surely he could not get the deer. " Yes, he will; he will follow him for days, and never leave the trail until he catches him." And, sure enough, in two days he came in with the deer slung over the pony's back in front of him.

On the lake shore were assembled about eight thousand

Indians, decorated with paint and wampum, armed with rifles, tomahawks, bows and arrows, war-clubs, scalping-knives, etc. Their squaws were armed with pappooses on their backs, and sometimes were decorated with ragged blankets; some, however, were dressed very fine.

The next day, after the sale had been completed, the place was filled with drunken Indians, in all stages of helplessness, and all wanting to fight. Under the influence of liquor, the Frenchman dances, the Italian sings, the American talks, and the Irishman and Indian want to fight. When dangerously drunk, the squaws would gather about them, throw them down, and sit upon their backs—often an unsteady and rocking seat. Three heavy squaws were sometimes sitting on one squirming, yelling Indian. I became frightened; I had heard how revengeful an Indian was, what little regard he had for his squaws. I thought, when they came to themselves and found their squaws had been sitting on their backs, there would be a terrible massacre, and so I told the Indian agent my fears. "You must be a tenderfoot," he said. "An Indian is always grateful to any one who restrains him when he is drunk; but let any one try it when he is not, and he will follow them as long as he lives to take his revenge." This proved to be true. When they awoke from their drunken sleep, all was peaceful and quiet.

[Chicago is noted for its rapid growth and wonderful rise in real estate, but the greatest rise recorded in history was in August, 1833.]

One day the land was bought for three cents per acre, and the next day it was sold for one hundred dollars per squire to the whites. We bantered each other to buy, for there was never a more unpromising location for a city than the low marshy ground of Chicago in 1833. We bought one squire of land.*

---

* This land that they bought was near where the College of Law of the Northwestern University now stands, at the southeast corner of Randolph and Dearborn streets. In later years they sold it for ten thousand dollars and thought they had done well, but it is now worth millions. At the time of the Columbian Exposition of 1893, in Chicago, Professor Turner, then in his eighty-eighth year, visited the Indian Department and talked with Poganon, the son of the Pottawatomie chief who had so unwillingly sold his heritage to the United States government in 1833, and learned that the land upon which Chicago and the beautiful "Dream City" then stood had never been paid for, even at the rate of three cents per acre. On his return home, Professor

Our ride from Chicago to Jacksonville was very trying; in fact, our whole exploring tour on the frontier settlements proved exceedingly tedious. We were worn out with nursing and were in no fit condition to take such a long and hard horseback tour. We rode from twenty to fifty miles per day every day—excepting the few days we were in Chicago—from August 28 to September 26, embracing a distance of from six to eight hundred miles through an unsettled region, most of it entirely destitute of roads and bridges, often twenty to thirty miles from one cabin to another, and generally from ten to twelve miles. So, you see, we were obliged to make roads for ourselves. Often we found ourselves galloping across an immense prairie covered with the most beautiful grass and flowers, sometimes as high as our heads, and of every hue and color under heaven. Anon we were in an almost impassable forest, or a mud-hole up to our horses' bellies, or plunging into the rapid current of the Illinois River. Sometimes we would lose our course and have to ride until twelve or one o'clock at night, then throw down our saddles for pillows and with the hewn logs of the hunter's cabin for a bed and our cloaks for our only covering. In the morning we ate with the backwoodsman his simple bread and water. We were obliged to lodge thus more than half the time we were away. A fine way, you will say, to recover from the exhaustion and fatigue of the cholera season. When I left Jacksonville I hoped I was done with nursing and doctoring, for a time at least; but, after two or three days out from Chicago, I was obliged to nurse both companions most of the way home. Professor Colton twice gave out entirely, saying he could not go another rod, if he died on the prairie.

I am busy now preparing for commencement next Wednesday, correcting compositions, drilling the seniors, and writing for the *Patriot*, etc.; and, with the groans of Professor Post and Colton in my ears, I bid you good night to camp down on the floor, napping with my ears open to their calls.

Yours truly,

J. B. TURNER

———————

Turner wrote this fact to Representative William M. Springer and Senator Shelby M. Cullom at Washington, urging them to redeem the fair name of Illinois from such injustice and shame. This they did, and the next Congress appropriated the sum, which, with all its accrued interest, amounted to only a little over five thousand dollars.

Before deciding a momentous question, Professor Turner consulted the wishes of Miss Kibbe:

ILLINOIS COLLEGE, November, 1833

Dear Rhodolphia:

. . . I have just received an invitation to join in an expedition over the Rocky Mountains to explore the country of the Flat Head Indians. Said expedition is to consist of ten men, if so many of sufficient intelligence, enterprise, and hardihood can be found. You are probably aware of the fact that four of this tribe came to St. Louis, a distance of four thousand miles, on foot, to hear of our religion. It has long been thought desirable to explore that region, but as yet little has been done, except by the government as related in the " Journal of Lewis & Clark." Now, did not my engagement here utterly forbid the idea, such a trip over the solitude of prairie and mountains would precisely fall in with my natural love of romantic adventure.

Mrs. Beecher invited me down to tea, when I met Dr. Finley and sister and a gentleman from Scotland, a graduate of Glasgow College. I have not yet decided that it is my duty to stay here more than the two years. I wish for all the light on this point you can give me, and I wish you would seriously and prayerfully inquire where we both, unitedly, can do the most good to our fellow men, and there we will go and stay, for there alone shall we be most happy and useful. Now, this is a question you are as deeply interested in as myself, and perhaps more so. I cannot, therefore, take upon myself the responsibility of deciding alone a question which will undoubtedly affect in no slight degree the happiness of each of us for time and eternity. Let us endeavor to do it in the light of eternity and as in the presence of God, so that we can claim Him as our Father and our Friend, wherever we may be or whatever may befall us.

Yours truly,

J. B. TURNER

March 20, 1834

Dear Rhodolphia:

This winter season has been far more moderate, as a whole, than any I have ever passed in New England—indeed, much more than I anticipated. The cold weather continued only about three weeks. The birds were singing and the geese flying in February, also until in December in the fall. This, I am told, is the usual course of things. There is a meeting of the trustees in session to-day, and they seemed determined that I shall wander no more. They have invited me to connect myself for life as a permanent professor in one of the departments, giving me my choice out of three, if I will stay.

COLLEGE HILL, May 24, 1834

Dear Rhodolphia:

. . . Since I wrote you last I have concluded to connect myself permanently with the college. The trustees were pleased to call me in the papers " Professor of Rhetoric and Belles Lettres," and I suppose that, for the remainder of my life, I shall go by that name. . . . My daily task is now Latin and Greek, as before, with the addition of hearing and revising the orations and compositions for commencement, which takes place the third Wednesday in August.

Friend Post and myself walk in our beautiful grove about ten rods back of the college buildings, on the crown of the hill, every eve a few moments, to study the stars and to catch the inspiring fragrance floating on the zephyrs. Our grove is full of all kinds of wild fruit, May-apples, cherries, plums, grapes, blackberries, raspberries, paw-paws, nuts, etc., by the bushel. I tell you, this is indeed a land " flowing with milk and honey "; for such is the abundance of wild bees and tame cows that scarcely a meal is made without an abundance of milk and honey. I never lived better in my life, even in old New England, or enjoyed better health and spirits, than I have this summer.

My secretary and things have all arrived safe, except one box of clothing worth about fifty dollars or seventy-five dollars; I do not know where that is. The others came about a month since, and I am beginning to be nearly naked for the want of it.

We contemplate erecting another building, four stories high, one hundred by forty feet, with wings, together with a chapel, as soon as we can make the necessary arrangements, and until that is done I do not expect to have much peace or leisure, except what I shall find in a continuous round of duties. About fifty thousand dollars will be requisite to complete our plans, and Mr. S. is now away to make the arrangements for the capital necessary. This, of course, throws an additional burden upon us who remain. But my health is good; never better.

Yours truly,

J. B. TURNER

ILLINOIS COLLEGE, January 1, 1835

. . . The weather for a few days has been excessively cold, about twenty degrees below zero, and one morning thirty-two degrees below—several degrees colder than I ever knew it in New England. There has been scarcely any snow, and the grapes continue to hang in clusters on the vines in the trees. Mr. Post and I continue to visit them, for we have no other fruit except occasionally an apple.

We have more students than we can accommodate in this country of limited means. Not much time for mischief for me. Dr. Post's eyes have laid him by for some weeks; besides, I have been examining the students, judicially, for some mischief committed on Christmas eve. Have detected the rogues and made them confess; four confessed and promised, and two are dismissed.

Yours truly,

J. B. TURNER

Another trip with Indians pleased the Professor's love of adventure.

ILLINOIS COLLEGE, April 26, 1835

My Dear Girl:

The trustees appointed me to an agency in behalf of the college, and within the three past weeks I have traveled something like a thousand miles to the north, mainly through a wild, romantic, and savage region, where, among things interesting and amusing to me, I had the pleasure of an introduction to Black Hawk and his son, Keokuk, Stabbing Chief, and the other chiefs and braves of the Sioux and Fox Indians. I played checkers with Black Hawk, and beat him. He jumped up and said, " Ugh! ugh! " I traveled on the Upper Mississippi River with about eighty of the head chiefs and braves for several hundred miles; had quite an opportunity to become acquainted with their habits of thought and life. Their manner of treating their squaws is brutal, and they are still more savage and disgusting towards one another when in liquor. I am glad to be among civilized beings once more and in my own "lonely cell." Term has commenced. Messrs. Beecher, Post, and Sturtevant are still away, and, of course, I have had no rest since I returned. I expect Mr. Sturtevant to-day or to-morrow. I send you a map of the State inclosed, upon which they have put our main building. Mr. Beecher lives in one wing and Mr. Sturtevant in the other wing; a prick of the pen designates the room I occupy in the third story front, south end. Where they will put you and me is uncertain; probably we shall be obliged to go down into some of the log huts in the town until another building can be erected similar to this. In fact, Messrs. Beecher and Sturtevant lived in "sucker style" [log houses] for two or three years, while this college was building.

Yours truly,

J. B. TURNER

As the day set for the wedding approached, the time began to drag for Professor Turner, as the following letter shows:

ILLINOIS COLLEGE, August 29, 1835

. . . Excessive rains have engendered an unprecedented number of bilious affections. Messrs. Beecher and Post are away; Mr. Sturtevant has been on his back three weeks or more; Mr. Catlin, the general agent in money matters, was away at the same time; and Mr. Graves, the superintendent of the farm and shops, and Mrs. Hitchcock, the chief cook, are also sick. Mr. S. is recovering, and I am somewhat relieved. Glad, glad shall I be to see the end of this term! I expect now to start for New England, September 21.

CHAPTER V

The Wedding Journey

In September, 1835, Professor Turner, for the sake of taking a trunk with him, hired a man to drive him and two ladies to Chicago in a two-horse wagon, instead of going in the usual way, on horseback. From Chicago, with several others, he started, late one afternoon, in a stage-coach for Detroit, Michigan. As they neared Lake Calumet, south of Chicago, he noticed that the driver, a boy about seventeen years of age, who was to drive the coach to the next station, was crying. Upon inquiry, it was found that he was afraid to attempt the ford, on account of the dangerous quicksands in Lake Calumet. The party had been delayed in leaving Chicago, and it was now so late that he was afraid he would not be able to recognize the landmarks. He wanted to turn back, and start again in the morning. But the passengers were unwilling to lose any more time. They tried to encourage him, and insisted upon proceeding. In his nervous fear he did partly miss the ford, and two wheels of the coach went down in the quicksands. The men leaped out and kept the stage from overturning, while the driver unhitched the horses and brought them to the stage door on the upper side, in order to get the women passengers out and on to dry land. Of this journey Professor Turner afterward wrote:

We worked for hours, but the horses could not move the stage; then the driver said that about ten miles away a man lived who owned two yoke of oxen; he was despatched to bring them and their owner, the men meanwhile holding on to the stage-coach, standing waist-deep in water, to prevent it from overturning. Hour after hour passed, and not until four o'clock in the morning did the driver return with the farmer and his oxen; then soon we were on our way.

We selected this route because it would take us over the famous government road then being built from Detroit to Chicago, and we had had delightful visions of bowling along a smooth highway built by government money and government engineers. But, alas! instead of being honest corduroy, as required in the contract and advertised in glowing colors, each tree felled and laid side by side with its neighbor tree, at right angles to the right of way, and all spaces carefully filled with dirt, the whole one unbroken, smooth surface, the trees were felled helter-skelter and left just as they happened to fall, but all were covered with dirt and rounded up smooth and even before the inspector came. The first spring rains had washed away the earth. Naked trunks of trees, at all angles and of all sizes, stretched over the impassable morasses of Indiana. By September the whole route was strewn with broken vehicles, wagon wheels, and parts of stage-coaches. The men walked behind, carrying rails on their shoulders to pry out the wheels, when skilful driving could not prevent their slipping between the tree-trunks and they were in danger of being wrenched off.

At one point Professor Turner ventured to say that he could have walked all the way, without carrying a rail on his shoulder, or working hard at prying out wheels, or paying money for his passage. " Yes," replied the driver, " but you could not have carried your trunk."

The bride's home in Somers, Connecticut, surrounded by great elm trees, and with the distant hills beautiful in their brown and purple glory, was, on October 22, 1835, the scene of a happy yet tearful wedding. The bride, an only child by her mother's first marriage (her father had died of typhoid fever, when she was only six weeeks old, before his first wedding anniversary), had all her life been cherished by her mother and uncles and aunts, who had protected her from every disappointment, and made every place smooth that love could foresee. And now she was to go to the Western wilds, that mysterious realm full of dangers and hardships, Indians and cholera. Pre-nuptial festivities had been many—visits to friends and relatives far and near. The wedding over, the guests departed; but the bride could not. Typhoid fever claimed her, and for weeks she hovered between life and death. No word reached the friends at Illinois College, and their anxiety became great, as the following letter from Professor Truman M. Post,* Professor Turner's room-mate at the college, shows:

ILLINOIS COLLEGE, December 7, 1835

My dear Brother Turner:

I have just received your anxiously expected epistle; I assure you, my dear friend, you have, as you well know, my most anxious sympathies and my prayers, and gladly would I be beside you at this moment to share in your—what shall I say, joys or sorrows? God grant it may be the former. Long and anxiously have we looked for you. At every stage all hands, students, professors, and professors' families, have run to the doors and windows to greet you and Mrs. Turner on your arrival. We have sympathized much with your supposed detention by accident and weather, and lamented the disagreeable traveling, in consequence of storms and extreme winter weather, that would introduce Mrs. Turner to her future home. A day or two since by intelligence from Mr. Gallaudette † (letter dated November 13), it was reported that your wife was dangerously ill. Your letter dated the 9th states that your wife was a little better. We feel uncertain whether Mr. G's information was posterior to your letter; you can see that our anxiety is still intense.

And now, I know not what to say to you; I know not how this may find you. As I write I think perhaps this may find you broken and bending over a fresh grave. All I can say is that if it is joy, no heart will more cordially rejoice with you; if in sorrow,

---

* A few years later Professor Post became the pastor of the First Congregational Church in St. Louis, Missouri.

† The well-known Dr. Gallaudet, of Hartford, Connecticut, who did so much for the deaf.

none shall more deeply sorrow with you than my own. In any event, my friend, do not despair; do not give way to hopeless grief. Come back to us. None will receive you with warmer hearts; come back and let us comfort you—at least, let us try. But I stop; in any case, I know all words, the words of friendship even, are idle.

At the end of six weeks it was thought that the bride was strong enough to start on the journey to Illinois. The fall had been unusually mild, the winter delayed. It was hoped that, if they started immediately, they could reach Jacksonville before the rivers and mountains became impassable from ice and snow.

They reached Philadelphia safely by stage, but were detained there six weeks by a severe snow and ice storm that made it impossible to cross the mountains. Many restless storm-bound passengers were there to keep them company. At the end of the six weeks one stage-coach driver said he thought he could cross the mountains; another said if any one could he could; another and another said the same. So, one clear morning in the last of January, 1836, thirteeen coaches, full of passengers and trunks, started on the perilous trip. The mountains were covered with ice, the roadways narrow, and the turns many and sharp. The only way that the drivers could keep their coaches from slipping off at the turns was to whip up their horses and pass on the run.

Mrs. Turner, who was not yet strong, sat on her husband's lap, her eyes shut tight and her face buried in his neck, with his cloak covering her head, while he kept one hand on the door-handle, ready to attempt a leap for safety, should any accident befall. The passage was made in safety by all except the last coach. The driver of this, losing his nerve while making one of the sharp turns, failed to keep his horses on a run fast enough to prevent the coach from slipping off. The six horses all fell on one side of a large maple tree, and the stagecoach on the other,—thus breaking the fall for the passengers,—and then rolled backwards down the mountain-side. Every horse was killed; but only one man was injured, and he only had a broken collar-bone.

At Wheeling Professor and Mrs. Turner had to wait two weeks for a thaw before they could take a boat down the Ohio River. Then one captain announced that he was ready, and would bring the first boat into St. Louis, or " bust the b'ilers." Two boats started side by side through the floating ice-cakes, plowing their way with equal speed until they neared the mouth of the Ohio River. Rivalry and pride had been gradually encroaching upon prudence and judgment, until now both boats were being driven at full speed, the passengers taunting each other as first one, and then the other, gained upon its rival. Ham, pork, barrels of lard, and tar were fed into the red-hot furnaces. Suddenly there was an explosion, and the air was full of steam, smoke, shrieking passengers, and shattered limbs. When the smoke and steam had cleared away, a mass of wreckage and groaning people floated alongside the boat Professor and Mrs. Turner were on, instead of their rival boat. Their captain safely reached St. Louis first.

After a few days of waiting there they took a boat up the Mississippi and Illinois rivers to Naples, the metropolis of Central Illinois, and traveled from there to Jacksonville by wagon, over roads of bottomless mud—" because the soil was so rich and free from stones and rocks," as the enthusiastic bridegroom assured his travel-worn bride. Near the " Mound," four miles west of the town, they stopped for rest and repairs at a blacksmith's shop. Professor Turner asked for news— was any one sick or had any one died? No, said the smith; not that he knew of. Anxious to make a good impression on the bride, and under the circumstances a little on the defensive,—for a wagon ride in March over Morgan County roads has never been considered a practical way of favorably impressing strangers with the beauty of an Illinois landscape,— Professor Turner asked, " Did you ever see a country or a climate so healthful, so free from sickness and death, no consumption or typhoid fever, nothing to fear? " " No," replied the smith; " none o' them things, but everybody is shaking so hard with the durn ague, they can't find time to die, no matter how much they want to." The bride smiled, and the wagon drove on.

Mrs. Turner had spent much of her life in boarding-schools and in visiting relatives, and knew nothing of housekeeping. Her mother, an energetic woman of unusual executive ability, whose home cares never caused a ruffle, and with whom everything moved as smoothly as clockwork, was dimly conscious that her daughter ought to receive some instruction in this line, and had begged for one more year, now that she was out of school, that she might receive it. But the impatient bridegroom had grandly assured her that her daughter would never have to keep house. The professors of Illinois College, he explained, were given so much for salary, with board and rooms for themselves and families in the dormitory; a housekeeper was employed, and the professors' wives had the care only of their own rooms.

The following extract from a letter, dated July 1, 1836, written by Mrs. Turner to her aunt, Mrs. Sumner Root, in Connecticut, gives an idea of the impressions made upon her by her first few months in Illinois:

The very bones and sinew of old New England are coming over to the help of this new country. A new State is the place for enterprise. A Mr. Baldwin, a clergyman of this place, was traveling a few weeks since in the northern part of this State. He stopped for the night at a small settlement. Some of the people expressed a desire for an academy. He selected a spot of ground, and three weeks after, when he returned, they had commenced a building and had written for a teacher. From the window where I write (southeast window in the front room of the south wing of the dormitory) I can see at least one thousand acres of corn. I must tell Uncle Root some stories, and then I expect he will set fire to his old mountain farm and run to Illinois by the light of it. A Mr. Tillson, one of the trustees of this institution, came to this State some twelve or fifteen years since to explore the country, with little or no property. For six weeks he entered no house, and with the help of a flint he cooked his meals, spreading his table on the prairies. He had no bed but his buffalo robe and the heavens above for a covering. He is

now worth from two hundred thousand to half a million dollars.
The Governor of this State, Joseph Duncan, came to this place
six years since with fifty thousand dollars, which he had by his
wife, and is now worth as much as Mr. Tillson.

A lot of land which was bought a year since for one thousand
dollars sold six months after for five thousand dollars, and probably now could not be bought for twenty thousand dollars. I
could mention other similar incidents. Mrs. Tillson, wife of the
gentleman mentioned, in writing friends, wrote that her house
was so open she could throw a cat through in any direction
between the logs. The friends were quite dissatisfied, as he had
described it as the best house in the county. In his reply he
wrote that it was the best, for it was the only one. She now has
a good house.

In a letter to her mother on the same date, Mrs. Turner
wrote:

We are pleasantly situated and contented; indeed, we should
be very ungrateful to be otherwise, surrounded as we now are
with all the comforts of life. Yes, I may say with all that heart
can wish, with the exception of our own dear friends. I hope,
whenever you think of me, you think of me as contented and
happy, and not as a great way off, but only as a journey of two
weeks or a little more, with a husband willing I should visit you
whenever I please, which is half the battle. I expect in a few
years we shall be able to take breakfast here Monday morning
and tea with you Saturday evening.

This last sentence was quoted far and near among the relatives, and thought to be perfectly absurd: " Rhodolphia's
husband is such a visionary man."

In September a little son came to share their love and care.
For many years he was known to the friends of the family
as " Tiny," though he lived to be six feet and two inches in
height and to weigh over two hundred and fifty pounds. He
was named Rhodolphus, for his grandfather. Weary of the
inconveniences of a large boarding-house, Professor and Mrs.
Turner determined to try their fortune by themselves. They
moved first into the eastern half of Mr. Graves' home on

Grove Street (now the first house west of the Old People's Home), then to a little house on College Avenue, just west of where the Congregational Church now is. Here, in the sudden cold snap of 1836, the ducks were caught swimming on the pond in the front yard, and frozen fast in the ice. The Turners' last move was to their own home on College Hill, 1152 West College Avenue.

In 1837 the contracts were being drawn up that would bring carpenters and lumber across the Alleghanies, to build their house; but, before the contracts were signed or the plans perfected, an enterprising carpenter appeared and furnished everything.

Soon after they were settled in the new home, Professor Turner went out after breakfast, one morning, to look around. He did not return. The young wife thought he had gone directly to his classes; but when he did not come back for dinner, nor in the afternoon, she became alarmed and called the neighbors. The Professor could not be seen in any direction, though neither tree nor house hid the view over the wide prairie. But the prairie-grass grew very high to the west of the house, and here, after searching for some time, they found him, holding on in a death struggle to the sprouting horns of a young deer. When he had started out in the morning, he had come unexpectedly upon the young fellow, and had caught him by the horns, thinking he could easily manage him, and that his wife would be interested in seeing the beautiful young creature. But he was mistaken; for once, his athletic strength did not suffice. All day they struggled round and round in the tall grass, the deer getting more and more angry, until it became a question whose life should pay the forfeit. Not a tree or a fence near, too far away for his shouts to be heard, his only hope was to hold on until both should be exhausted or help should come. His friends arrived none too soon. The deer was taken to the house, but not in the beauty and graceful vigor of its young life. Professor Turner's bleeding hands bore witness to the contest.

And now let us draw a veil over the trials and tribulations of the inexperienced young couple. No competent domestic help was to be had for love or money. Not a garment of any description could be purchased for man, woman, or child; not a loaf of bread, not a biscuit or a cracker, not a particle of ready-made yeast, and not a cook-book in the land with any practical directions for preparing food. And no relative near to counsel or help.

Three little boys came before they had been married four years, the third before the two older could walk. But Mrs. Turner proved a most conscientious and devoted mother to the seven little ones that in time came to her arms, and she became a model housekeeper, whose bread was known to her many guests and relatives as most delicious; but this was not until many years had passed, and, as she often said, " tears enough to drown herself had been shed." Often had she seen her husband take a slice of bread and enthusiastically exclaim, " Why, Rhodolphia, how you have improved! This is the best you have made." And then, when it would not go down, he would slip it from his mouth under the edge of his plate, and when he left the table hide it in his hand until he could throw it out of sight in the yard when he thought she was not looking. The only good wheat bread they had for years was when their kind neighbor, Mrs. Graves, brought them a loaf. Many a time did the young housekeeper cry for joy over the gift, and then cry for shame because she could never return a like favor. Often sick and weary with the quickly multiplying cares of motherhood, she found too little strength left to learn the complicated details of housekeeping in a pioneer land.

CHAPTER VI

Illinois College in the '30's

Illinois College in the '30's consisted of one small brick building forty feet square—the north half of what is now called Beecher Hall. It contained a school-room furnished only with a teacher's desk and benches for the students—not a sign of a library or apparatus of any kind. A little to the east was a large dormitory, four stories high, with two wings, one on the north and one on the south. The south wing, which is now the college club-house, is all that is left of the dormitory, which was destroyed by fire in January, 1853. Southwest of the present Beecher Hall was the home of Mr. Graves, the superintendent of farming. Across Mound Avenue and a little farther west was the college barn, at that time believed to be the largest barn in the state of Illinois. East of the barn, at the west corner of Lincoln and Mound Avenues, a part of the building still standing was the cabinet-shop, presided over by Mr. Beal; for Illinois College was a manual training school as well as a college of literature and arts. Much of the furniture used in the college and in its vicinity was made here (Professor Turner had some pieces in his home) —excepting mahogany furniture, which was shipped from the East by way of New Orleans. After a few years the cabinet-shop was turned into a medical school, under charge of Dr. David Prince, a surgeon, and a philanthropist greatly beloved by the people of Jacksonville. At this time the college land, nearly half a mile square, extended from State Street on the north over the brook on the south, and from City Place on the west to Prospect Street on the east. It was nearly all one vast corn-field, worked by the students under the superintendency of Farmer Graves; but later the student labor was given up as unprofitable. The boys were not very fond of this part of the curriculum, and, at the first sound of the bell that ended the period at plow or harrow, would drop the reins and hasten back to the class-room, leaving the horses or oxen either to return to the barn or run away. It was finally decided that the damage to animals and implements far outweighed the profit to the students or the college.

It was customary for the professors, in vacation time, to ride over the prairies, visiting the cabins of pioneers in the timber along the streams, and trying to persuade the fathers and mothers to send their children to the college. Some of the settlers were eagerly waiting for this good news; but the professors sometimes were met with, " I never had any book-l'arnin', and they kin git along as well as I kin." In the '20's and '30's there was much antagonism to this " book-l'arnin'." Not until 1835, nearly twenty years after Illinois became a State, were the friends of Illinois College—by combining with the friends of McKendree at Lebanon, and Shurtleff at Alton, and the college at Jonesboro—able to influence their Representatives in the Legislature to secure a charter. The charter at Jonesboro was never used.

One day Professor Turner, before starting on one of these trips, hired a young horse of high life but bad reputation. He thought he could manage him, and after considerable trouble the horse was saddled and the Professor was on his back, bucking over the prairie. Suddenly the girths gave way, and saddle, saddle-bags, and Professor lay upon the ground. When he opened his eyes and saw the stars overhead and darkness all around, he wondered what it could mean. He tried to move, and then he remembered. In the distance a dim light shone from a settler's cabin. He crawled toward it on his hands and knees until he was near enough to make himself heard. Finally some of the occupants came out and found him, carried him in, and laid him on their only bed. They were very kind. They helped him to cut his veins for bleeding—which was then the universal remedy for every ailment—and nursed him for weeks; for he was very ill.

The settler's wife seemed to be distressed because he could not eat and one day she said: "You can't git strong without food. I will cook you anything. Can't you think of something that you would like—something your mother used to cook?"

Professor Turner, in telling about it afterward, used to say:

"After seeing the skillet, the one and only household utensil, do service for cooking the food, then as a dish-pan, and finally as a foot-tub, I had not much appetite; but, after much importuning, I said, 'I would like a piece of my mother's pumpkin pie'—thinking that it was the one thing that could not possibly be obtained.

"To my astonishment, she replied: 'You shall have it.'

"I had noticed crescent-shaped strips of something strung on a string and suspended from the top of the cabin, and had wondered what they could be; I had finally decided that they were intended to attract and furnish a roosting-place for the innumerable flies.

"The kind woman made her crust, covered the bottom of the skillet with it, and then climbed up and took down a number of these strips of pumpkin, black with dust, smoke, and flies. After washing them, she laid them closely side by side all over the crust, and baked it in the coals of the fireplace. What could I do? She was so sure she had something I would like! Nature came to my relief—the sight of it made me deathly sick. I told her I could not eat yet, to save it for her family; but she truthfully replied, 'Our men-folks don't like pumpkin pie.'"

Professor Turner was glad indeed when, presently, he was able to travel and return to his home in Jacksonville.

Prayers were held at Illinois College at six o'clock in the

morning, one hour later than had been the custom at Yale, and sometimes a recitation was held an hour before prayers.

Students came to the college from near and far, many of them walking across the prairies. In 1833, Joseph Trotter Mills, whose father had taken his slaves across the river into Ohio to free them, and for this was compelled to leave his home in Kentucky, walked from Bond County to Jacksonville to attend Illinois College, but he did not graduate. General Zachary Taylor sent to President Beecher for a tutor for his children, and Joseph Mills was recommended, and accepted the offer. On his way by boat to Fort Crawford at Prairie du Chien, Wisconsin, he passed a young couple in a boat coming down the river who seemed to be attracting the attention of travelers. Later he learned that it was Jefferson Davis eloping with the old General's daughter.

William G. Green and his brother, sons of a widow living in Menard County, Illinois, also walked to Illinois College, carrying their few books and clothes and luncheon. At noon they laid their burdens down and went in search of water; when they returned they found that the prairie-wolves had already enjoyed their luncheon.

At the end of the school year they walked home, and found that their mother had hired a tall, rawboned man to help in the harvest fields. His name was Abraham Lincoln. After supper he said, " Well, boys, what did you learn at college? Will you let me see your books? " They told him of their college life, and gave him their books. He selected the one on English grammar, and every night, for weeks, he studied it, sometimes asking questions, which they answered as well as they could—quoting as their authority Jonathan B. Turner, Professor of Belles Lettres, Latin, and Greek at Illinois College.

Professor Turner taught all the branches included in the curriculum, except chemistry, but his specialty was belles lettres, rhetoric, Latin, and Greek. He did double duty often-times, as all the professors did when one or more of their number were away on college work. In addition to teaching, the disciplining of the students was left to him.

The good old Bible doctrine, " Spare the rod and spoil the child," was still followed strictly. It is said that one teacher in the neighborhood of Jacksonville opened his school each morning, not by calling the roll, but by whipping every boy, big and little, in order to make him mindful of the duties of the day.

One student at Illinois College had given the faculty a great deal of trouble. He was incorrigible in mischief in school, as he was in fun and frolic out of school. The fact that he was the son of the Rev. Thomas Lippincott, one of the trustees of the college, and its devoted friend, made the situation embarrassing; but, when patience had ceased to be a virtue, Professor Turner was told to discipline the boy in any way he thought best, as long as he did it well.

The Professor took the boy up the four flights of stairs to the attic in the old dormitory, placed him, face down, upon a table, and tied his hands and feet to the four corners of the table. Then he took up a long blacksnake whip which he had provided for the occasion—laid it down, and took it up again. Finally, instead of thrashing the boy, he began to talk to him, telling him how hard it was to strike his noble father's son, as he had been directed to do, not only for the good of the school, but for his own good. The boy did not seem very deeply impressed. Laying the whip on the floor, in plain view, Professor Turner then said he would have to go away for a while, but would return soon.

All that day he left the boy stretched upon the table, with the whip in sight upon the floor. By the time he returned, late in the afternoon, the boy did not need to be punished further. He had pondered long and well upon the Professor's words, and, with the whip suggestively before him, had decided to promise to do better.

Years afterward, Professor Turner was invited to Chandlerville, Illinois, to officiate at the wedding of this same boy.* After the wedding dinner, the groom arose and told the

---

* Later the Hon. Charles E. Lippincott, a Civil War veteran, Auditor of the State of Illinois for two terms, and, at the time of his death, superintendent of the Soldiers' Home at Quincy.

guests why he had been determined to have Professor Turner at his wedding: " I knew he would start me on the right road in matrimony, for he guided me, years ago, into the right road of true manhood, when all others had failed." Then he related the story of the whipping, which by that time the Professor had forgotten.

Professor Turner's duties as disciplinarian did not seem to affect his standing with the students. For many years, until enfeebled by old age and blindness, he was the favorite toastmaster at their Sigma Pi and Phi Alpha reunions and banquets.

Judge T. J. C. Fagg, who was an Illinois College student in the '30's, was a devoted friend and admirer of Professor Turner, as well as a true friend of the college. After a visit to his alma mater in 1896, Judge Fagg wrote a letter from which the following paragraph is quoted:

LOUISIANA, MISSOURI, November 17, 1896

My dear Friend:

I have just returned from Jacksonville. I was sorry not to find you at home when I called. I wandered over to the college grounds, and located the spot at which the gate stood through which we drove up to the old college building on the third day of April, 1837. I found Albert Shaw of Marshall, Illinois, and Hendershott, on that chilly morning, engaged in setting out the trees that now stand between the old college site and the foundation of the new library building.

The trees planted that morning in 1837 form the beautiful grove in the southern part of the campus where the commencement exercises are now held every June. The gate referred to stood where the carriage road now enters the campus on College Avenue between Whipple Academy and the Gymnasium.

Besides his college duties, Professor Turner gave some attention to business matters, and found time to invest considerable money for his friends in the East. Among the men who trusted him with funds were Dr. Osgood, of Greenfield, Massachusetts, a boyhood and lifelong friend, with whom he always corresponded, and Dr. Gallaudet, of Hartford, Connecticut, who wrought such wonders in the instruction of the deaf and dumb. At one time he had an open account of thirty thousand dollars belonging to these men, and it was all repaid to the last cent.

Land speculation was as uncertain in that day as it is now, and Professor Turner's investments were not always successful. When the removal of the capital from Vandalia was first suggested, Governor Duncan bought a tract of land in the exact geographical center of the State, had it surveyed into town lots, with broad avenues and streets, and gave it the appropriate name of Illiopolis. Many of the Governor's friends bought these lots, believing the new town would become the capital of the State. But the enterprising citizens of Springfield were able to secure more votes for their little settlement, and the capital went to that city. Several years afterward, Professor Turner, while traveling in that part of the State, decided to stop and see if he could locate his corner lots. It was midwinter; the ground was covered with snow and landmarks were difficult to find. Finally, after much floundering about on horseback, he found his plot, and on it a wolf-trap that had captured a prairie wolf—the only living thing in that wilderness of snow. Illiopolis, however, is now a thriving town.

In 1837, when the presidential " bee " was buzzing in Daniel Webster's ears, he made a tour of the Western States, and stopped at Jacksonville to visit his friend, Governor Duncan. A platform was built around the trunk of a great elm tree in Duncan Grove, and trenches were dug and half filled with wood for the great barbecue feast of whole oxen to be roasted on the live coals.

The first thing on the program that day was the speech. President Beecher of Illinois College introduced the distinguished orator. Daniel Webster rose to his feet, and for a moment stood silent upon the platform; then haltingly he began to speak, clearing his throat, coughing, and hesitating. Finally he said, " Is there any water convenient? I am very thirsty." A friend in the audience, catching the cue, handed up a glass of pure alcohol, which the assembled multitude believed to be water. Webster drank it, and soon the lightning began to flash and the thunder to roll in the brilliant speech of the great American orator. The next morning he appeared at the college chapel to speak to the future fathers of our country, and, what was of more interest to him, the future voters. He began with some hesitation, and looked around helplessly. But this time there was no friend at hand with a glass of alcohol. He made a few commonplace remarks and sat down.

The students were surprised and not a little chagrined, believing that Webster was unwilling to waste his oratory on mere students. President Beecher followed with an appropriate address, occupying the rest of the time that it had been expected the great Webster would use. The students cheered their president, and later comments proved that they thought Daniel Webster a greatly overestimated man. He might be a great man in the East, but he could not compare in the West with their own beloved president.

Illinois College had received many gifts in land which had been added to the original fifty-one and one half acres bought of Judge Lockwood; but, at the same time, the college often needed money for current expenses. At one time the outlook was so promising and the gifts so generous that President Beecher frequently prayed, in faculty meeting, that the Lord would remove their worldly possessions (a prayer which the faculty, for a short time in later years, believed had been literally answered) if they were in danger of becoming proud-spirited and overbearing.

But in the panic of 1837 prices and values dropped, and the college was unable to meet expenses. After two years of teaching with no salary, Professor Turner accepted college lots at the " boom " price set before the panic, and for the remainder of his life lived upon the beautiful seventeen and one half acres on College Hill.

CHAPTER VII

The Slavery Question at Illinois College

Jacksonville was the Mecca of all the early emigrants to Illinois, the one garden spot in the prairie State, before Springfield was dreamed of as its capital, or Chicago, now the metropolis of the Middle West, was thought of. The graceful and easy Southerner and the energetic Yankee came by river and stage-coach, ox-teams, or with horses, ambitious for greater opportunities of personal gain or greater service to their Master and mankind. They formed two distinct elements of opposition and antagonism in the early years of the little village, but later became one united whole of grace and energy when the question of slavery had passed away and the younger generation had joined hearts and hands.

In those early years the intensity of opposition was increased when home friends and relatives came to visit in the village, bringing with them their slaves as nurse-girls, waiting-maids, and men-servants. The question of slavery in the Northwest Territory was fought over again with tongue and pen. Neighbor was divided against neighbor, friend against friend, even parents against children and children against parents; and when it was rumored that a man slave had been whipped to death in a house on West State Street, just west of Grace Methodist Church, because he attempted to run away, and when Mr. Samuel Willard and others had been caught helping a Negro girl on her way to Canada by the underground railroad, excitement was at fever heat. Although Professor Turner was a member of the underground railroad, he was never very zealous in its work, believing that the true and only successful way to attack the curse of slavery was by openly fighting with tongue and pen for the enforcement of the laws upon the statutes of the State and the enactment of new laws, if necessary—rather than by individual effort in helping a few poor creatures to Canada. Yet he never refused his personal aid when called upon.

One experience of his own Professor Turner describes in " Historic Morgan ":

One bitter cold night in December, the fall after we so nobly welcomed the Portuguese to our city, Mr. Henry Irving, who was one of the bravest of men connected with the Underground Railroad, came to me while in my barn feeding my horse, and said that there were three colored women, who had escaped from the St. Louis slave market, concealed in an old abandoned cabin southwest of " Negro Town " in the fields. If left there, they would freeze to death or be captured, as their pursuers and our police were close after them. He wished me to go to their rescue, while he returned to the city to watch the police. What could I do? But one thing was possible. I at once cut me a heavy hickory bludgeon from the wood-pile, which I could then wield far more fearlessly and unscrupulously than now, hid it under my camlet cloak, and proceeded to the rescue. Arriving at the cabin door, I rapped. No one stirred. I repeated my raps, but all was still, and I supposed they had been captured or had fled in fear. I bethought me to say, " I am your friend." At once there was a slight rustle, and soon the crack of the door was cautiously opened. I quickly reassured them, and three trembling, frozen, and half-dead women stood around me—all, as I afterwards learned, regular members of the orthodox Methodist Church in St. Louis, who had been out of doors for a week, trying to escape from a sale down South, away from all their families and friends, which they deemed in those days worse than death. Seeing the lanterns of the police glancing about " Negro Town," as we called it, I told them to follow me one after the other, within sight of each other, as I led them out of the bright starlight under the shadows of the trees and fences, and, if anything happened to me or to them, to scatter and hide in the corn-fields. By this time my blood was up. I was ready for business, and determined to defend my charges at all hazards. But it soon occurred to me I had got " an elephant on my hands," and that it would be impossible to conceal them at my house, or in that of any known anti-slavery man.

Dr. Pierson then lived on the Post place, one mile or more west of town.* He was an elder in the Presbyterian Church, a good Christian man, but regarded as pro-slavery in his sympathies. I resolved to take them to him; for I thought I knew the bottom of the old man's heart better than he did himself. So I proceeded to pilot them to the gate that led to his house, and waited for them to come up. Only two of the three came. I supposed the last one had been nabbed, or from her excessively frozen feet had missed her way. I therefore hid the two in the shelter of a fence and brush, and ran back at full speed for the third. I found she could not keep in sight of the others from excessive lameness— her feet were cut and bruised by the ice and snow. I then took them up to Dr. Pierson's door, rapped, and called for the doctor, and said to him, " Here we all are, Doctor. I found these strangers so and so. You know I cannot protect them. I have brought them to you. You must either protect or betray us." " Come in, come in, Mr. Turner. We won't betray you. We will do the best we can for them. Wife, these people need some hot coffee and something to eat." On went the tea-kettle, open flew the larder, as if the king himself had knocked at the door—as, indeed, he had. The Lord's children got their supper, and left the devil outdoors to feed on creeds, orthodoxies, conservatisms, and wind, to his heart's content.

They were kept in Dr. Pierson's barn for two weeks; then a man took my horses and sleigh and carried them off towards the Canada line. I heard they got through safely. The first of January, after this, we had one of our old-fashioned annual union dress-parade prayer meetings in the basement of the same church in which we had before welcomed the Portuguese. In these meetings all the sects united, except the Campbellites, who had not then got fully on their orthodox pinafores. For then, as now, no faith was deemed orthodox that had not been salted down long enough

---

* Now Fair View, Dr. Pitner's home.

to begin to petrify and turn to stone. Any true description of those union prayer meetings would now be resented as a caricature. On this occasion a most excellent Christian man, now in heaven, but then too orthodox for either heaven or earth, quoted freely from an Assembly's catechism to show the exceeding danger and peril of all heretics, and especially of all Unitarians, or men so inclined. I stood the first round very comfortably in silence. But when he again renewed the assault, so vigorously that all eyes were turned over to my corner, I could not resist the temptation to reply. I quoted from Christ's creed instead of the church creeds; narrated my experience in detail as given above, in an effort to conform to Christ's creed, only taking care to implicate no one in it but myself; commended them for their noble reception of the Portuguese in that church but little before, who had been deprived by the tyranny of the Catholics of the privilege of reading only one book, the Bible. But here were American-born citizens, orthodox church members, whom the tyranny of our laws and votes and churches had deprived of the privilege of reading all books whatever, from God or man, and had sealed their immortal souls in total midnight darkness, denying them the right to their own wages, husbands, and children—nay, to their own souls and bodies; and when, about to be sold from all these, fleeing from lusts more dreadful to them than death, with frozen feet and starved bodies, they appealed to me for aid, I was compelled to skulk away, through the darkness of midnight, from all our courthouses and officers, our churches and creeds and orthodoxies, as though I was a whipped dog, or was perpetrating some infamous crime. "We have had enough of creeds that were never anything but the bastard and leprous progeny of the old Papists and despots of Europe. Let us Americans return to the creed of Him who alone is the son of man, son of God, and Saviour of the world, and alone competent to give us a creed." Of course, I do not remember the exact words of this little speech, but its spirit I can never forget; for at that time I felt that more fines than all my property was then worth, and a possible term in the State's prison, in which my old and much-beloved class-mate Torrey * gloriously died, hung on every word of its utterance. The next morning the town was astir. Esquire Smith, a

---

* Charles Turner Torrey, an author and zealous anti-slavery reformer, was arrested for aiding fugitive slaves to escape and imprisoned in Baltimore, Maryland, where he died in prison May 9, 1846.

Southern man, one of our grandest old men and a leading lawyer, was at the prayer meeting and heard all that was said. The proslavery party naturally went to him to get out writs for me, on my own confession. He said to them: " You go home and keep quiet. The less you have to say about that meeting, the better it will be for you and for us all."

In 1843 and 1844 Professor Turner was editor of the Illinois *Statesman*, a local paper. Elijah Lovejoy's paper in Alton was the first anti-slavery paper published in Illinois, and Professor Turner's was the second. In its columns appeared the first notice of a Negro wedding. No advertisement of runaway slaves was ever permitted in its columns, and so boldly was slavery denounced that Professor Turner's neighbor and friend, Dr. Samuel Adams, and sometimes others, followed him as he went to and from his office at night, for fear that he would be assassinated. A few extracts from letters are of interest in this connection.

Albert Hale of Springfield, while deeply deploring his friend's scathing language as un-Christian, wrote:

In the meantime, be assured that, in reference to the opinions maintained in the *Statesman*, I do not hesitate to say that I know of no Western political paper teaching as much truth with as little error. So far, then, as its doctrines are concerned, my estimate of the *Statesman* is high enough.

Silas Reed wrote:

Dear Sir:
I had intended to do myself the pleasure of calling on you and thanking you in person—but was prevented—for the manly, impartial manner in which you have rebuked the unjust revilers of President Tyler on several occasions in your paper, and to express the gratification derived from the perusal of your pamphlet on the subject of currency, also addressed to Mr. Tyler.

Edward R. Tyler, a publisher in New Haven, Connecticut, wrote:

Rev. and dear Sir:

I want to say how grateful I feel to you for the reading of the *Statesman*, a paper which excels all others with which I am acquainted for sound statesmanlike views of the public interest, for honest, untrammeled independence. Can it be that party vehemence will prevent a just appreciation of such a valuable journal and its wide circulation among the best population of your State? I hope not.

In a letter addressed to a friend in New York, dated June 7, 1836, Professor Turner's brother Asa, a trustee of Illinois College, wrote from Quincy, Illinois:

Dr. Nelson has been driven here by a mob; excitement very great. Cause, holiness in the form of Presbyterianism and abolition. Mobs are threatened here. What will be the end I know not.

In 1842 the following letter was received by Professor Turner, warning him of his threatened assassination on account of his opposition to slavery:

LOUISVILLE, KENTUCKY
September 10, 1842

J. B. TURNER, Esq.

Sir:

Although a stranger to you personally, I am well acquainted with your character as professor and as a writer against the Mormons. I feel interested in you for these accounts as well as from the precepts of religion, and we are told that we should do to others as we should like them to do for us, and now, sir, for the matter in view.

I have just returned from Missouri, where I was looked upon as a slaveholder, being from Kentucky. I am not a slaveholder, however. I had the entire confidence of some whose names I am in honor bound not to name. But it is sufficient for me to warn you against the evil that hangs over your head and the heads of others; a hint to the wise should be sufficient. Be assured, then, the evil is determined against you, through an association of slaveholders in Missouri, and that the destruction of your college, the kidnapping of yourself and some others will be attempted;

that, if that fails, a little poison, or a hemp cord on your neck, or a messenger of lead, or a bowie-knife will be certain in their time.

It is whispered that Governor T. Carlin is a hypocrite and connives at abolitionism, and might as well have a ball through him; they have determined the secret death of every abolitionist they can find. You may see that, should I give my name and it be found out, I would lose my life by it; but you may depend on the truth of the above.

Hoping this may reach you in time, I am,

Yours, etc.,

FRIEND

P. S. The Quincy Institute is under the same threats as yours. Dr. Nelson is aware, I suppose, that his life is not safe. As to Carlin, I think they are mistaken about him; for, from what I can learn, he is in favor of slavery; but he is rather two-faced.

The writing in this letter, when compared with the writing in letters from Cassius M. Clay, with whom Professor Turner corresponded in later years, is easily identified.

In 1845 Mr. Cassius M. Clay was threatened by a mob in Lexington, Kentucky. His printing-press and office were destroyed. His wife defended him and her home so courageously and so well that she was able to parley with the mob until her husband had escaped through a back door. The papers in the North were filled with the account. Professor Turner so admired her womanly devotion, good judgment, and courage that he wrote Mr. Clay, and received permission to name his only daughter Mary, in honor of Mrs. Clay.

CHAPTER VIII

The Close of College Life

Ecclesiastical and political disturbances grew more and more intense at Illinois College. Students from the South, Mississippi, Alabama, and all the States between gave a decided pro-slavery tone to the student life, and the wealth and social activity of the village was led by the Southern element. But the New England element was true to its Pilgrim ancestry and the great work to which the " Yale Band " had consecrated themselves; and, while not wealthy, they were really the aristocracy of the place.

Commencement was the great event of the year at Jacksonville. Friends and strangers came from far and near, by stage and private teams, and Professor Turner's little home was full to overflowing. Father, mother, and babies were glad to find a resting-place on the floor, while guests filled every bedroom.

Illinois College was poor, and the trustees and faculty were afraid of offending its Southern patrons. But fear and poverty could not silence the tongues of President Beecher and Professor Turner. In 1844 President Beecher resigned. He had gone East to raise funds for the college; a letter followed him to Boston, telling him he need not return. It was a great sorrow to his friend. Their recreation hours had been spent together. Their gardens adjoined, being separated by a Virginia rail fence. Often they were seen leaning on their hoes, earnestly talking, forgetful of their work and the dinner hour, and unmindful of the housekeepers' voices reminding them that it was time the vegetables were cooking. Frequently they would lean on the fence, President Beecher with a jack-knife in his hand, whittling. At one time—so the story is told— about the time of the Lovejoy excitement, he whittled away so furiously that the top rail fell apart, cut entirely in two before either had noticed the progress of the knife.

Professor Turner had been admitted to the ministry after coming West, and for several years had charge of the Congregational churches in Waverly and Chandlerville. But he was not in sympathy with the theology of that day, especially the doctrine of election and predestination.

In 1844 the Synod of Illinois ordered an investigation into the religious teachings and influences at Illinois College, which was under the Presbyterian denomination. The trustees and faculty thought this was due to Professor Turner's peculiar views. Dr. Samuel Adams and Professor Turner, neighbors and friends as well as professors in the same college, were called upon to state their views, as were all the members of the faculty. Dr. Adams, a noble, generous-hearted man and an able and successful teacher, was greatly beloved by his students in as well as out of the class-room. A teacher of science, he had also the true love and appreciation of all that was beautiful in poetry, art, and general literature. Naturally orthodox and deeply religious, he was not in sympathy with his friend's radical views. He stated his own beliefs in writing, clearly, concisely, and reverently. They were perfectly satisfactory to the committee and to the public. Not so with Professor Turner. His statement was more lengthy, but not so satisfactory. However, this was smoothed over. But Professor Turner's anti-slavery principles, together with his advanced religious views, continued to make the relations with the college unpleasant, and in 1848, he resigned—" more feeble and broken in health," as he afterward wrote to his daughter, " at forty-five than I now am at ninety-one years of age."

Just at the time in a man's life when he most enjoys being

a leader among men, and having his opinions respected and his actions approved, Professor Turner left his chosen field of labor. A few friends remained staunch and true, but the majority of his co-workers and acquaintances heaved a sigh of relief over his departure in July, 1848.

Worn with anxiety and strife, in debt, with a wife and five little children, no capital for new ventures, and no heart for the old pursuit, it was as balm to his wounded spirit when he received the following petition:

COLLEGE HILL, January 10, 1850

We, the undersigned persons, respectfully request Professor Turner to commence a Bible class at the Congregational Church, and will agree to attend.

It was signed by many of the students of Illinois College. This petition was continued each year for several years, with the addition of new names, in spite of the frowns and opposition of the so-called orthodox class. From a letter written in 1906 by the Rev. O. C. Dickerson, pastor of the Earlville Congregational Church, is taken the following extract:

In the old Congregational Church on the east side of the Square, Professor Turner held a Bible class. One Sunday morning, as I was passing, I remembered this class, and went in. I slipped in at the end of a seat, and so became a member. It was principally composed of Illinois College students; yet some months later I brought in, and added to my beloved teacher's responsibilities, twelve young men from about town. I was a blacksmith apprentice. The Professor always expressed himself very strongly upon topics that moved him profoundly. It was through him, in a prayer-meeting talk, that I first heard about the Fugitive-Slave law. I caught the latter sentences only of this talk: " We are told this institution of which we are all to become defenders is authorized by the Bible. Well, if this is the Bible, I say, take away the Bible. We do not want it. Give us the Book of Mormons, the Koran, the Hindoo Shasters. Anything is better. But, thank God, this infamy is not from the Bible. ' Whom the Son maketh free is free indeed.' " Once, in a class, he had occasion to denounce fore-ordination, which he characterized as omnipotence, " chaining men down by decree, and then damning them for not being free." " I tell you," he said, " nothing could equal my utter detestation of such a God as that; but, thank Heaven, such is not the God of the Bible!" One can easily see how any controversialist opposed, by emphasizing the beginning and forgetting the close of his denunciatory sentences, could bring out a form of error of which the great heart of our departed thinker was wholly innocent. I have, through all my gospel preaching of fifty-three years, held and defended the great doctrine of the evangelical system of the strictest sort, an orthodox Congregationalist. It would be no easy thing to make me believe my spiritual father, J. B. Turner, had one fiber in his great heart that was not loyal to the blessed Christ and the kingdom of God.

For a time after he resigned the chair of belles lettres and literature, Professor Turner thought of studying medicine, as he had a remarkable talent for caring for the sick, and in cases of great emergency and distress was often sent for by friends far and near. Finally, however, he decided upon horticulture and Osage orange culture. He laid out the home place in hedge fields, vegetable and flower gardens, and orchards. A grass walk four feet wide extended from the house on College Avenue straight north to State Street. On either side were flower-beds of the same width, filled with every variety and color of crocus, tulips, hyacinths, crown imperials, jonquils, daffodils, and narcissus. Back of these were roses, spiræas, and all kinds of shrubs; then, farther east and west, were the apple, peach, pear, and small-fruit orchards, and the vineyards. On the land where now stands the beautiful residence of Colonel John Robertson was a melon-patch, which was the delight of the children in the neighborhood, and the scene of many an escapade when Professor Turner's older sons lay in ambush at night, with guns loaded with salt, to fire at the legs of trespassers. To the west, part of what is now included in the front yard of the State School for the Deaf, were the Osage orange hedge fields. The small plants with their glossy leaves, in rows as straight as a line, running the full length of the fields, were a pleasing sight, and they furnished work for many a boy with a three-cornered hoe in the summer, and in winter in counting the plants stored in the barn cellar. The beginning of more than one honored career was laid in the hedge-rows, and in the cellar of the old plant-house, of Professor Turner.

Professor Turner was the originator of the Turner red raspberry, which is still the standard raspberry in other countries as well as in the United States. He planted every tree that would grow in this climate. In 1862 he had a greater variety than could be found in the Smithsonian Gardens at Washington. Evergreen seeds were sent to him from the Sierra Madre and Sierra Nevada, from the Rocky and White Mountains, the Himalayas, and from the cedars of Lebanon in Palestine.

CHAPTER IX

The Osage Orange

" What can public schools do for families so widely scattered? " was the query that was ever ringing in Professor Turner's ears as he rode over the great, uncultivated prairies, with not a wagon or bridle-path to mark the way, not a bridge over creek or river. " How can they be peopled—how can they be cultivated? " There was not enough timber to build fences, no way of protecting crops or corralling stock. What could be done to tempt the pioneer from his home in the East to settle upon the fertile lands in the West? The first problem was to get something for fences. It must be " horse-high, bull-strong, and pig-tight "; it must be grown from the soil, for Illinois must furnish not only crops, but the material to protect her crops. He experimented with barberry, box, hawthorn, and many other plants, even sending to England and other countries for varieties—a proceeding attended with no little expense. But not one of these would answer.

In the summer of 1835 Professor Turner attended a camp-meeting at Pisgah, on Charles Drury's farm, where the first log church of Pisgah was built. Logs had been cut for benches, and a rude platform built for the speakers. The preacher, a man from New York, dressed in the clerical style of the time, broadcloth coat, white tie, and high silk hat, precise and formal, was addressing the people, but did not seem to interest them. The young people were wandering through the woods, picking blackberries, while the older men stayed in the background, discussing the questions of the day. Late in the afternoon, a man walked up the grassy aisle. His clothes were dusty and worn and his whole appearance so unkempt that Professor Turner put out his hand to stop him, thinking he must be some wayfarer who did not know what he was doing. To his surprise, the preacher stopped speaking and came forward to greet the newcomer. It proved to be the Rev. Dr. David Nelson,* who had for his circuit Illinois, Kentucky, Tennessee, Arkansas, and Missouri. No wonder that his clothes were dusty and worn, and that he wore one shoe and one boot, both of which had holes in them. He began to address the camp-meeting. Soon they gathered round until there was not one vacant seat, and for three hours he held this great audience.

After the meeting, Professor Turner, in talking with him, told him of his experiments in trying to find some plant that would make good fences, and asked him if he had seen anything, on his journeyings, that could be grown into a hedge. Dr. Nelson replied that he had seen a thorny plant growing on the banks of the Osage River in Arkansas, and that he would bring some of the seed when he came again. Professor Turner said afterward:

He gave such an interesting account of this plant that I immediately determined to send for it. I wrote to every one in the Southwest I heard of that would be likely to give me any information about it; but, as the Doctor had failed to give me the name *bois d'arc*, by which it was known farther West, these inquiries were pushed for years without any satisfactory results. Finally an answer came from a correspondent, who sent me a few plants, which I put out, and found to grow well.

I now turned my attention to propagating from them, with pretty good success; but with a new supply of plants came a few seeds taken from the orange ball. The planting of these showed

---

* Rev. David Nelson afterward had an Institute at Marion, Missouri, from which he had to flee on account of his anti-slavery sympathies, pursued by an angry mob. Later he had an institute at Quincy, Illinois, of which General O. O. Howard wrote such interesting reminiscences.

that from the seed it could be propagated with great ease and facility. I procured a quantity of seed, but the first proved worthless. The second time, however, I was more fortunate, and succeeded in growing some plants. Experience soon convinced me that the object of my search was found at last. But the preparation of the soil, the planting of the seed at what time and depth, how to cultivate the plants and how to take them from the ground, how to keep them from the frost until spring, all had to be learned by years of experiment and study. The return for all this was usually the incredulous laugh of the passer-by. Even the Osage orange, for the first year or two, had the pretty appellation of " Professor Turner's Folly."

The cultivation by hand was too slow and expensive. The cost of raising prohibited their general use; so I invented and patented a cultivator to grind the dirt very fine by means of circular disks; also a drill and a planter to plant the Osage orange seed; and a corn-planter and wheat-drill where the driver could ride as well as drive.

In 1847 I issued my first circular to the people, offering the Osage orange plants for sale. In describing the plants the circular stated:

" It is a native of Arkansas and Texas, and will grow on any soil where common prairie-grass will grow. Overflowing the land does not harm it. It will live for weeks, even months, entirely under water. It endures all climates, from Boston to New Orleans, perfectly well. Prairie fires will not destroy it or often injure it. It is armed with a very stout thorn under every leaf. Its dense iron branches soon become so interlocked that no domestic animal, not even a common bird, can pass through it. Both its thorns and its bitter acrid juice prevent all animals and insects from browsing or feeding on its branches. Its seed is like the orange seed and its root like the hickory. Consequently it can never spread into the field. One hedge around a farm secures orchards, fruit-yards, stables, sheepfolds, and pasture-grounds from all thieves, rogues, dogs, wolves, etc. One good gate, well locked, makes the whole farm secure against all intruders. It may be trained so high as to afford shelter to stock and break the rough prairie winds."

Dr. H. W. Milligan, in an address upon " Scholarly Horizons," delivered before the senior class of Illinois College, December 19, 1898, said:

We know a college professor who devoted himself to fencing prairies, and who made the *Maclura aurantiaca* (Osage orange) known in two hemispheres. In the Mississippi Valley he made forty-acre and quarter-section farms possible, where otherwise there would have been broad plantations, or still larger baronial estates.

And so the State of Illinois and all the neighboring States were divided into fields by fences of living green. Farms were inclosed, the prairies cultivated, schools organized, and the future of Illinois as one of the great educational States of the Union was assured. For many years Professor Turner kept a man in the South to gather Osage orange balls and prepare the seed. In 1861 he wrote to Washington, D. C., to ask if he could continue that part of his business and not be considered disloyal to the government. The officials replied that he could so continue, but that it would have to be at his own risk; the government would not be responsible for any loss. The demand for hedges increased rather than diminished during the dark days of the Civil War. Plants sold for ten dollars a thousand. But the risk and difficulty of getting the seed from Arkansas increased, and finally the agent wrote that he could not remain there; the fact of his having business relations with the North endangered his life.

One day, at the close of business hours, this man left everything as usual, collecting nothing, taking nothing, and started in a southerly direction, not daring to go directly north. The second night out, he stopped at a little hotel, paid in advance for his night's lodging, saying that he wished to start early in the morning and would not wait for breakfast. When he went to his room, he found two other beds in it. He rather demurred, but the landlord told him that it was the best he could do. About midnight three men came and occupied the beds. At daylight he awoke and started on his way his three roommates had already gone. As he passed the outskirts of the village, he saw the bodies of those three men swinging from the limb of a tree. With great fear he continued on his way, traveling only at night, and finally reached Jacksonville, glad to escape with his life.

Professor Turner wrote a great deal for agricultural papers, and he now urged the farmers to let Osage trees grow in their hedges, twenty-five feet apart, and to bring their oranges to him—that he would pay a good price for them. This they did, Professor Turner often paying as high as from three to five dollars a bushel for oranges, and the problem of getting Osage seed for hedges was again solved.

CHAPTER X

Early Work for Education in Illinois

Even before Illinois became a State, it was planning for its future needs in the way of education. An ordinance by the general government of 1785 had granted that one section in each township in the Northwest Territory should be designated as "school land," and the proceeds of the sale of this land should go to the support of public schools. Later, by the acts of Congress of 1804 and 1818, other government lands, within the Territory of Illinois, were granted for the endowment and support of a seminary, college, or university; this was usually called the "Seminary Fund."

Professor Turner early became identified with the educational movement which later developed into public schools by taxation and State universities, as will be seen by the following extract from letters to Miss Kibbe, his future wife:

ILLINOIS COLLEGE, November 12, 1834

My dear Girl:

Soon after writing my last, I determined to spend the vacation in looking into the state of common schools in Illinois. I have been absent about seven weeks, have passed through some dozen or fifteen counties, and delivered public addresses in all the county-seats and principal villages.

The result is that in all the counties I have visited, and many others to which I have written, they have resolved to call county meetings and elect delegates to the State convention to be held at Vandalia next December to discuss the subject of common schools, and lay the subject before the people and the Legislature. My success has been better than I expected, and I hope great good will result.

Yours truly,

J. B. TURNER

ILLINOIS COLLEGE, January 1, 1835

Dear Girl:

As to common schools, things are going on well. The convention met, as proposed, at Vandalia. I was appointed a member from Morgan County, but could not attend. Therefore I cannot give you all the particulars at present. In general, however, they presented a memorial to the Legislature, which is now under consideration by that body, and also an address to the people, now in press; and the friends of education believe that it will at last result in a good system of common schools established by law throughout the State—which is undoubtedly at present a great desideratum.

Yours truly,

J. B. TURNER

On November 13, 1834, Professor Turner delivered an address in Springfield, Illinois, on the subject of " Common Schools." During the summer he had traveled about five hundred miles through the central part of the State, lecturing on the same subject. He gave a clear and concise account of the common schools in the United States, dividing them into two groups, " poor schools " and " free schools," proving the justice of the classification by quoting statistics and by what he had learned during his trip over the State the previous summer. He explained the necessity for good schools in Illinois, and suggested ways in which they could be secured. In the following extract from another lecture, on " The American System of Education as Regards Its Application to Illinois," delivered in September, 1837, it may be seen that already the plan of concentration and coöperation was in his mind. He said:

While others are still contesting the boundaries of human freedom and adjusting the restraints of human depravity, we would give unlimited scope to the one by exterminating the other from the face of the earth. With these ends in view, it devolves on us to augment the facilities, the resources, and the completion of knowledge, until a royal road shall be paved from the threshold of every cabin in the land to the open doors and waiting honors of our most magnificent temples of science. If by council, concert, and coöperation we concentrate our energies and husband our resources to the utmost, who can overestimate the final results? But if we fling the experience of the past and the advantages of the present to the winds, and each for himself rushes on in his own solitary career of experiment and effort,—beleaguering and jading the public mind and exhausting the public resources with our own isolated and selfish schemes,—what a fearful retribution awaits both us and those who are to come after us!

In 1840 Mr. John S. Wright of Chicago, editor of an agricultural paper that later developed into the *Prairie Farmer*, advocated a normal school. In 1843 the Legislature of Illinois passed the following legislation concerning the handling of money received by the State from its sale of government lands:

An act to provide for the receipt of the distributive share of this State of the proceeds of the sale of the public lands.

Sec. 1. *Be it enacted by the People of the State of Illinois, represented in the General Assembly,* That the Governor of this State be, and he is hereby authorized and empowered, by himself, or by his accredited agent, to receive from the treasury of the United States any and all sum or sums of money now due, or which may become due, to this State under the provisions of an act of the Congress of the United States of America, entitled "An act to appropriate the proceeds of the sales of the public lands, and to grant preëmption rights," approved September fourth, one thousand eight hundred and forty-one, and to execute any needful and proper voucher therefor.

Approved, February 21st, 1843.

In 1844 an educational convention was held in Peoria, when the subject of greatest interest under discussion was the support of public schools by taxation. In 1846 another educational convention was held in Chicago, where the first Teachers' Institute was organized. It still continues, under the name of the Illinois Teachers Association, and is attended by its members from all over the State—university and college presidents and professors, as well as teachers in the public schools—during the holidays each year, to discuss subjects and questions of interest to students and teachers.

During these years Professor Turner took an active part in these meetings, and corresponded with many prominent educators in various parts of the United States, among the number being Henry L. Tappan of Norfolk, Virginia, later President of the University of Michigan, and John Blatchford of Chicago. An extract from a letter to Professor Turner from Jonathan Blanchard, President of Knox College, Galesburg, Illinois, illustrates how the minds of these men were already turned toward industrial education:

KNOX COLLEGE, Galesburg, Illinois, October 19, 1848

Dear Brother:

I am just returning from the East, and find your letter with others awaiting my return. I saw nothing of Mr. Kingsbury. I wish you would advise him to come here and see us. I cordially wish he would endow a Professorship of Agriculture, Horticulture, and Pomology for you here, or at least pay you for a course of lectures. I pine for a professorship of the blessed green earth. If I could get the endowment I would move the Legislature to adopt it as a State agricultural foundation, though it would raise a tumult of sect if I should move them for funds.

Very truly, yours in Christ,

J. BLANCHARD

CHAPTER XI

Griggsville, May 13, 1850
"A State University for the Industrial Classes"

In 1850 Professor Turner had been at work for nearly twenty years promoting the cause of general education in Illinois, observing the especial needs of the State, and considering how they could best be filled. On May 13 of that year he formulated his idea in an address entitled "A Plan for a State University for the Industrial Classes," which he gave, as president of the Illinois Teachers Institute, at the annual meeting of that body in Griggsville, Illinois. In this address he proposed not only the foundation of a State university for the agricultural and general industrial classes in Illinois, but a system in all the States of the Union. A few years later, in delivering an address at the dedication of a new high school building at Griggsville, he spoke of this first public announcement of his idea as follows:

Citizens of Griggsville: Some here will recollect that a few years ago I delivered an address to you in this place, the first that I ever did deliver on industrial education. For several years the advocates of that scheme were branded in the public print with all sorts of opprobrious epithets by the long-eared guardians of our faith, our morals, and our civilization. We were denounced as ruthless and visionary agitators and outlaws. The bill for richly and appropriately endowing such institutions, involving the expenditure of millions of money, is now favorably and hopefully before Congress, and great sovereign States are disputing, through the press, about the honor of having originated the scheme. It is my own firm belief that *you* are the first people in the Union, and the first in the civilized world, that ever gave to that scheme a warm, earnest, and decided support. Certainly, the reception you gave it led me first to regard it as practically hopeful as well as truly needful.

This speech,* which gave the first impetus to the movement that established the great State land-grant universities of this country, was as follows:

All civilized society is, necessarily, divided into two distinct coöperative, not antagonistic, classes: a small class, whose proper business it is to teach the true principles of religion, law, medicine, science, art, and literature; and a much larger class, who are engaged in some form of labor in agriculture, commerce, and the arts. For the sake of convenience, we will designate the former the *professional*, and the latter the *industrial* class; not implying that each may not be equally industrious, the one in their intellectual, the other in their industrial pursuits. Probably in no case would society ever need more than five men out of one hundred in the professional class, leaving ninety-five in every hundred in the industrial; and, so long as so many of our ordinary teachers and public men are taken from the industrial class, as there are at present, and probably will be for generations to come, we do not really need over one professional man for every hundred, leaving ninety-nine in the industrial class.

The vast difference, in the practical means, of an *appropriate liberal education*, suited to their wants and their destiny, which these two classes enjoy, and ever have enjoyed the world over, must have arrested the attention of every thinking man. True, the same general abstract science exists in the world for both

* Editor's note: The speech quoted here is identical to the one which Turner made at Granville in November, 1851. It is possible that Mrs. Carriel has mistaken the date and the occasion.

classes alike; but the means of bringing this abstract truth into
effectual contact with the daily business and pursuits of the one
class does exist, while in the other case it does not exist, and
never can till it is new created.

The one class have schools, seminaries, colleges, universities,
apparatus, professors, and multitudinous appliances for educating
and training them, for months and years, for the peculiar profession which is to be the business of their life; and they have
already created, each class for its own use, a vast and voluminous
literature that would well-nigh sink a whole navy of ships.

But where are the universities, the apparatus, the professors,
and the literature specifically adapted to any one of the industrial classes? Echo answers, Where? In other words, society has
become, long since, wise enough to know that its *teachers* need
to be educated; but it has not yet become wise enough to know
that its *workers* need education just as much. In these remarks
I have not forgotten that our common schools are equally adapted
and applied to all classes; but reading, writing, etc., are, properly,
no more education than gathering seed is agriculture, or cutting
ship-timber navigation. They are the mere rudiments, as they
are called, or means—the mere instrument of an after education;
and, if not so used, they are and can be of little more use to the
possessor than an ax in the garret or a ship rotting upon the
stocks.

Nor am I unmindful of the efforts of the monarchs and aristo-
crats of the Old World in founding schools for the " fifteenth
cousins " of their order, in hopes of training them into a sort of
genteel farmers, or rather *overseers* of farmers; nor yet of the
several " back fires " (as the *Prairie Farmer* significantly designates them) set by some of our older professional institutions
to keep the rising and blazing thought of the industrial masses
from burning too furiously. They have hauled a canoe alongside of their huge professional steamships and invited all the
farmers and mechanics of the State to jump on board and sail
with them; but the difficulty is, they will not embark. We thank
them for even this courtesy. It shows that their hearts are
yearning toward us, notwithstanding the ludicrous awkwardness
of their first endeavors to save us.

An answer to two simple questions will perhaps sufficiently
indicate our ideas of the whole subject, though that answer on

the present occasion must necessarily be confined to a bare out-line. The first question, then, is this:

I. WHAT DO THE INDUSTRIAL CLASSES WANT?

II. HOW CAN THAT WANT BE SUPPLIED?

The first question may be answered in few words. They want, and they ought to have, the same facilities for understanding the true philosophy, the science and the art of their several pursuits (their life business), and of efficiently applying existing knowl-edge thereto, and widening its domain, which the professional classes have long enjoyed in their pursuits. Their first labor is, therefore, to supply a vacuum from fountains already full, and bring the living waters of knowledge within their own reach. Their second is, to help fill the fountains with still greater sup-plies. They desire to depress no institution, no class whatever; they only wish to elevate themselves and their pursuits to a position in society to which all men acknowledge they are justly entitled, and to which they also desire to see them aspire.

II. HOW, THEN, CAN THAT WANT BE SUPPLIED?

In answering this question, I shall endeavor to present, with all possible frankness and clearness, the outline of impressions and convictions that have been gradually deepening in my own mind, for the past twenty years, and let them pass for whatever the true friends of the cause may think them worth.

And I answer, first, negatively, that this want cannot be sup-plied by any of the existing institutions for the professional classes, nor by any incidental appendage attached to them as a mere secondary department.

These institutions were designed and adapted to meet the wants of the professional classes, as such—especially the clerical order; and they are no more suited to the real wants of the indus-trial class than the institution we propose for them would be suited to the professional class.

Their whole spirit and aim is, or should be, literary and intellectual—not practical and industrial; to make men of books and ready speech—not men of work, and industrial, silent thought. But the very best classical scholars are often the very worst prac-tical reasoners; and that they should be made workers is contrary to the nature of things, the fixed laws of God. The whole interest, business, and destiny for life of the two classes run in opposite lines; and that the same course of study should be equally well adapted to both is as utterly impossible as that the same pursuits and habits should equally concern and benefit both classes.

The industrial classes know and feel this, and therefore they do not, and will not, patronize these institutions, only so far forth as they desire to make professional men for public use. As a general fact, their own multitudes do, and *will forever*, stand aloof from them; and, while they desire to foster and cherish them for their own appropriate uses, they know that they do not, and can not, fill the sphere of their own urgent industrial wants. They need a similar system of *liberal education* for their own class, and adapted to their own pursuits; to create for them an *industrial literature*, adapted to their professional wants; to raise up for them *teachers* and *lecturers* for subordinate institutes; and to elevate them, their pursuits, and their posterity to that relative position in human society for which God designed them.

The whole history of education, both in Protestant and Catholic countries, shows that we must begin with the higher institutions, or we can never succeed with the lower; for the plain reason that neither knowledge nor water will run uphill. No people ever had, or ever can have, any system of common schools and lower seminaries worth anything until they have first founded their higher institutions and fountains of knowledge from which they could draw supplies of teachers, etc., for the lower. We would begin, therefore, where all experience and common sense show that we must begin, if we would effect anything worthy of an effort.

In this view of the case, the first thing wanted in this process is a National Institute of Science, to operate as the great central luminary of the national mind, from which all minor institutions should derive light and heat, and toward which they should also reflect back their own. This primary want is already, I trust, supplied by the Smithsonian Institute, endowed by James Smithson, and incorporated by the United States Congress at Washington, D. C.

To coöperate with this noble institute, and enable the industrial classes to realize its benefits in practical life, we need a University for the Industrial Classes in each of the States, with their consequent subordinate institutes, lyceums, and high schools in each of the counties and towns.

The objects of these institutes should be to apply existing

knowledge directly and efficiently to all practical pursuits and professions in life, and to extend the boundaries of our present knowledge in all possible practical directions.

Plan for the State University.—There should be connected with such an institution, in this State, a sufficient quantity of land, of variable soil and aspect, for all its needful annual experiments and processes in the great interests of agriculture and horticulture.

Buildings of appropriate size and construction for all its ordinary and special uses; a complete philosophical, chemical, anatomical, and industrial apparatus; a general cabinet, embracing everything that relates to, illustrates, or facilitates any one of the industrial arts, especially all sorts of animals, birds, reptiles, insects, trees, shrubs, and plants found in this State and adjacent States.

Instruction should be constantly given in the anatomy and physiology, the nature, instincts, and habits of all animals, insects, trees, and plants; their laws of propagation, primogeniture, growth, and decay, disease and health, life and death; on the nature, composition, adaptation, and regeneration of soils; on the nature, strength, durability, preservation, perfection, composition, cost, use, and manufacture of all materials of art and trade; on political, financial, domestic, and manual economy (or the saving of labor of the hand) to all industrial processes; on the true principles of national, constitutional, and civil law, and the true theory and art of governing and controlling or directing the labor of men in the State, the family, shop, and farm; on the laws of vicinage, or the laws of courtesy and comity between neighbors, as such, and on the principles of health and disease in the human subject, so far at least as is needful for household safety; on the laws of trade and commerce, ethical, conventional, and practical; on bookkeeping and accounts; and, in short, in all those studies and sciences, of whatever sort, which tend to throw light upon any art or employment which any student may desire to master, or upon any duty he may be called to perform, or which may tend to secure his moral, civil, social, and industrial perfection as a man.

No species of knowledge should be excluded, practical or theoretical; unless, indeed, those specimens of " organized ignorance " found in the creeds of party politicians and sectarian ecclesiastics should be mistaken by some for a species of knowledge.

Whether a distinct classical department should be added, or

not, would depend on expediency. It might be deemed best to leave that department to existing colleges as their more appropriate work, and to form some practical and economical connection with them for that purpose; or it might be best to attach a classical department in due time to the institution itself.

To facilitate the increase and practical application and diffusion of knowledge, the professors should conduct, each in his own department, a continued series of *annual experiments*.

For example, let twenty or more acres of each variety of grain (each acre accurately measured) be annually sown, with some practical variation on each acre, as regards the quality and preparation of the soil, the kind and quantity of seed, the time and mode of sowing or planting, the time and modes and processes of cultivation and harvesting, and an accurate account kept of all costs, labor, etc., and of the final results. Let analogous experiments be tried on all the varied products of the farm, the fruit-yard, the nursery, and the garden; on all modes of crossing, rearing, and fattening domestic animals, under various degrees of warmth and light, with and without shelter; on green, dry, raw, ground, and cooked food, cold and warm; on the nature, causes, and cure of their various diseases, both of those on the premises and of those brought in from abroad; and advice given, and annual reports made on those and all similar topics. Let the professors of physiology and entomology be ever abroad at the proper seasons, with the needful apparatus for seeing all things visible and invisible, and scrutinizing the latent causes of all those blights, blasts, rots, rusts, and mildews which so often destroy the choicest products of industry, and thereby impair the health, wealth, and comfort of millions of our fellow men. Let the professor of chemistry carefully analyze the various soils and products of the State, retain specimens, give instruction, and report on their various qualities, adaptions, and deficiencies.

Let similar experiments be made in all other interests of agriculture and mechanic or chemical art, mining, merchandise, and transportation by water and by land, and daily practical and experimental instruction given to each student in attendance in his own chosen sphere of research or labor in life. Especially let the comparative merits of all labor-saving tools, instruments, machines, engines, and processes be thoroughly and practically tested and explained, so that their benefits might be at once enjoyed, or the expense of their cost avoided by the unskilful and unwary.

It is believed by many intelligent men that from one third to one half the annual products of this State are annually lost from ignorance on the above topics. And it can scarcely be doubted that in a few years the entire cost of the whole institution would be annually saved to the State in the above interests alone, aside from all its other benefits, intellectual, moral, social, and pecuniary.

The apparatus required for such a work is obvious. There should be grounds devoted to a botanical and common garden, to orchards and fruit-yards, to appropriate lawns and promenades, in which the beautiful art of landscape-gardening could be appropriately applied and illustrated, to all varieties of pasture, meadow, and tillage needful for the successful prosecution of the needful annual experiments. And on these grounds should be collected and exhibited a sample of every variety of domestic animal, and of every tree, plant, and vegetable that can minister to the health, wealth, or taste and comfort of the people of the State; their nature, habits, merits, production, improvement, culture, diseases, and accidents thoroughly scrutinized, tested, and made known to the students and to the people of the State.

There should also be erected a sufficient number of buildings and out-buildings for all the purposes above indicated, and a *repository*, in which all the ordinary tools and implements of the institution should be kept, and models of all other useful implements and machines from time to time collected, and tested as they are proffered to public use. At first it would be for the interest of inventors and vendors to make such deposits. But, should similar institutions be adopted in other States, the general government ought to create in each State a general patent office, attached to the universities, similar to the existing deposits at Washington, thus rendering this department of mechanical art and skill more accessible to the great mass of the people of the Union.

I should have said, also, that a suitable industrial library should be at once procured, did not all the world know such a thing to be impossible, and that one of the first and most important duties of the professors of such institutions will be to create, at this late hour, a proper practical literature and series of text-books for the industrial classes.

As regards the *professors*, they should, of course, not only be
men of the most eminent, practical ability in their several departments, but their connection with the institution should be
rendered so fixed and stable as to enable them to carry through
such designs as they may form, or all the peculiar benefits of the
system would be lost.

Instruction, by lectures and otherwise, should be given mostly
in the colder months of the year, leaving the professors to prose-
cute their investigations, and the students their necessary labor,
either at home or on the premises, during the warmer months.

The institution should be open to all classes of students above
a fixed age, and for any length of time, whether three months
or seven years, and each taught in those particular branches of
art which he wishes to pursue, and to any extent, more or less.
And all should pay their tuition and board bills, in whole or in
part, either in money or necessary work on the premises—regard
being had to the ability of each.

Among those who labor, medals and testimonials of merit
should be given to those who perform their tasks with most
promptitude, energy, care, and skill; and all who prove indo-
lent or ungovernable excluded at first from all part in labor,
and speedily, if not thoroughly reformed, from the institution
itself; and here, again, let the law of nature, instead of the law
of rakes and dandies, be regarded, and the true impression ever
made on the mind of all around, that *work alone is honorable*,
and indolence certain disgrace, if not ruin.

At some convenient season of the year, the commencement,
or *annual fair*, of the university should be holden through a
succession of days. On this occasion the doors of the institution,
with all its treasures of art and resources of knowledge, should
be thrown open to all classes, and as many other objects of agricultural or mechanical skill gathered from the whole State as
possible, and presented by the people for inspection and pre-
mium on the best of each kind; judgment being rendered, in all
cases, by a committee wholly disconnected with the institution.
On this occasion all the professors, and as many of the pupils as
are sufficiently advanced, should be constantly engaged in lecturing and explaining the divers objects and interests of their
departments. In short, this occasion should be made the great
annual *gala day* of the institution, and of all the industrial
classes, and all other classes in the State, for the exhibition of

their products and their skill, and for the vigorous and powerful diffusion of practical knowledge in their ranks, and a more intense enthusiasm in its extension and pursuit.

As matters now are, the world has never adopted any efficient means for the application and diffusion of even the practical knowledge which does exist. True, we have fairly got the primer, the spelling-book, and the newspaper abroad in the world, and we think that we have done wonders; and so, comparatively, we have. But if this is a wonder, there are still not only wonders, but, to most minds, inconceivable miracles, from new and unknown worlds of light, soon to break forth upon the industrial mind of the world.

Here, then, is a general, though very incomplete, outline of what such an institution should endeavor to become. Let the reader contemplate it as it will appear when generations have perfected it in all its magnificence and glory; in its means of good to man, to *all men* of *all classes*; in its power to evolve and diffuse practical knowledge and skill, true taste, love of industry, and sound morality—not only through its apparatus, experiments, instructions, and annual lectures and reports, but through its thousands of graduates, in every pursuit in life, teaching and lecturing in all our towns and villages; and then let him seriously ask himself, is not such an object worthy of at least an effort, and worthy of a State which God himself, in the very act of creation, designed to be the first agricultural and commercial State on the face of the globe?

Who should set the world so glorious an example of educating their sons worthily of their heritage, their duty, and their destiny, if not the people of such a State? In our country we have no aristocracy, with the inalienable wealth of ages and constant leisure and means to perform all manner of useful experiments for their own amusement; but we must create our nobility for this purpose, as we elect our rulers, from our own ranks, to aid and serve, not to domineer over and control us. And, this done, we will not only beat England and beat the world in yachts and locks and reapers, but in all else that contributes to the well being and true glory of man.

I maintain that if every farmer's and mechanic's son in this State could now visit such an institution but for a single day in the year, it would do him more good in arousing and directing the dormant energies of mind than all the cost incurred, and far more good than many a six months of professed study of things he will never need and never want to know.

As things now are, our best farmers and mechanics, by their own native force of mind, by the slow process of individual experience, come to know, at forty, what they might have been taught in six months at twenty; while a still greater number of the less fortunate, or less gifted, stumble on through life almost as ignorant of every true principle of their art as when they began. A man of real skill is amazed at the slovenly ignorance and waste he everywhere discovers on all parts of their premises, and still more to hear them boast of their ignorance of all " book farming," and maintain that " their children can do as well as they have done "; and it certainly would be a great pity if they could not.

The patrons of our university would be found in the former, not in the latter, class. The man whose highest conception of earthly bliss is a log hut in an uninclosed yard, where pigs of two species are allowed equal rights, unless the four-legged tribe chance to get the upper hand, will be found no patron of industrial universities. Why should he be? He knows it all already.

There is another class of untaught farmers who devote all their capital and hired labor to the culture, on a large scale, of some single product, which always pays well when so produced on a fresh soil, even in the most unskilful hands. Now, such men often increase rapidly in wealth, but it is not by their skill in agriculture, for they have none—their skill consists in the management of capital and labor; and deprive them of these, and confine them to the varied culture of a small farm, and they would starve in five years, where a true farmer would amass a small fortune. This class are, however, generally the fast friends of education, though many a looker-on will cite them as instances of the uselessness of acquired skill in farming, whereas they should cite them only as a sample of the resistless power of capital even in comparatively unskilful hands.

Such institutions are the only possible remedy for a caste education, legislation, and literature. If any one class provide for their own liberal education in the State, as they should do, while another class neglect this, it is as inevitable as the law of gravitation that they should form a ruling caste or class by themselves, and wield their power more or less for their own exclusive interests, and the interests of their friends.

JONATHAN BALDWIN TURNER

THE TURNER HOMESTEAD, TEMPLETON, MASSACHUSETTS

JONATHAN BALDWIN TURNER'S HOME, JACKSONVILLE, ILLINOIS

THE BALDWIN HOMESTEAD, BALDWINSVILLE, MASSACHUSETTS

ILLINOIS COLLEGE, JACKSONVILLE, ILLINOIS, IN 1833

GOVERNOR RICHARD YATES

BRONSON MURRAY

THE TURNER BROTHERS: EDWARD, ASA, AVERY, JONATHAN

PROFESSOR TURNER AND HIS SON HOWARD,
FROM A DAGUERREOTYPE TAKEN IN 1854

Ho. of Repr.
Washington D.C Dec 30. 1861

Dear Sir:

I was delighted to find you firm, by the letter of the 15th inst. had not all burned out. I presume I recognize Prof Turner an old prisoner in the cause of Ag. education.

I have only to say that, amid the fire, smoke, and embers I have faith that I shall get my bill into a law at this session.

I thank you for your continued and interest and am

Very sincerely yours

Justin S. Morrill

J. B. Turner Esq.
Jacksonville
Ills

FACSIMILE OF A LETTER FROM JUSTIN S. MORRILL
TO PROFESSOR TURNER IN 1861

DR. H. F. CARRIEL

MRS. MARY TURNER CARRIEL

If the industrial were the only educated class in the State, the caste power in their hands would be as much stronger than it now is as their numbers are greater. But now industrial education has been wholly neglected, and the various industrial classes left still ignorant of matters of the greatest moment pertaining to their vital interests, while the professions have been studied till trifles and fooleries have been magnified into matters of immense importance, and tornadoes of windy words and barrels of innocent ink shed over them in vain.

This, too, is the inevitable result of trying to crowd all liberal practical education into one narrow sphere of human life. It crowds their ranks with men totally unfit by nature for professional service. Many of these, under a more congenial culture, might have become, instead of the starving scavengers of a learned profession, the honored members of an industrial one. Their love of knowledge was indeed amiable and highly commendable; but the necessity which drove them from their natural sphere in life, in order to obtain it, is truly deplorable.

But such a system of general education as we now propose would (in ways too numerous now to mention) tend to increase the respectability, power, numbers, and resources of the true professional class.

Nor are the advantages of the mental and moral discipline of the student to be overlooked; indeed, I should have set them down as most important of all, had I not been distinctly aware that such an opinion is a most deadly heresy; and I tremble at the thought of being arraigned before the tribunal of all the monks and ecclesiastics of the Old World, and no small number of their progeny in the New.

It is deemed highly important that all in the professional classes should become writers and talkers; hence, they are so incessantly drilled in all the forms of language, dead and living, though it has become quite doubtful whether, even in their case, such a course is most beneficial, except in the single case of the professors of literature and theology, with whom these languages form the foundation of their professions and the indispensable instruments of their future art in life.

No inconsiderable share, however, of the mental discipline that is attributed to this peculiar course of study, arises from daily intercourse, for years, with minds of the first order in their teachers and comrades, and would be produced under any other course, if the parties had remained harmoniously together. On the other hand, a classical teacher who has no original, spontaneous power of thought, and knows nothing but Latin and Greek, however perfectly, is enough to stultify a whole generation of boys and make them all pedantic fools like himself. The idea of infusing mind, or creating or even materially increasing it, by the daily inculcation of unintelligible words—all this awful wringing to get blood out of a turnip—will, at any rate, never succeed except in the hands of the eminently wise and prudent, who have had long experience in the process; the plain, blunt sense of the unsophisticated will never realize cost in the operation. There are, moreover, probably, few men who do not already talk more, in proportion to what they really know, than they ought to. This chronic diarrhœa of exhortation, which the social atmosphere of the age tends to engender, tends far less to public health than many suppose. The history of the Quakers shows that more sound sense, a purer morality, and a more elevated practical piety can exist, and does exist, entirely without it, than is commonly found with it.

Indeed, I think the exclusive and extravagant claims set up for ancient lore, as a means of disciplining the reasoning powers, simply ridiculous when examined in the light of those ancient worthies who produced that literature, or the modern ones who have been most devoted to its pursuit in this country and in Europe. If it produces infallible practical reasoners, we have a great many thousand infallible antagonistic truths, and ten thousand conflicting paths of right, interest, duty, and salvation. If any man will just be at the trouble to open his eyes and his ears, he can perceive at a glance how much this evasive discipline really does, and has done, for the reasoning faculty of man, and how much for the power of sophistical cant and stereotyped nonsense; so that if obvious facts, instead of verbose declamation, are to have any weight in the case, I am willing to join issue with the opposers of the proposed scheme, even on the bare ground of its superior adaptation to develop the mental power of its pupils.

The most natural and effectual mental discipline possible for any man arises from setting him to earnest and constant thought about things he daily does, sees, and handles, and all their connected relations and interests. The final object to be attained, with the industrial class, is to make them *thinking laborers*;

while of the professional class we should desire to make *laborious thinkers*; the production of goods to feed and adorn the body being the final end of one class of pursuits, and the production of thought to do the same for the mind the end of the other. But neither mind nor body can feed on the offals of preceding generations. And this constantly recurring necessity of reproduction leaves an equally honorable, though somewhat different, career of labor and duty open to both, and, it is readily admitted, should and must vary their modes of education and preparation accordingly.

It may do for the man of books to plunge at once amid the catacombs of buried nations and languages, to soar away to Greece and Rome, or Nova Zembla, Kamchatka, and the fixed stars, before he knows how to plant his own beans, or harness his own horse, or can tell whether the functions of his own body are performed by a heart, stomach, and lungs, or with a gizzard or gills. But for the man of work thus to bolt away at once from himself and all his pursuits in after life contravenes the plainest principles of nature and common sense. No wonder such educators have ever deemed the liberal culture of the industrial classes an impossibility; for they have never tried nor even conceived of any other way of educating them except that by which they are rendered totally unfit for their several callings in after life. How absurd would it seem to set a clergyman to plowing and studying the depredations of blights, insects, the growing of crops, etc., in order to give him habits of thought and mental discipline for the pulpit; yet this is not half as ridiculous, in reality, as the reverse absurdity of attempting to educate the man of work in unknown tongues, abstract problems and theories, and metaphysical figments and quibbles.

Some, doubtless, will regard the themes of such a course of education as too sensuous and gross to lie at the basis of a pure and elevated mental culture. But the themes themselves cover all possible knowledge and all modes and phases of science, abstract, mixed, and practical. In short, the field embraces all that God has made, and all that human art has done; and if the created universe of God and the highest art of man are too gross for our refined uses, it is a pity the "morning stars and the sons of God" did not find it out as soon as the blunder was made. But, in my opinion, these topics are of quite as much consequence to the well being of man and the healthful development

of mind as the concoction of the final nostrum in medicine, or
the ultimate figment in theology and law, conjectures about the
galaxy, or the Greek accent; unless, indeed, the pedantic professional trifles of one man in a thousand are of more consequence
than the daily vital interests of all the rest of mankind.

But can such an institution be created and endowed? Doubtless it can be done, and done at once, if the industrial classes so
decide. The fund given to this State by the general government,
expressly for this purpose, is amply sufficient, without a dollar
from any other source; and it is a mean if not an illegal per-
version of this fund to use it for any other purpose. It was given
to the people, the whole people, of this State—not for a class,
a party, or sect, or conglomeration of sects; not for common
schools, or family schools, or classical schools; but for " an university," or seminary of a high order, in which should, of course,
be taught all those things which every class of the citizens most
desire to learn—their own duty and business for life. This, and
this alone, is an university in the true, original sense of the term.
And if an institution which teaches all that is needful only for
the three professions of law, divinity, and medicine is, therefore,
an university, surely one which teaches all that is needful for all
the varied professions of human life is far more deserving of the
name and the endowments of an university.

But in whose hands shall the guardianship and oversight of
this fund be placed, in order to make it of any real use for such
a purpose? I answer, without hesitation and without fear, that
this whole interest should, from the first, be placed directly in
the hands of the people, and the whole people, without any
mediators or advisers, legislative or ecclesiastical, save only their
own appointed agents, and their own jurors and courts of justice,
to which, of course, all alike must submit. It was given to the
people, and is the property of the people, not of legislators,
parties, or sects; and they ought to have the whole control of it,
so far as is possible consistently with a due security of the funds
and needful stability of plans of action and instruction. This
control I believe they will be found abundantly able to exercise;
and more than this no well-informed man would desire.

The reasons for placing it at once and forever beyond all legislative and ecclesiastical control are obvious to all. For if under
the former it will continually exist as the mere tool of the domi-
nant party, and the object of jealous fear and hatred of their

opponents; or else it will become the mere football of all parties, to be kicked hither and thither as the party interests and passion of the hour may dictate. We well know how many millions of money have been worse than thrown away by placing professed seminaries of learning under the influence of party passion, through legislative control. And it is surely a matter for devout gratitude that our legislators have had wisdom enough to see and feel this difficulty, and that they have been led, from various causes, to hold this " Seminary Fund " free from all commitment to the present hour, when the people begin to be convinced that they need it, and can safely control it; and no legislator but an aristocrat or a demagogue would desire to see it in other hands.

The same difficulty occurs as regards sects. Let the institution be managed ever so well by any one party or sect, it is still certain their opponents will stand aloof from it, if they do not oppose and malign it for that very reason. Hence, all will see at once that the greatest possible care should be taken to free it from not only the reality but even from the *suspicion* of any such influence. Should the party in power, when the charter may be granted, appoint a majority of the board of trustees from the parties in the minority, it would show a proper spirit, and be, in all coming time, an example of true magnanimity, which their opponents could not fail to respect and to imitate, and which the people at large would highly approve. A victorious hero can afford to be generous as well as brave—none worthy of a triumph can afford to be otherwise. In all future appointments, also, the candidates should be elected with such an evident regard to merit, and disregard of all political and sectarian relations, as ever to carry the conviction that the equal good of the whole alone is sought. There can be no great difficulty in accomplishing all this, if it is well known in the outset that the people will keep their eye closely upon that man, whoever he may be, who, by any bargaining for votes, or any direct or indirect local, sinister, or selfish action or influence, or any evasion or postponement, or by any desire to tamper and amend merely to show himself off to advantage, shall in any way embarrass or endanger this greatest of all interests ever committed to a free State—the interest of properly and worthily educating all the sons of her soil. Let the people set on such a man, if the miscreant wretch lives, for all future time, a mark as much blacker than the mark set on Cain as midnight is darker than noonday. This is a question, above all others, that a man who is a man will desire to meet openly and frankly, like a man. Will our legislators do it? I, for one, believe they will. I shall not believe the contrary till it is proved; and I will even suggest, in general, a mode by which the great end may be safely gained. Let others, however, suggest a better one, and I will cheerfully accord with it.

Let the Governor of the State nominate a board of trust for the funds of the institution. Let this board consist of five of the most able and discreet men in the State, and let at least four of them be taken from each of the extreme corners of the State, so remote from all proximity to the possible location of the institution, both in person and in property, as to be free from all suspicion of partiality. Let the Senate confirm such nomination. Let this board be sworn to locate the institution from a regard to the interests and convenience of the people of the whole State. And, when they have so done, let them be empowered to elect twelve new members of their own body, with perpetual power of filling their own vacancies, each choice requiring a vote of two thirds of the whole body, and, upon any failure to elect at the appointed annual meeting, the Governor of the State to fill the vacancy for one year, if requested by any member of the board so to do. Let any member of the board who shall be absent from any part of its annual meetings thereby forfeit his seat, unless detained by sickness, certified at the time, and the board on that occasion fill the vacancy, either by his reëlection, or by the choice of some other man. Let the funds then, by the same act, pass into the hands of the trustees so organized, as a perpetual trust, they giving proper bonds for the same, to be used for the endowment and erection of an industrial university for the State of Illinois.

This board, so constituted, would be, and ought to be, responsible to no legislature, sect, or party, but directly to the people themselves—to each and every citizen, in the courts of law and justice, so that, should any trustee of the institution neglect, abuse, or pervert his trust to any selfish, local, political, or sectarian end, or show himself incompetent for its exercise, every other member of the board and every citizen at large should have the right of impeaching him before the proper court, and, if guilty, the court should discharge him and order his place to be filled by a more suitable man. Due care should be taken, of course, to guard against malicious prosecutions.

Doubtless objections can be urged against this plan, and all others that can be proposed. Most of them may be at once anticipated, but there is not space enough to notice them here. Some, for example, cherish an ardent and praiseworthy desire for the perfection of our common schools, and desire still longer to use that fund for that purpose. But no one imagines that it can long be kept for that use, and, if it could, I think it plain that the lower schools of all sorts would be far more benefited by it here than in any other place it could be put.

Others may feel a little alarm when, for the first time in the history of the world, they see the millions throwing themselves aloof from all political and ecclesiastical control, and attempting to devise a system of liberal education for themselves; but, on mature reflection, we trust they will approve the plan—or, if they are too old to change, their children will.

CHAPTER XII

Granville, November 18, 1851
The Farmers' Move for a State University

Several bills to regulate the disposition of the Seminary Fund were introduced in the Illinois Legislature, from time to time, but none passed. The one most difficult to resist was proposed in 1850 by Newton Cloud of Jacksonville, who recommended that the fund be divided among all the colleges of the State. The income and equipment of these colleges were inadequate to enable them to compete with Eastern colleges in securing students from the wealthier families of the West, and consequently their many friends were favorably impressed by Mr. Cloud's bill.

In the summer of 1851 Professor Turner was invited to attend the last quarterly meeting of Buel Institute at Granville, Illinois, but could not accept. Later in the fall of 1851 he received an invitation to attend, in the northern part of the State, a convention of farmers from the counties of Putnam, Bureau, Henry, La Salle, Whiteside, Grundy, Fulton, Lake, and Winnebago.

GRANVILLE, PUTNAM COUNTY, October 29, 1851

REV. J. B. TURNER
Dear Sir:

We regret that you were not able to meet with us. We had a very interesting fair; the largest body of men were present that I have ever seen in Illinois, and a general feeling of satisfaction was expressed by those present. I write at this time mainly to inform you of a convention of farmers that is to meet at Granville the third Tuesday of November next, at two o'clock P. M., for the purpose of adopting some measures to establish an agricultural school, or agricultural department in some school, in northern Illinois. We should be glad to see you at this convention and wish your assistance to help us to start the plan.

Yours respectfully,
Ralph Ware, on Committee

Professor Turner accepted this invitation, and took an active part in the discussions. This convention proved to be the birthplace of all active measures taken to interest the people of Illinois in industrial education. The proceedings were afterward prepared for publication by Professor Turner, at the request of the convention; for he there gave again his plan for an industrial university, substantially as he had given it a year and a half before at Griggsville. This farmers' convention at Granville, called to consider the establishment of a local agricultural school, resulted in the first practical appeal to the State Legislature for the establishment of an agricultural university for Illinois. The formal minutes of the business and resolutions of this meeting, as given in the pamphlet published in 1853 by the Illinois Industrial League, which was formed to further the movement, are worth reproducing:

In accordance with previous notice, a convention of farmers was held at Granville, Putnam County, on Tuesday the eighteenth day of November, 1851. The attendance was quite large, and from various parts of the State.

The convention organized by appointing Hon. Oaks Turner,

of Hennepin, chairman *pro tem.*, and Mr. M. Osman, of Ottawa, secretary *pro tem.*

Mr. Ralph Ware moved that a committee of three be appointed by the chair to nominate permanent officers for the convention; which was agreed to; whereupon the chair appointed Messrs. Ralph Ware, John Hise, and Sidney Pulsifer said committee.

The committee, after a few minutes' absence, returned and reported the following persons as permanent officers of the convention:

Hon. Oaks Turner, President.

Hon. Wm. Reddick, of Ottawa, and Professor J. B. Turner of Jacksonville, Vice-Presidents.

Mr. M. Osman, Recording Secretary.

Mr. Ralph Ware, of Granville, Corresponding Secretary.

On motion, the report was adopted and the committee discharged.

The President then stated that he was not fully advised as to the real objects of the convention, and suggested that some one better qualified should make them known.

Mr. Ware then stated that, according to the call, they had met to take into consideration such measures as might be deemed most expedient to further the interests of the agricultural community, and particularly to take steps towards the establishment of an agricultural university.

On motion of Mr. Greble, a committee of three was appointed to report business upon which the convention should act. The committee consisted of Mr. John Greble, Professor J. B. Turner, and Mr. Lewis Weston.

During the absence of this committee, short addresses were delivered by Messrs. Hise, Greble, Ware, and others.

The committee returned and stated that they would not be fully prepared to report before evening, and suggested that the afternoon be devoted to a general discussion of such subjects pertaining to agriculture as might present themselves.

A lively discussion was then commenced on various subjects, in which Powell of Mount Palatine, Butler of Spoon River, Greble of Putnam County, Weston, of La Salle County, Gilmer of Granville, Reddick of Ottawa, and others participated.

After which the convention adjourned until half past six o'clock in the evening.

EVENING SESSION

The convention was called to order by the chairman.

Professor Turner, as chairman of the Committee on Business, reported the following resolutions for the future action of the convention:

" *Resolved*, That we greatly rejoice in the degree of perfection to which our various institutions, for the education of our brethren engaged in professional, scientific, and literary pursuits, have already attained, and in the mental and moral elevation which those institutions have given them, and their consequent preparation and capacity for the great duties in the spheres of life in which they are engaged; and that we will aid in all ways consistent for the still greater perfection of such institutions.

" *Resolved*, That as the representatives of the industrial classes, including all cultivators of the soil, artisans, mechanics, and merchants, we desire the same privileges and advantages for ourselves, our fellows, and our posterity, in each of our several pursuits and callings, as our professional brethren enjoy in theirs; and we admit that it is our own fault that we do not also enjoy them.

" *Resolved*, That, in our opinion, the institutions originally and primarily designed to meet the wants of the professional classes, as such, cannot, in the nature of things, meet ours, any more than the institutions we desire to establish for ourselves could meet theirs. Therefore,

" *Resolved*, That we take immediate measures for the establishment of a university in the State of Illinois expressly to meet those felt wants of each and all the industrial classes of our State; that we recommend the foundation of high schools, lyceums, institutes, etc., in each of our counties, on similar principles, so soon as they may find it practicable so to do.

" *Resolved*, That, in our opinion, such institutions can never impede, but must greatly promote, the best interests of all those existing institutions."

After reading the above resolutions, Professor Turner proceeded, in an able and interesting manner, to unfold his plan for the establishment and maintenance of the Industrial University.

The convention then adjourned till nine o'clock to-morrow morning.

Met pursuant to adjournment.

On motion, the resolutions were again taken up and read, and, after some deliberation, severally adopted.

Mr. Hise offered the following resolutions:

"*Resolved*, That we approve of the general plan for an Illinois state university for the industrial classes, presented by Professor J. B. Turner, and request him to furnish the outlines of his plan, presented to this convention, to the Committee of Publication, for publication in the *Prairie Farmer* and all other papers in this State which will publish the same; and that one thousand copies be published in pamphlet form for gratuitous distribution.

"*Resolved*, That W. A. Pennell, M. Osman, L. L. Bullock, and Ralph Ware be a Committee of Publication.

"*Resolved*, That the Committee of Publication forward to each editor in every county in the State a copy of the publications of this convention, with a request that they should republish the same; and also send a copy to our Governor, Senators and Representatives, and State officers, and to all others who may be interested in the same.

"*Resolved*, That each member of this convention do all in his power to promote the circulation and reading of the above publications, and, through this and other means, to secure, as far as practicable, speakers to lecture on the subject in each of the counties in the State.

"*Resolved*, That Messrs. J. B. Turner and Marcus Morton, of Morgan County; James McConnell, Elijah Iles, and David L. Gregg, of Sangamon County; John Davis, of Decatur; John Woods, of Quincy; John Hise, of La Salle County; Aaron Shaw, of Lawrence County; John Dougherty, of Union County; L. S. Pennington, of Whiteside County; W. J. Phelps, of Elm Wood, Peoria County; and Dr. Ames, of Winnebago County, be a Central Committee to call a State convention, to meet at Springfield at an early hour of the next session of the Legislature, or at such other time and place as they and the friends of the cause may deem most expedient.

"*Resolved*, That this convention earnestly solicit the Governor of this State [A. C. French] to enumerate in the call for an extra session of the Legislature, should one be held before the next regular session, the objects of this convention in the establishment of an industrial university, as business to be acted upon by that body at that time.

" *Resolved,* That a memorial and petitions be prepared and furnished by the publishing committee for the purpose of petitioning the Legislature upon this subject."

During the discussion of these resolutions the convention adjourned till 1 o'clock P. M.

AFTERNOON SESSION

Met pursuant to adjournment.

Mr. Hise's resolutions were again taken up and severally passed.

Mr. Lofflin introduced the following resolution, which was adopted:

" *Resolved,* That we earnestly solicit the people of this State to meet in their primary assemblies and discuss the objects of this convention as shall be made known by our published proceedings, and join with us in asking the Legislature to grant to the people of this State the fund which belongs to them, to aid them in establishing an institute for the industrial classes of this State, instead of dividing that fund among the different colleges now in the State, as contemplated by those institutions."

In compliance with a request made by Mr. Thomas Ware and others, Professor Turner gave a short history of a number of experiments he had made in reference to the blight upon fruit trees.

The convention then adjourned *sine die.*

M. OSMAN, *Sec'y*   OAKS TURNER, *Pres't*

The newspapers in the State became interested and took up the subject. Many approved, but more were in opposition to the plan. Among the latter was Professor Turner's own home paper, the *Morgan Journal.* He replied to its editorials, closing his last article with these words:

But is it to be treated as a crime that I have expended voluntarily time and money to propose frankly, over my own name and signature, my honest views of the best plan for the use of the State fund? Let any other man or body of men—who are

men—come out and give the public the details of another plan;
then let the State choose, and I am content.

My appeal, and the appeal of the Farmers' and Mechanics'
Convention at Granville, is to the interest and common sense of
the laboring and industrial classes, and before them we are
willing to stand or fall. Meantime, all anonymous scribblers may
answer their own objections if they choose.

A few friends were favorable to the plan when first proposed, as the following extracts from letters testify:

MOUND NURSERY, February 6, 1852

PROFESSOR TURNER

My dear Sir:

The copy of Proceedings of Farmers' Convention, together
with your plan of industrial university, was also received—for
which I thank you very much. In relation to your " plan," no
Illinoisian who has true greatness and glory of his country at
heart could disapprove of it. The only objection I find is that
it is *too good a thing* for its accomplishment to be hoped for
very soon. The immobility of the masses is such that it seems to
me it will take years of hard *hammering* to force them out of the
old routine their forefathers chalked out for them.

Your friend,

C. R. OVERMAN

HENNEPIN, February 11, 1852

PROFESSOR J. B. TURNER

My dear Sir:

Your favor of the 5th inst. I received last evening. The cause
with us goes bravely on. I hear scarce a breath against it, nor
do I expect any real opposition in this part of this State to it.
I will see that the Buel Institute petitions Congress as you have
suggested.

Pardon this hasty note, and believe me,

Yours truly,

OAKS TURNER,
President of Farmers' Convention at Granville

SPRINGFIELD, March 11, 1852

Dear Sir:

My absence has prevented an earlier reply to your letter of the 3d inst., on the subject of the Industrial University.

I am satisfied that the best period for holding a convention of the friends of education will be on or about the commencement of the special session of the General Assembly. The seat of government [Springfield], if the time requested is agreed on, is undoubtedly the proper place of meeting. Many advocates will arise from the opportunity which will thus be afforded of personal explanations with the members of the Legislature.

I suppose the Governor will present the matter of the University in such a way that it can come up for consideration. As chairman of the committee appointed by the Granville Convention, you will no doubt feel called on to prepare a public notice at the proper time, and I authorize you to use my name in connection therewith, at your discretion.

Very respectfully yours,

D. L. GREGG *

PEORIA, ILLINOIS, March 21, 1852

PROFESSOR TURNER

Dear Sir:

I beg leave to send you this paper, which I have the honor to publish. You will please find therein that I hastened as soon as possible to translate your excellent plan of an industrial university and to bring it to the knowledge of the German public. I am very sorry that the circulation of this paper, because a few weeks since started, is very small, and that not every member of my language can read it.

You would very much oblige me if you would let me know the state of the matter, and if you would please to give me directions what to do to promote the realization of the plan.

Yours most respectfully,

A. ZOTZ,
Co-Editor of the Illinois "Banner"

The following letter, from one of the Ohio members of

---

* Secretary of State.

the House of Representatives, shows that the subject early attracted attention outside of the State of Illinois.

HOUSE OF REPRESENTATIVES

WASHINGTON, April 26, 1852

Dear Sir:

I received your letter of the 3d, and the pamphlet, both of which I read with great pleasure. During my service here I shall take great pleasure in aiding and in forwarding every measure to promote universal education, believing there is no surer means of promoting human happiness and our national renown.

In haste,

Very truly yours,

L. D. CAMPBELL

CHAPTER XIII

Springfield, June 8, 1852
The First Proposal of General Federal Land Grants

A second convention to promote the movement of industrial education in Illinois was held Tuesday, June 8, 1852, at Springfield. The Industrial League report of it said:

Pursuant to a call by the committee appointed for that purpose by the Granville convention last autumn, a number of gentlemen met at the courthouse at Springfield on Tuesday, the 8th inst., at nine o'clock, to consider the subject, appropriate education for the industrial classes. The meeting was temporarily organized by the appointment of Professor J. B. Turner as president and W. H. Powell as secretary. Dr. Kennicott offered the following resolution:

" *Resolved*, That all persons be considered members of this convention who, by their own showing, are the friends of practical industrial education, and who desire the concentration of the means and influences for that purpose."

The resolution was adopted.

Following the opening of the convention to the general public, a controversy arose between the members of the Industrial Convention and the advocates and representatives of some few of the old classical and theological colleges, who were admitted by courtesy to participate in the debates of the convention, which consumed most of the time of the convention, and but little, if any, impression for good was made upon the public mind.*

These colleges desired themselves to be made the instruments through which the funds of the State should be applied to the education of the industrial classes. This the representatives of these classes have at all times, in all their conventions, unanimously and steadfastly opposed.

At that meeting, however, the following memorial was presented to the Legislature:

ILLINOIS INDUSTRIAL CONVENTION

MEMORIAL OF THE INDUSTRIAL CONVENTION TO THE SENATE AND HOUSE OF REPRESENTATIVES OF THE STATE OF ILLINOIS

The convention of the friends of the Industrial University, proposed to the consideration of the people of Illinois by the Granville convention, whose report is alluded to in the message of the Governor of the State, beg leave to submit to the consideration of the Senators and Representatives of the people the following memorial:

But three general modes have been publicly proposed for the use of the College and Seminary funds of the State.

I. The *perpetual continuance* of their use for common-school

---

* " Guests by courtesy " took possession of the meeting, and, by preconcerted plans, attempted, through ridicule and sarcasm, to break it up. Not knowing that Professor Turner was present, or perhaps forgetting that he was a university graduate, they hurled at the audience a volley of questions relating to abstract and classical subjects, thinking that no one in that audience would be able to answer them, and that in the confusion and mortification of their ignorance they would prove their unfitness to organize or to conduct an educational institution. Professor Turner rose in his seat and respectfully answered all questions. Then he returned the compliment by asking them the practical questions of the day, which they could not answer without convicting themselves of incompetency; and when they had been utterly confused and confounded, he turned upon them and in the most scathing language depicted their ungentlemanly conduct as guests of an organization to which they had been invited, until they were glad to take refuge in flight, amid the laughter and jeers of their intended victims.

purposes is not seriously expected by any one, but only their temporary use as a loan for this noble object.

II. The equal distribution of their proceeds among the ten or twelve colleges in charge of the various religious denominations of the State, either now in existence or soon to arise and claim their share in these funds, and the equally just claim of medical and other institutions for their share, it is thought by your memorialists, would produce too great a division to render these funds of much practical value either to these institutions or to the people of the State. Nor do they consider that it would make any practical difference, in this regard, whether the funds were paid directly by the State over to the trustees of these institutions, or disbursed indirectly through a new board of overseers or regents, to be called the University of Illinois. The plan of attempting to elect by State authority some smaller number of these institutions, to enjoy the benefit of the funds, on the one hand, to the exclusion of others, or attempting to endow them all so as to fit them for the great practical uses of the industrial classes of the State, we trust your honorable bodies will see at once to be still more impracticable and absurd, if not radically unequal and unjust in a free State like ours.

III. Your memorialists, therefore, desire, not the dispersion by any mode, either direct or indirect, of these funds, but their continued preservation and concentration for the equal use of all classes of our citizens, and especially to meet the pressing necessities of the great industrial classes and interests of the State, in accordance with the principle suggested in the message of his Excellency the Governor of the State [A. C. French] to your honorable bodies; and also in the recent message of Governor Hunt of New York to the Legislature of that State, and sanctioned by the approval of many of the wisest and most patriotic statesmen in this and other States.

The report of the Granville convention of farmers, herewith submitted and alluded to, as above noticed in the message of our Chief Magistrate, may be considered as *one*, and as *only* one, of the various modes in which this desirable end may be reached, and is alluded to in this connection as being the only published document of any convention on this subject, and as a general illustration of what your petitioners would desire, when the wisdom of the Senators and Representatives of the people shall have duly modified and perfected the general plan proposed, so as to fit it to the present resources and necessities of the State.

We desire that some beginning should be made, as soon as our statesmen may deem prudent so to do, to realize the high and noble ends for the people of the State proposed in each and all of the documents above alluded to. And if possible on a sufficiently extensive scale to honorably justify a successful appeal to Congress, in conjunction with eminent citizens and statesmen in other States, who have expressed their readiness to coöperate with us, for an appropriation of public lands for each State in the Union for the appropriate endowment of universities for the liberal education of the industrial classes in their several pursuits in each State in the Union.

And in this rich and, at least prospectively, powerful State, acting in coöperation with the vast energies and resources of this mighty confederation of united republics, even very small beginnings, properly directed, may at no very remote day result in consequences more wonderful and beneficent than the most daring mind would now venture to predict or even conceive.

In the appropriation of those funds your memorialists would especially desire that a department for normal school teaching, to thoroughly qualify teachers for county and district schools, and an appropriate provision for the practical education of the destitute orphans of the State, should not be forgotten.

We think that the object at which we aim must so readily commend itself to the good sense and patriotism both of our people, rulers, and statesmen, when once fully and clearly understood, that we refrain from all argument in its favor.

We ask only that *one* institution for the numerous industrial classes, the teachers and orphans of this State, and of each State, should be endowed on the same general principles and to the same relative extent as some *one* of the numerous institutions now existing in each State for the more especial benefit of the comparatively very limited classes in the three learned professions. If this is deemed immoderate or even impracticable, we will thankfully accept even less.

As to the objection that States cannot properly manage literary institutions, all history shows that the States in this country, and in Europe, which have attempted to manage them by proper methods, constituting a vast majority of the whole, have fully succeeded in their aim. While the few around us which have attempted to endow and organize them on *wrong* principles, condemned by all experience, have, of course, failed. Nor can a State charter originate railroads, or manage any other interest, except by proper methods and through proper agents. And a people or a State that cannot learn, in time, to manage properly and efficiently all these interests, and especially the great interest of self-education, is obviously unfit for self-government, which we are not willing as yet to admit in reference to any State in the Union, and least of all our own.

With these sentiments deeply impressed on our hearts, and on the hearts of many of our more enlightened fellow citizens, your memorialists will never cease to pray your honorable bodies for that effective aid which you alone can grant.

Respectfully submitted,

By order of the Committee of the Convention,

J. B. TURNER, *Chairman*

The movement was now well launched. Governor French, in his message of 1852, had discussed the general subject of industrial education. The Representatives of Illinois in Congress were immediately interested. The constituency of the State was, of course, largely agricultural, and movements in its peculiar interests were naturally given attention by its political agents. In addition, Richard Yates, then a member of Congress and afterward a Senator and Governor of Illinois, had been a student under Professor Turner in Illinois College, and was at once put in touch with the plan. The following letters from Mr. Yates, dated just after the second convention, show the early interest of himself and Senator Douglas:

WASHINGTON, June 25, 1852

PROFESSOR J. B. TURNER

Dear Friend:

I send you by to-day's mail a copy of the Proceedings of the National Agricultural Convention, held in Washington yesterday. The *Republic* does not set forth my real motion. I presented your address to the Granville convention, and moved that it be referred to the Committee on Business, with instructions to report the subject of National and State Industrial Universities as one of the subjects which should be proposed for the consideration of the convention. I took occasion to refer to the plan proposed by you, with proper commendations, and referred to the message of the Governor of Illinois and the action of the Legislature in relation to the same. I have but little doubt that the Legislature will, at the present or next session, adopt the plan you have proposed. Although but little has been done in relation to the subject of an Agricultural Bureau,* I still hope something will yet be done. There is a good feeling in its behalf, and could it be got up in order (without a motion to suspend the rules, which requires a two-thirds vote, which seems impossible), it would pass the House, and the Senate also, without trouble.

I received yours, Dr. Kennicott's, and other letters in his behalf for his appointment at the head of the Agricultural Bureau, should that be established. I have not answered him, for the reason that, should the same be created, I have another name to be presented, and had that name in my mind a long time before the reception of the letters. To be plain, that name is yours, and you need not write declining, for my mind is made up and I will not be moved from my purpose. Your address to the Granville convention would aid me much, and I think I could bring an influence from the West, and also from the East, which perhaps you are not aware of. I say I will not be moved from my purpose, because I have personal reasons to influence me as well as public interests in view—the elevation of one of the instructors of my youth and one of the professors of my alma mater to a post where he would receive honor and profit, and the country great advantages.

Your friend,

RICHARD YATES

P. S. Senator Stephen A. Douglas, who is one of the Committee of the Agricultural Convention to prepare *business*, told me (I having to have the convention to vote and act on William Bennett's Railroad Bill) that he would try and embrace the subject of your address.

---

* The organization of this Agricultural Bureau, the forerunner of the Agricultural Department, by Congress had been delayed from year to year until the farmers all over the country were very indignant.

WASHINGTON, July 10, 1852

Dear Sir:

If you have a spare copy of your address to the Granville convention on the subject of a State Agricultural University, please forward it to me. The only copy which I had was published in the *Valley Farmer* of St. Louis, and some of the Committee at the Agricultural Convention took that off. I had the promise of Mr. Ewbanks to have it published in the Patent Office Report, but, for fear he may overlook it, I have drawn up a request, to be signed by Stephen A. Douglas and myself, which I will forward him to-morrow. The *Republic* has not gone to press yet.

Very respectfully, your friend,

RICHARD YATES

CHAPTER XIV

February 8, 1853
Illinois Petitions Congress for Land-Grant Universities

In the fall of the same year—on November 24, 1852—another general convention was held at Chicago, at which it was decided formally to organize the movement as the " Industrial League of Illinois." The Legislature was petitioned for a charter, which was received in the next winter. The Proceedings of this convention are given in the pamphlet of the League as follows:

At this convention much important business was transacted, and many interesting views suggested, and speeches thereon, made and reported. Among other things, it was resolved to organize The " Industrial League of the State of Illinois," which has since been chartered by our Legislature, empowered to raise a fund, by subscriptions from the members of ten cents each per annum, and by voluntary contributions, to be applied to the forwarding of the objects of the convention, and promoting the interests of the industrial classes.

I. By disseminating information both written and printed on this subject.

II. By keeping up a concert of action among the friends of the industrial classes.

III. By the employment of lecturers, to address citizens in all parts of the State. Professor J. B. Turner of Jacksonville was appointed principal director.

John Gage of Lake County, Bronson Murray of La Salle County, Dr. L. S. Pennington of Whiteside County, J. T. Little of Fulton County, and William A. Pennell of Putnam County, associate directors.

It was also " *Resolved*, That this convention memorialize Congress for the purpose of obtaining a grant of public lands to establish and endow industrial institutions in each and every State in the Union."

The plan for an industrial university, submitted by Professor Turner to the Granville convention, was then called for, and a motion passed to discuss its principles by sections; whereupon, after thus reading and discussing of its various sections, the general principles of the plan were approved.

It was also "voted unanimously that a department for the education of common-school teachers be considered an essential feature of the plan."

Professor J. B. Turner of Jacksonville, William Gooding of Lockport, and Dr. John A. Kennicott of Northfield were appointed a committee to report a plan to the next convention, and to memorialize the Legislature for the application of the College and Seminary funds to this object, in accordance with the acts and ordinances of Congress, etc.

J. B. Turner, L. S. Bullock, and Ira L. Peck were also appointed a committee to prepare an address to the citizens of this State on the subject of industrial education and the establishment of an Industrial Institution.

The following extract is taken from the Ottawa *Free Trader* of November 24, 1852:

INDUSTRIAL EDUCATION CONVENTION

In pursuance of a resolution of the Chicago Industrial Education Convention, a similar body will meet at Springfield on the 8th of January next.

It is manifestly important that those who are friendly to this enterprise should exhibit their interest by attending this convention. The next Legislature may make a final decision of the disposition of the Seminary Fund, and if our mechanics would have a word in the matter, the Springfield convention may be their last opportunity.

But the "immobility of the masses" was frequently demonstrated in the early days of the movement, and was most discouraging. They would not attend the meetings especially planned for them. Great efforts were made to interest them through personal interviews, as well as by the public press, as can be seen by the following extract from newspapers:

November 24, 1852

To the Editor of the Springfield "Journal":

You ask for the opinion of your readers as regards the propriety of another convention of the friends of the Industrial University at Springfield, Illinois.

I have been informed that the members of the former convention held in this place felt somewhat surprised and aggrieved at the seeming utter indifference of the people of Springfield and Sangamon County to the interests of these conventions and their cause. They propose to commence an institution in this State, and, if possible, in every State in the Union, in which every man, especially every member of the great industrial classes, has a deep personal interest. Now, if the great masses of teachers, merchants and mechanics, and farmers of Sangamon County cannot be made to see and feel that *one* institution in this great State, devoted primarily to their interests and the interests of their industrial and teaching professions, is needful and desirable for them and their children; if they cannot be induced to spend a single day or a single dime to turn out and listen to the subject, or to those who propose to advance their best interests in this way; if they are determined that they will not take time to hear about it—it can be of little use to try to hold conventions. But if they will come together and talk the matter over, as do the people in some other counties, they will soon be convinced of their duty and their *rights,* and they will soon take the matter into their own hands, and conventions will be found not only to be interesting to them, but to do good. The only argument now against commencing at once such an enterprise in their behalf is derived from the interests of the common schools. But there is no desire on the part of any one to meddle with any of the common-school funds of the State. The friends of the industrial classes only wish for the University and Seminary Fund given them by the general government for this purpose. They ask only for their own.

J. B. TURNER

After the organization of the Illinois Industrial League at the Chicago convention, the whole history of this educational movement in favor of industrial education was published, in compliance with a resolution adopted at the Springfield and Chicago conventions, in a little pamphlet called " The Industrial League of Illinois." Professor Turner was chairman of the Committee on Publication. In the Introduction Professor Turner said:

Is it said that farmers and mechanics do not and will not read?

Give them a literature and an education, then, suited to their actual wants, and see if it does not reform and improve them in this respect, as it has done their brethren in the professional classes. As a matter of fact, all know they now have no such practical, congenial literature to read; and still, as a general rule, they read more and know more about the proper pursuits of the professional classes than those classes do about theirs, in proportion to the opportunities they have.

Suppose you should supply the libraries of the divine and the lawyer with practical treatises on the raising of crops, the resuscitation and improvement of soils, and the management of stock, or the navigation of the polar seas, instead of books treating of the peculiar nature and duties of his own profession. Does any man suppose that these professions would exhibit the same love of reading and study or attain the same mental discipline which they now do? The idea is absurd.

Give a divine or a lawyer a book on agriculture, and how soon it is thrown aside! And is it surprising that the farmer and mechanic treat other books on the same principle, and in the same way, for the same reason? But how greedily they devour, in all our periodicals and pamphlets, the few scraps that directly pertain to their own interests, and how soon new implements of life and power start up from their practical and creative minds out of every new idea in philosophy that dawns upon the race and claims its place in the crystal palaces and its reward at the industrial fairs of the world! And are such minds on this great continent to be longer left, by the million, without a single university or school of any sort adapted to the peculiar wants of their craft, while the whole energies of the Republic are taxed to the utmost to furnish universities, colleges, and schools adapted to the wants of the professional and military classes, who constitute not the hundredth part of the population, and represent not the thousandth part of the vital interests of any civilized and well-ordered community?

Are these pursuits, then, beneath the dignity of rational and accountable man? God himself made the first Adam a gardener or farmer, and kept him so till he fell from his high estate. The second Adam, sent to repair the ruin of this fall, he made a poor mechanic called " the son of a carpenter," who chose all his personal followers from the same humble class. Deity has pronounced his opinion on the dignity and value of these pursuits by the repeated acts of His wisdom and grace, as well as by the inflexible laws of His providence compelling industrial labor as the only means of preserving health of body, vigor, purity of mind, and even life itself.

Where did Socrates, the wisest of the Greeks, and Cincinnatus, the most illustrious of the Romans, Washington, the father of America, and Franklin, and Sherman, and Kossuth, and Downing, and Hugh Miller, and a whole host of worthies too numerous to mention, get their education? They derived it from their connection with the practical pursuits of life, where all other men have got theirs, so far forth as it has proved of any practical use to themselves or the world.

What we want from schools is to teach men, more dull of apprehension, to derive their mental and moral strength from their own pursuits, whatever they are, in the same way and on the same principles, and to gather from other sources as much more as they find time to achieve. We wish to teach them to read books, only that they may the better read and understand the great volume of nature ever open before them.

Can, then, no schools and no literature, suited to the peculiar wants of the industrial classes, be created by the application of science to their pursuits? Has God so made the world that peculiar schools, peculiar applications of science, and a peculiar resultant literature are found indispensable to the highest success in the art of killing men, in all states, while nothing of the kind can be based on the infinitely multifarious arts and processes of feeding, clothing, and housing them? Are there no sufficient materials of knowledge and of the highest mental and moral discipline in immediate connection with these pursuits? This is to suppose that God has condemned the vast majority of mankind to live in circumstances in which the best and highest development of their noblest faculties is a sheer impossibility, unless they turn aside from those spheres of duty to which His providence has evidently consigned them. Such an assumption is as pedantic and shallow as it is wicked and blasphemous. For what, but for this very end of intellectual discipline and development, has God bound, the daily labors of all these sons of toil, in the shop and on the farm, in close and incessant contact with all the mighty mysteries of his own creative wisdom, as displayed in heaven above, and on earth beneath, and in the waters and soils that are under the earth? Why are there more recondite and profound principles of pure mathematics immediately connected with the sailing of a ship, or the molding and driving of a plow, or an ax, or a jack-plane, than with all three of the so-called learned professions together, if it be not intended that those engaged in these pursuits should derive mental culture as well as bodily sustenance and strength from these instruments of their art and their toil? Why has God linked the light, the dew-drop, the clouds, the sunshine and the storm, and concentrated the mighty powers of the earth, the ocean and the sky, directed by that unknown and mysterious force which rolls the spheres and arms the thunder-cloud—why are all these mystic and potent influences connected with the growing of every plant, and the opening of every flower, the motion of every engine and every implement, if he did not intend that each son and daughter of Adam's race should learn, through the handicraft of their daily toil, to look through nature up to nature's God, trace His deep designs, and derive their daily mental and moral culture, as well as their daily food, from that toil that is ever encircled and circumscribed on all hands by the unfathomed energies of his wisdom and his power? No foundation for the development and culture of a high order of science and literature, and the noblest capacities of mind, heart, and soul, in connection with the daily employments of the industrial classes! How came such a heathenish and apostate idea ever to get abroad in the world? Was God mistaken when He first placed Adam in the garden instead of the academy? or when He sentenced him to toil for his future salvation, instead of giving him over to abstract contemplation? when He made his Son a carpenter instead of a rabbi? or when he made man a man instead of a monk? No; God's ways are ever ways of wisdom and truth; but Satan has, in all ages, continued to put darkness for light—sophistry and cant for knowledge and truth; cunning and verbiage for wisdom and virtue; tyranny and outrage for government and law—and to fill the world with brute muscles and bones in one class, luxurious, insolent, and useless nerves and brains in another class, without either bodies or souls, and to call the process by which the result in the latter case is reached, education. From the possibility of such an education as this, God has, in His mercy, hitherto sheltered his defenseless poor. And if such hotbed processes are alone to be dignified with the name of education, then it is clearly impossible that the laboring classes should ever be educated: God has interdicted it. Or, even if no other system of education is ever to be devised or attempted, except that alone which is most fit for the professional and the military man, it is equally clear that this cannot be made available to any considerable portion of the industrial classes.

Following is the report of the meeting to appoint delegates to the Fourth Convention:

ILLINOIS JOURNAL

Vol. V   No. 49

SPRINGFIELD

Tuesday Morning, Jan. 4, 1853

INDUSTRIAL CONVENTION

Pursuant to public notice, a meeting was held in the courthouse for the purpose of appointing delegates to the Industrial Convention, to be held in this place on the 4th inst.

Mr. John Armstrong was called to the chair, and John W. Gray appointed secretary.

Mr. Lumsden explained the object of the meeting, and concluded his very appropriate remarks by offering the following resolutions, which were separately considered and unanimously adopted:

" 1st. *Resolved*, That in view of the vast influence that mechanics have had in all ages in the upbuilding and progress of the world in all the useful and enduring, equalizing and ennobling properties of humanity, which have given to history all that it is worth being known, to latest recorded time; we fearlessly assert that they are entitled in this land to some share in the special education of the age, and demand it as a right to ourselves and posterity.

" 2d. *Resolved*, That, in the opinion of this meeting, the time has come when the people of the State of Illinois are called upon by every consideration to awaken to the subject of the education of the masses, and that the plan of a permanent college for the special benefit of the industrial class in the State, now deeply engaged in the public mind, meets with our hearty approval.

" 3d. *Resolved*, That we are in favor of the appropriation by the Legislature of our State, of the College and Seminary Fund for the endowment of such an institution."

On motion, delegates were appointed to attend the convention, and also that the Proceedings be published in each daily paper of this city.

JOHN ARMSTRONG, Chairman

JOHN W. GRAY, *Secretary*

The fourth convention [records the Industrial League's pamphlet] was holden at Springfield on the 8th of January, 1853.

At this meeting, also, a great many items of a miscellaneous character were brought before the convention, and discussed and decided upon—in almost every case by a unanimous vote.

The greatest harmony and good feeling prevailed among all the members and delegates, and the Representatives and executive officers of the people in the Legislature; many of whom, from all parts of the State, took the deepest interest in the subject, and made noble and eloquent speeches at their evening session in the Senate chamber in its behalf. It was

Resolved, That, inasmuch as any detailed plan of public instruction can only be decided and acted upon by the trustees, directors, or other officers of the desired institution, when created, it is not expedient to attempt to fix upon any such details in any preliminary convention of the people; and that the committee appointed to report on that subject be discharged from further duty.

The duties and terms of office of the League were also prescribed by this convention.

After the adjournment of the convention, the following
memorial was written, at the request of the committee, by
Professor Turner and signed by the president (Bronson Murray) of the convention and presented immediately to the
Legislature, in accordance with a resolution passed by the
convention. The idea of a chain of State universities for the
industrial classes throughout the United States had been
growing in Professor Turner's mind since his first illusion
to the matter at Griggsville in 1850. It appears in this petition in the very definite form of a demand for grants of
government lands for that purpose. The text of the petition
follows:

MEMORIAL
OF THE FOURTH INDUSTRIAL CONVENTION OF
THE STATE OF ILLINOIS

*To the Honorable Senate and House of Representatives of the
    State of Illinois:*

We would respectfully represent: That we are members of
the industrial classes of this State, actively and personally engaged in agricultural and mechanical pursuits. We are daily
made to feel our own practical ignorance, and the misapplication of toil and labor and the enormous waste of products, means,
materials, and resources that result from it. We are aware that
all this evil to ourselves and our country results from a want of
knowledge of those principles and laws of nature that underlie
our various professions, and of the proper means of a practical
application of existing knowledge to those pursuits. We rejoice
to know that our brethren in the several learned professions have
to a good degree availed themselves of these advantages, and have
for years enjoyed their benefit. They have universities and colleges, with apparatus, libraries voluminous and vast, able and
learned professors and teachers, constantly discovering new facts,
and applying all known principles and truths directly to the
practical uses of their several professions and pursuits. This is
as it should be. But we have neither universities, colleges, books,
libraries, apparatus, nor teachers adapted or designed to con-

centrate and apply even all existing knowledge to our pursuits; much less have we the means of efficiently exploring and examining the vast practical unknown that daily lies all around us, spreading darkness and ruin upon our best-laid plans, blighting our hopes, diminishing our resources, and working inevitable evil and loss to ourselves, to our families, and to our country. Some think one half—no intelligent man thinks that less than one third or one fourth—of the entire labor and products of our State are made an annual sacrifice to this needless ignorance and waste. Knowledge alone here is power, and our relief is as clearly obvious as our wants. We need the same thorough and practical application of knowledge to our pursuits that the learned professions enjoy in theirs, through their universities and their literature, schools, and libraries that have grown out of them. For, even though knowledge may exist, it is perfectly powerless until properly applied, and we have not the means of applying it. What sort of generals and soldiers would all our national science (and art) make if we had no military academies to take that knowledge and apply it directly and specifically to military life?

Are our classic universities, our law, medicine, and divinity schools, adapted to make good generals and warriors? Just as well as they are to make farmers and mechanics, and no better. Is the defense, then, of our resources of more actual consequence than their production? Why, then, should the State care for the one and neglect the other?

According to recent publications, only one in two hundred and sixty of the population of our own State is engaged in professional life, and not one in two hundred in the Union generally. A great proportion even of these never enjoyed the advantages of our classical and professional schools. But there are in the United States two hundred and twenty-five principal universities, colleges, and seminaries, schools, etc., devoted to the interest of the professional classes, besides many smaller ones, while there is not a single one, with liberal endowments, designed for the liberal and practical education of the industrial classes. No West Point as yet beams upon the horizon of their hope. True, as yet, our boundless national resources keep us, like the children of Japhet emigrating from the Ark, from the miserable degradation and want of older empires; but the resources themselves lie all undeveloped in some directions, wasted and misapplied in others, and rapidly vanishing away as centuries roll onward, under the ignorance and unskilfulness that directs them. We, the members of the industrial classes, are still compelled to work empirically and blindly, without needful books, schools, or means, by the slow process of that individual experience that lives and dies with the man. Our professional brethren, through their universities, schools, teachers, and libraries, combine and concentrate the practical experience of ages in each man's life. We need the same.

In monarchical Europe, through their polytechnic and agricultural schools, some successful effort has been made, in some departments and classes, to meet this great want of the age.

But in our democratic country, though entirely industrial and practical in all its aims and ends, no such effort has been efficiently made. We have in our own State no such institutions, and no practical combination of resources and means, that can ever produce one worthy of the end. We have not even a normal school for the education of our teachers, nor half a supply of efficient teachers even for our own common schools—and never can have without more attention to the indispensable means for their production. Hence, our common schools are, and must continue to be, to a great extent, inefficient and languishing, if not absolute nuisances on our soil, as in some cases they now are. But the common-school interest is the great hope of our country, and we only desire to render it efficient and useful, in the only way it can be done: by rearing up for it competent and efficient teachers, in the normal department of our industrial universities. Knowing that knowledge, like light and water, runs downward, not upward, through human society, we would begin with the suns and fountains, and not with the candles and puddles, and pour the light and water of life down through every avenue of darkness below, and not begin with the darkness and drought, and attempt to evolve and force it upward. No State ever did, or ever will, succeed by this latter process. The teacher is the first man sought, and the life and light of the whole thing, from the university downward.

To this end, concentration is the first indispensable step. Leaving all our common-school funds untouched, as they now are, the proposed distribution of our University Fund, amounting to about $150,000, will illustrate this point. The annual interest of this, at six per cent, is about $9,000. If this should be divided among our ten or fifteen colleges, it would give them only from $600 to $900 each per annum. Divided among our hundred counties, it would give $90 to each county, for a high school or any other purpose. Divided as it now is among the million of our people, it gives nine mills, or less than one cent, to each person. Concentrated upon an industrial university, it would furnish an annual corps of skilful teachers and lecturers, through its normal school, to go through all our towns and counties, create, establish, and instruct lyceums, high schools, and common schools of all sorts, and, through its agricultural and mechanical departments, concentrating and diffusing the benefits of practical knowledge and experience over all our employments and pursuits, our farms and shops. Here, as elsewhere, the sun must exist before the diamonds and dew-drops can shine. The mountain heights must send down their rills and their torrents, gathered from their own flood and the boundless resources of the ocean and the sky, before the desert can blossom as the rose. Money, however much or little, concentrated in logs, clapboards, and brick, inclosing a herd of listless, uneasy, and mischievous children, cannot make a common school. The living teacher must be there—living, not dead; for dead teachers only make dead scholars the more dead. Nor can grammar, language, metaphysics, or abstract science, however accurate, voluminous, and vast, ever diffuse new life and new energy into our industrial pursuits. There practical apparatus, the thorough and accurate needful experiments, as well as the living and practical teachers, are needed in order even to begin the great work. This is necessarily expensive, quite beyond even the anticipated resources of our existing institutions. Hence, again, we need concentration, and not a miserable, useless, and utterly wasteful diffusion of our resources and means.

Throughout our State,—and throughout the whole civilized world in all ages,—where there has been most neglect of universities and high seminaries, and most reliance placed by the people in the miserable pittance doled out to them by the State, like so many paupers, for the support of common schools— precisely there the common school will be found, for the inevitable reasons above indicated, most inefficient, weak, and worthless, if not positive nuisances to society; and whenever the reverse is found, the reverse influences of life, light, animation, and hope beam forth from the schools at once.

We repeat it, the common school is our great end, our last hope and final joy. But we would reach and reanimate it under the guidance of practical common sense, as all experience shows it must be done, as it only can be done, and we would reach the vital, practical interests of our industrial pursuits by precisely the same means and on precisely the same well-known and thoroughly tried plans and principles. We seek no novelties. We desire no new principles. We only wish to apply to the great interest of the common school and the industrial classes precisely the same principles of mental discipline and thorough scientific practical instruction, in all their pursuits and interests, which are now applied to the professional and military classes.

The effect this must have in disciplining, elevating, and refining the minds and morals of our people, increasing their wealth and their power at home and their respect abroad, developing not only the resources of their minds, but their soil and treasures of mineral, and perfecting all their materials, products, and arts, cannot but be seen by every intelligent mind.

No other enterprise so richly deserves and so urgently demands the united effort of our national strength.

We would, therefore, respectfully petition the honorable Senate and House of Representatives of the State of Illinois, that they present a united memorial to the Congress now assembled at Washington to appropriate to each State in the Union an amount of public lands not less in value than $500,000, for the liberal endowment of a system of industrial universities, one in each State in the Union, to coöperate with each other, and with the Smithsonian Institute at Washington, for the more liberal and practical education of our industrial classes and their teachers, in their various pursuits, for the production of knowledge and literature needful in those pursuits, and developing to the fullest and most perfect extent the resources of our soil and our arts, the virtue and intelligence of our people, and the true glory of our common country.

We would further petition that the Executive and Legislature of our sister States be invited to coöperate with us in this enterprise, and that a copy of the memorial of this Legislature be forwarded by the governors and Senates of the several States.

We would also petition that the University Fund of this State, if not at once applied to these practical uses, be allowed to remain where it now is, and its interest applied to present uses, until such time as the people shall be prepared to direct it to some more efficient use.

By order of the convention.

BRONSON MURRAY, *President*

A similar memorial was submitted to the convention by the committee—consisting of his Excellency Governor French, the Hon. David L. Gregg, and Dr. L. S. Pennington—appointed by the Chicago convention, and accepted and forwarded to Congress, as ordered by that convention.

These memorials were presented to the Senate and Representatives of Illinois then in session, and the merits of the plan fully discussed by able and eloquent advocates, and the following resolutions were unanimously passed by both houses, and received the approbation of the Executive within a month after the memorials were received. The official record of the Legislature's action is as follows:

Mr. Denio offered the following preamble and resolutions:

Of the General Assembly of the State of Illinois, Relative to the Establishment of Industrial Universities, and for the Encouragement of Practical and General Education among the People—Unanimously Adopted.

Whereas, The spirit and progress of this age and country demand the culture of the highest order of intellectual attainment in theoretic and industrial science: and *whereas,* It is impossible that our commerce and prosperity will continue to increase without calling into requisition all the elements of internal thrift arising from the labors of the farmer, the mechanic, and the manufacturer, by every fostering effort within the reach of the government: and *whereas,* A system of industrial universities, liberally endowed in each State of the Union, coöperative with each other and the Smithsonian Institution at Washington, would develop a more liberal and practical education among the people, tend the more to intellectualize the rising generation, and eminently conduce to the virtue, intelligence, and true glory of our common country; Therefore, be it

Resolved, by the House of Representatives, the Senate concurring herein, That our Senators in Congress be instructed, and our Representatives be requested, to use their best exertions to

procure the passage of a law of Congress donating to each State
in the Union an amount of public lands not less in value than
five hundred thousand dollars, for liberal endowment of a system
of industrial universities, one in each State in the Union, to
coöperate with each other, and with the Smithsonian Institution
at Washington, for the more liberal and practical education of
our industrial classes and their teachers; a liberal and varied
education adapted to the manifold want of a practical and enterprising people, and a provision for such educational facilities,
being in manifest concurrence with the intimations of the popular will, it urgently demands the united efforts of our national
strength.

Resolved, That the Governor is hereby authorized to forward
a copy of the foregoing resolutions to our Senators and Representatives in Congress, and to the Executive and Legislature of
each of our sister States, inviting them to coöperate with us in
this meritorious enterprise.

JOHN REYNOLDS
Speaker of the House of Representatives

G. KOERNER
Speaker of the Senate

J. A. MATTESON
Governor

Approved, February 8, 1853.
A true copy: Attest,

ALEXANDER STARNE, *Sec'y of State*

CHAPTER XV

The Fight of the Industrial League

It was a year before the resolution of Illinois was formally brought before Congress. In the meanwhile the new Industrial League of Illinois, and Professor Turner, its moving spirit, were hard at work to secure public support for the State Industrial University plan, both in Illinois and in the nation. It was chartered by the Illinois Legislature February 8, 1853, and Professor Turner started at once lecturing, securing other lecturers, and circulating the pamphlets which the League had authorized him to prepare and publish. The story of the hard struggle of that year is well told by extracts from his letters, and by notices appearing in the newspapers of Illinois.

The following letters, written by Professor Turner, were addressed to the Hon. Bronson Murray of Ottawa, Illinois, an enthusiastic friend of the Industrial University plan, and a most generous contributor to the daily growing expenses through all the dark days of this early struggle. At this time Professor Turner was very anxious to start Dr. Rutherford on a lecture tour over the State.

B. MURRAY

Dear Sir:

I wrote you last week, and must bore you again. I wish your advice as regards Dr. Rutherford. He proposes to start out at once and lecture through the State, and give his whole time and strength to the League, for $600 per annum and found, and take the risk of gathering the dimes or have other agents gather them after him as he goes.

I cannot but regard this as a God-send to us, but it may strike you differently. I have never known a man in the State so successful as a popular lecturer as Dr. Rutherford has been, or so acceptable to all classes. He can also give, in connection with his University and League lectures, an occasional lecture on his favorite theme of physiology with his charts, when deemed best as a ticket lecturer, the profit of which shall go to the League. What say you to this move? Please advise me.

The old Hunker presidents and pedants are figuring away again at Springfield, I learn, for the University Fund slyly. I threw a bomb-shell among them by mail this morning. Please write your friends to be on their guard against them.

They now propose to divide up the fund with the Catholics and four other sects—to the exclusion of all others, and of the industrial classes, too; give it to them on this odious and partial union of church and state.

Yours truly,

J. B. TURNER

ILLINOIS COLLEGE, February 5, 1853

B. MURRAY, Esq.

Dear Sir:

I am in distress again. I was just exulting in our complete triumph when I heard, through Lumsden, that a bill was pending for a charter for the University. He and others may have alluded to this before to me, but, if so, I always supposed they referred to a charter for the League. I know nothing definitely—I only know the fact that somebody there at Springfield has drawn a bill of some sort for the incorporation of the University.

We needed no such movement now—it can only do us harm. I did not dream it was possible so important a matter could come up, as it was not recommended by the convention, or alluded to, as I heard.

I am sorry for this, but we must bear it as well as we can and make the best of it. We must ever expect to take the evil with

the good, and our success at Springfield (aside from this) , I
admit, was almost too good for mortals to expect.

Yours truly,

J. B. TURNER

Mr. Lumsden immediately afterward explained his motive
for introducing a university bill in the Legislature at this
time, in a letter to Mr. Murray:

SPRINGFIELD, ILLINOIS, February 16, 1853

To B. MURRAY, Esq.

My dear Friend:

Yours of the 12th reached me to-day. I have just finished
writing some dozen letters and mailing some forty circulars. I
intend to forward them to all the States and Territories, even
that of Utah. I called upon Governor Matteson to-day, and gave
him some forty or fifty to send into the several States. I asked
his opinion of the project of industrial universities. He is quite
favorable. The funds in the hands of this State obtained from
the sales of lands appropriated by the United States expressly for
the use of a college or university, and the two townships for the
establishment of a seminary of learning, cannot by the law and
compact of the grant be ultimately used for any other purpose.
The State can loan the funds to any purpose, but cannot apply
them for any other purpose than for what they were given. The
law is imperative on this point, and is similar in Missouri and
other States. But the latest notion which the " priests of Baal "
have deigned to utter is that the " state is incompetent to control
the subject of education. Where it has been tried it has signally
failed. That the church alone is competent to educate the
people " !!! I told the Protestant priest who said this to me that
he had better keep such thoughts to himself or else we should
know where to place him. This is the very argument of the
Papists. If our modern Protestants are going back in principle,
they had better assume the name with full honors.

Well, you seem to express alarm at the work I have been about,
when there really is no occasion for any whatever. I knew that
the only way to get at our object was to bring the subject right
up in the Legislature, have it discussed, and let it be referred to

some committee. But you need not fear but what I had all the matter in my mind. The rough outline was passed straight through the House, the amendment stuck on to it in the Senate, and, had it been adopted and gone into the House, I should have had it there made perfect and just to our notion. The discussion alone was worth all the trouble. In fact, it was primarily for no other object than this, and to have its title go out among the Proceedings of the House and Senate. This would make the citizens of Zion quake with very fear! And, I tell you, I have had my own sport over the long and wry faces manifested by those "presidential and college men."

The "Northern Industrial College" is the title of that charter. It was amended on its passage, and will incite to a greater attention on the subject. "My bill" was referred to the Judiciary Committee of the Senate, and was reported back and laid on table, for want of time to give it that consideration the subject merited. Mr. Judd attended to it for me, and did with it as I requested. Year in and year out shall we make appeals to the people, and to the Assembly in their behalf. Next time we shall have a good bill, fully submitted to all the friends, with their approval and the recommendation of the Governor. I have written to Messrs. Yates, Seward, Gibbings, Shields, and Douglas [in Congress], besides to the Patent Office and the Secretary of the Interior, and sent them circulars; also to Governor Seymour of New York and to many agricultural, mechanical, and general papers and associations. Horace Greeley of the New York *Tribune* comes out very flatteringly about the resolutions. It will devolve on you to send one of them to each of the governors of the States. You will find their names all in the Whig Almanac for 1853, second page on cover. If you write me, address at St. Joseph, Missouri. I leave to-day.

Yours truly,

GEORGE LUMSDEN

Professor Turner confirms my fears that we have nothing to hope positively from Governor M. [Matteson]. There is something rotten in Denmark.

Professor Turner's letters to Mr. Murray continue the story of the work of 1853:

ILLINOIS COLLEGE, February 23, 1853

B. MURRAY, Esq.

Dear Sir:

Your welcome letter of February 12 is at hand. I have concluded a contract with Dr. Rutherford to lecture, and to commence about the first of May at his own risk, he to have the privilege of withdrawing therefrom whenever he chooses, or, if he can make it go, of continuing two years.

The cost of our pictorial certificate is going to be too much unless we continue to use vignettes already engraved at the banking-house. But I leave the matter wholly to your judgment. Dr. Rutherford is quite desirous to have something of the kind in readiness when he first starts out in May, if possible. Can it be done?

You mentioned that I could draw on the funds of the Chicago Convention for a certain amount—I forget how much, and whom besides yourself. I would like now to make the draft, so as to get Stephens hold of the work for the League—the address records, copying, printing, etc. This cannot be done without money, and my own business and collections have been so much neglected this past year that I shall not be able to collect or advance anything of my own, in all probability, till after payments for next sales come in, in the fall, nor then if I neglect it as much as I have been obliged to for months past. A line from Dr. Kennicott shows him to be in good heart still; same of other friends.

Yours truly,

J. B. TURNER

ILLINOIS COLLEGE, March 15, 1853

B. MURRAY, Esq.

Dear Sir:

Yours of the 9th is at hand, with extracts, for which many thanks. Mr. Lumsden has been here and explained the matter of the charter all fully and satisfactorily. He has managed the thing well in the end—they did not catch him in any of the traps I was fearful they would try to. He was quite too wide awake to be caught napping, and, when he had done all he could with his bill by way of agitation, killed it off himself, and escaped all danger. Was not that very well done?

I have some hopes of getting Mr. John Davis to lecture in the south of the State. He will do it and feed his own horse for $500 per annum, and possibly $400. He is one of five to guarantee his own pay for the first trial. I would be one of the five also, but do not know how to do it—burning colleges, and events of business, have picked me so bare this year. Besides, we must not use up this pledge fund in this way, for if we do we shall not have the means of our lectures operating successfully. I wish Lumsden could be kept in Springfield, or in the State; he is useful there; but I fear we shall lose him.

If we could manage to start Rutherford north and Davis south to lecture, I think we could make it go. Please express your mind.

Yours in haste, truly,

J. B. TURNER

B. MURRAY, Esq.   May 8, 1853
Dear Sir:

Yours of April 30 is at hand. I have only time to say that we have made no progress with the League matters since I last wrote you—not a bit. Not one of the gentlemen to whom I wrote remitted, and, of course, there are no funds to do anything with, and I have had no time to push the matter this spring.

I do not like this design as well as the other, but, as it is so much cheaper, I suppose we must do with it for the present.

The lecturers are not ready yet to enter upon the field—nor do I know that they will do it unless something as an outfit can be collected with which to start them.

These and other things are very discouraging, and no progress can be made; nor ought any debts of the League to be incurred so long as things are so. My address to the people of the State is ready (or nearly so), and approved by those who have seen it; but there are no funds to publish it, and it lies still-born.

I like the suggestion as regards fees. My present business, as usual in spring, has used me up for months past until now. Our friends elected me to go to Ottawa on the 18th of May to the Free-Soil Convention, and if I can get away I shall go, so as to see some of the friends there of the University. I hope to see you, but it seems almost impossible for me to get away. Kind regards to family and friends. In haste,

Yours truly,

J. B. TURNER

JACKSONVILLE, ILLINOIS, August 1, 1853

BRONSON MURRAY, Esq.

Dear Sir:

Your sketch for the League came to hand. I think it will answer for the present, though not at all equal to the other. Those familiar with the public feeling say the people are too much engrossed with railroads just now to render much attention to our project, and think it is not expedient to try to push it with great vigor just yet. What say you to this?

The opposition dynasty we are using up as fast as we can on another score. I think we shall effectually lay them cold without even mentioning university, which is much to be desired, if possible. I have spent half my time at it this summer, and will send you the final issues of the controversy as soon as out of the press—which I hope you will see scattered far and wide; for this clique are our most formidable enemies, and it is better for us to destroy their corrupt power in the State on other grounds, if we can *justly*, rather than wait and have to fight them again directly over the University, as we shall surely have to do if we do not put them down now on the grounds of the existing institutions. With this in view, I have directed my whole energies this summer toward that result, and have had a hard time of it, too. But we have got them at bay finally now, and shall soon use them up. They, of course, have done all they could to ruin me, in return; but it has all returned upon their own heads here, so far. We have at least nine tenths of the people with us, and the whole of the law and the courts, and the whole of the old Governor French administration and their friends.

We are all in fine health and tolerable spirits. Mrs. Turner and little Mary are still in the East.* Please tender our kind regards to Mrs. M. and your family friends.

Yours truly,

J. B. TURNER

In the next letter Professor Turner refers to the controversy described later in Chapter XXVI. The people could not understand his long contest with the " clique " over the management of the State Hospital funds. It is very doubtful

---

* Mrs. Turner had been sent last to her mother, to remain during the controversy over the Board of the Hospital for the Insane.

if many of them ever knew his motives, but the following extract from a letter to his friend Bronson Murray shows the far-reaching effect he thought the victory would have in the management of State institutions, not only of this institution in this State, but of all institutions that might come after it.

JACKSONVILLE, ILLINOIS, August 9, 1853

B. MURRAY, Esq.

Dear Sir:

Yours of August 3 is at hand. I wrote you a week ago, stating the causes of existing delay, and intimating the "war to the knife" in which I have been involved, together with the other friends of the Insane Hospital, every week since you were here. This war has had a direct bearing upon our League and industrial interests, and must necessarily delay them all till it is through, or ruin them, for the present at least, if our opponents are not thoroughly defeated. This we all see here, but it is too long and complicated a story to explain in a letter. We feel that they are pretty well used up now, and they feel it more than we do. Now I hope for a clear sea, fair wind, and sailors' rights ever after this most desperate fight, for all admit it has been the most desperate fight ever had in the State. We have given them the grape to their hearts' content, and now I hope they will let us alone. If this job is thoroughly done up, as we intend it shall be, and think it now is, the University and other State institutions will hereafter have fair play.

Yours truly,

J. B. TURNER

The hard fight was showing results. In the meantime, every method of reaching the people was being used. The following notice from the Ottawa *Free-Trader* during this year illustrates the painstaking effort to reach the whole population:

The Industrial League have made a report to the people of this State upon the movement in favor of the Industrial University. It is for sale at the post-office in Ottawa, at the cost of printing and paper, and purchasers who have read it may, if they choose, return it and take up their money if they do not seriously deface the copy.

The terms are fair, ten cents, and every person who has a son or daughter to educate should read it.

Now that the United States Government has some ten or twenty millions of surplus moneys, which politicians are at a loss how to dispose of constitutionally, it strikes us that this little pamphlet provides a desirable solution of the difficulty. Farmers and mechanics are especially invited to attend to this.

The Illinois State Agricultural Society was incorporated at the same session of the Legislature as the Industrial League, and was organized on February 5, 1853, three days before the League's incorporation. On February II a fund of two thousand dollars was appropriated by the Legislature for its use. A committee of the society met in Springfield on May 25, to make plans for the first State Fair, which was held near that city from the 11th to the 14th of the following October. Professor Turner was invited to deliver the address. In this address Professor Turner referred to the university land-grant movement in the following words:

Doubtless you are aware that several conventions of farmers and mechanics have been held in our State, and in other States, to secure this great end. You are also aware that the Legislature of our State had the high honor to be the *first* in this great confederation of republics to invoke our sister States to unite in a petition to the general government for an appropriation of five hundred thousand dollars' worth of our vacant lands for the endowment in each State in the Union of an industrial university suited to their wants.

Our friends in New York have already reprinted our reports—without honoring them with quotation-marks—and thus, with our stolen thunder, aroused their industrial population and called for munificent endowments for an industrial university. She has already her funds and her university in full blast, and is now calling upon her people, on this basis, for a second munificent endowment for the same end.

Michigan many years ago established a State Agricultural College, but she has never made any effort for agricultural colleges outside of the boundaries of her own State.

Illinois is the first to advocate a national appropriation for every State and Territory.

Many extracts from editorials in newspapers opposing this plan of Professor Turner's for industrial universities could be given which, in the light of history as written to-day, would make very interesting reading. Professor Turner became weary of these criticisms, and wrote a sarcastic reply which silenced them for a time; but a few courageous friends were tried and true.

The following extract is from a letter from W. H. Powell, the candidate for State Superintendent of Schools, to B. Murray:

PEORIA, February 12, 1856

One correspondent requested me to plant myself fair and square on the "anti-Professor Turner platform," and concluded a long letter by saying that I "can have no possible hope of success unless I do." I have replied to it saying what I mean: that "between the two alternatives of being Superintendent of Illinois and retaining the respect and esteem of Professor Turner, I should unhesitatingly and unequivocally choose the latter." Professor T. may, like all men, sometimes be in the wrong, but in his education ideas I believe, if I rightly comprehend them, he is right—though somewhat in the advance of some by whom he is surrounded. The day has gone by when class interests are the only ones to be subserved. Our American civilization demands a more comprehensive and liberal system. We must educate the whole people as the only enduring foundation upon which our republican institutions can rest.

Professor Turner's friend, President Tappan of the University of Michigan, sent this invitation on February 13, 1856:

My dear Sir:

The Executive Committee of the Association for the Advance of Education have instructed me to invite you to read a paper on some subject related to their great object, at the next annual meeting, which will be held in Detroit on the second Tuesday of August next. Will you reply to this at your earliest convenience, and if you accept this invitation, which we earnestly hope you will, inform me of the subject you have selected.

I am, very respectfully and

Truly yours,

HENRY P. TAPPAN,
President of the Association

Professor Turner accepted this invitation and wrote the following letter home after he had delivered the address:

DETROIT, MICHIGAN, August, 1856

My dear Wife and Children:

The convention here has been an important and interesting one, and I have made the acquaintance of several interesting and distinguished men and heard several spirited discussions on the subject of education. My own discussion took them all aback as I expected, but it was listened to with profound attention and respect, and characterized by one distinguished member of the convention from Brooklyn, New York, as a discussion " in strong thought and strong language, strongly expressed, a thing not easy to get by."

Some further discussion of it may take place this morning; and, if so, I presume the old fogies and dough-faces in the convention will (if there are any such) try to pick it to pieces. But they will find the bones very hard to pick, for the majority of the convention evidently received it not only with profound respect but with heartfelt satisfaction, and *know* that it is just what ought to be both said and done.

Affectionately yours,

J. B. TURNER

A letter from United States Senator Stephen A. Douglas reads:

CHICAGO, ILLINOIS, October 12, 1857

My dear Sir:

Accept my thanks for your kind note enclosing the pamphlet on Industrial Universities which I will take pleasure in reading with the view of forming a favorable judgment on the proposed movement.

I shall be happy to receive your work on " The Races " when completed.

Very respectfully, your obedient servant,

S. A. DOUGLAS, U. S. S.

At the meeting of the State Teachers' Association, held in Chicago in December, 1856, Professor Turner addressed a letter to the Association which was read by the late Dr. Newton Bateman. This letter exerted a great influence in securing the passage of the bill in the Legislature to establish the State Normal School toward which the " Seminary Fund " had been applied.

By the establishment of the State Normal School at Bloomington a nucleus was formed, around which gathered all the practical educational interests of the State. A correspondent of the Chicago *Times*, June 27, 1860, gave an interesting account of the commencement week; for, besides the anniversary exercises of the Normal School and the Illinois Natural History Society, a State convention was organized to consider the best method of advancing the agricultural educational interests of the State:

Captain James N. Brown was unanimously elected president of the convention. Mr. C. T. Chase of Chicago, being called for, said that, at the request of his associates of the Horticultural Society, he had visited, in person, the greater number of the agricultural schools in the country. He had found many manual training schools, schools of agriculture, and farm schools, the latter near the great cities, for the purpose of reclaiming younger children who had fallen under evil influences. In New York on Lake Geneva, and in Michigan, a large tract of land had been purchased and each State had appropriated money, but as yet nothing practical had resulted. In Iowa the matter was still in embryo. The State had gone so far as to buy, for the purpose, seven hundred acres, located a day's ride from Des Moines, the capital. The result was, nothing had as yet been effectively done; and it remained for the State of Illinois, ignoring all sectional and political jealousies, simply striving for the best manner and men to carry forward this noble work to a successful and prosperous issue.

Professor McChesney of Springfield, being called for, said that the University of Chicago, in receiving its charter had incorporated within it a provision for an agricultural department. He had accepted a professorship in the college proper, but he was interested in the work of the State also, and hoped there would be no feeling of jealousy; in enterprises like these there should be a common sympathy of brotherhood for a common object. He then gave an interesting account of the plans contemplated.

Professor Turner was then called for, and said, in part:

"I see an omen for the future in the present gathering. I remember well when we could not get out a single farmer at a convention for this purpose, though repeated calls and drumming had been made, and though the convention was held at the capital during the session of the Legislature. The world moves, Mr. President. If I might be allowed to use a homely farmer's simile, while sitting in my own door-yard, I have seen the immense droves of Missouri cattle coming by, and as the heavy, clustered tramp of the pawing, bellowing herd came near, all left their irresistible, onward path; and so now I feel, when I see the farmers coming up in masses, bent on the accomplishment of an object—I feel the presence of a mighty, irresistible power."

He suggested the necessity of union, and the entire abandonment of sectional interests. He deemed the failure of agricultural societies heretofore to be due to making manual labor schools of them, to entanglement with State and political interests, and to the placing at their head some one whose taste and spirit was not agricultural. To put an elderly clergyman at the head of an agricultural school was like placing General Scott in charge of a theological seminary. The speaker advocated, as a source of endowment, the procuring of the passage of what *is known as the Morrill Bill*. The speaker deprecated any jealousy of the school located at Chicago. The State was a broad one, and he was only sorry that the noble work commenced in Chicago was not fourfold in its extent. He suggested the placing of the agricultural school in charge of men appointed by the two great and permanent organizations who are chosen by the farmers and mechanics at large—the State Agricultural Society and the State Horticultural Society.

CHAPTER XVI

Letters from Home

For fear that some reader may think the head of the household, engaged in this long and arduous fight, was the only one who was anxious and weary, a glance into the home may not be without profit. In all great movements, it is the wife and mother, at home with the little ones, beyond the line of excitement, enthusiasm, or danger, as the case may be, who bears the heavier burden and deserves the greater honor. Mrs. Turner was a timid woman, afraid of the storm, afraid of the dark, afraid of the enemies of her husband, who threatened, ridiculed, and annoyed—a conservative woman, holding in honor and reverence the thoughts and customs of her day, and viewing with apprehension and dismay the revolutionary movements in which her husband was constantly engaged, first in one field of thought and then in another, but always fifty years in advance of his time, and, therefore, never on the topmost wave of honor and respect. It seems incredible now, in view of the many State universities all over our broad land, that such bitter strife could have arisen over the founding of anything so useful and so splendid. At first the plan was assailed from pulpit and rostrum. Ministers and judges vied with each other in using it as an illustration of all that was most visionary and absurd. They christened it " Turner's folly." Cartoons appeared in the daily and weekly papers, showing professors, in high silk hats and kid gloves, out in the fields, holding plow-handles in the most awkward and ungainly way, teaching the students, standing around, how to plow.

At the beginning of the second year of the fight, Professor Turner wrote to his family of his successful lecturing tour:

EDWARDSVILLE, ILLINOIS, January 8, 1853

My Own Wife and Family:

We have met but one continued triumph so far. We have carried all before us in Upper and Lower Alton, without the least opposition from any source. Mr. Norton and all other *good men* who may have differed with me in time past on other matters, like true Christian men seem rejoiced that I have at last found a sphere of labor and action in which they can heartily coöperate with me and bid me God-speed.

I will write you again from Chicago.

Yours as ever,

J. B. TURNER

His wife's experiences were not so pleasant. After reaching Chicago Professor Turner received the following letters:

JACKSONVILLE, ILLINOIS, January 13, 1853

My dear Husband:

We did not receive your letter until yesterday. I began to think surely some evil had befallen you. The boys have generally done well. We have not been burnt out yet, but I do not know but that we shall freeze out, for it is terribly cold. We shall be glad when you are back again.

Seven days later she wrote:

. . . We are so constituted we can get accustomed to almost anything, and it is well that it is so; but there are a good many things here that need your presence. However, I am willing you should stay until you think it best to come home.

Evidently the wife's letter of the 13th had not been received when Professor Turner wrote from Chicago:

January 16, 1853

My dear Wife:

I was exceedingly disappointed in not hearing from you by to-day's mail.

I have lectured here two evenings, Friday and Saturday. Our cause, here as at all other places, is carrying all before it. We have got almost the entire press and the most influential men in the city and church and the State, including the Mayor and Council of the city.

The Mayor is greatly interested, and invited me to make his house my home so long as I remained in the city, which I am doing.

My arrival here was announced in the city papers, and the editors of the daily papers are all giving us a strong and flattering aid, as you will see. The rich men and the railroad men are strong for us, and we are attacked from *no quarter,* nor do *any treat* us with indifference who know our plans. My own health is good; I have lectured almost every night somewhere since I left home, on some subject connected with our theme.

I am engaged for Tuesday and Wednesday nights positively, and conditionally for some evenings after that, if I do not hear from home. The principal railroad men here are so deeply interested in our views that they have given me a pass over their railroad wherever I wish to go till next July.

I am so anxious to hear from you, and know how you all get on and what you all desire. I hope to hear by mail to-night. I shall bend my steps homeward as soon as all our interests are secured in Chicago, and leave Dr. Rutherford to finish the northern part of the State. Our friends, however, wish me to take Peoria and the largest towns in my route, if I hear nothing from you to prevent. We have not yet met with one single resistance or a discouraging fact.

In haste,

Yours as ever,

J. B. Turner

Chicago, ever alert to see and to receive any new thought or plan that might react to her advantage, received the lecturer most cordially and indorsed his ideas with enthusiasm. The city papers contained reports of the meetings and lectures.

The City Council requested the Mayor to call a special meeting to consider " the founding of an industrial university and State normal school, and to petition the Legislature to appropriate the Seminary Funds for that purpose."

The Board of Directors of the Mechanics' Institute, a literary association, took similar action.

The next letter from his wife, however, formed the one cloud over the success of Professor Turner's stay in Chicago:

JACKSONVILLE, ILLINOIS

Sabbath Evening, January 22, 1853

My dear Husband:

I hope you will come directly home. Patrick [the hostler] has been drinking badly all the last week. I do not think he is fit to have charge of the team. He came down this noon (Sunday) and said he was going to the country to get a cow for us. I knew he had been drinking, and persuaded him not to go until to-morrow; but he took one horse in the afternoon, unbeknown to us, and went out sleigh-riding. When the boys went out to the barn, Bally was gone. The boys found him harnessed with one of Mr. McEver's horses to a sled up in front of the hostler's house. Rhodolphus brought him home. They were mad—there were several Irishmen there; they were all more or less drunk. They swore so that I could hear them down to our house. I started to go up, not knowing what might happen (you know young blood is hot) ; but I met the boys with the horse, which looked as if he had seen hard times. Pat was very drunk. I regret very much indeed that this happened. The children are afraid, and we have, as you well know, many causes of anxiety before this happened. It is severely cold here. Good night. From your affectionate wife, who feels somewhat of cares, consisting of fires within and without, boys, horses, and drunken Irishmen,

R. S. TURNER

So the words " industrial university " and the little black valise in the father's hand brought only fear and sorrow to the loved ones left behind. One picture stands out clear on memory's walls. The father, ready to start for the train, the mother and six little children standing near. The mother's

voice still rings in our ears, though more than fifty years have
come and gone: " Mr. Turner, *must* you go—*must* you go? "
" Yes, Mother." And I can see, even now, the tender look in
my father's eyes and hear his trembling voice. " But I will
take the first train home, after my lecture." And so the husband and father departed from home, taking with him all the
sunshine and happiness, and, as it seemed to our childish
minds, all the safety, too.

The discussion in the press and public assemblies continued. The working classes and the agricultural papers grew
more and more convinced of the practical features of the
" plan " and its great advantages for them; while the literary
and professional classes attacked it with ever-increasing venom.
The secret of this was not so much opposition to the " plan,"
or lack of interest in the working classes, as that each college
and seminary hoped to get hold of the College and Seminary
Fund, or a part of it—which now, with its accumulated interest, amounted to some hundred and fifty thousand dollars—
for their own endowment fund. To see springing up a new
university which promised to be so strong a competitor in
their own line of work was bad enough; but to see it also
swallowing up all the funds they had been endeavoring for
so many years to get a part of was even more dismaying.

Requests for newspaper articles and letters of inquiry came
from all over the United States; this, in addition to his own
line of work and of lecturing, wore heavily upon Professor
Turner, for he was a poor man with a large family dependent
upon him. After working all day in his nursery and Osage
orange hedge fields, he would write at night, often with his
little children playing around him. The only reproof that
can be remembered is the following mild one—when they
climbed upon the table to jump down: " Sho, sho! you joggle
me." Little things did not disturb him. So interested was
he in the success of this university, and so oppressed by his
correspondence and lecturing, that sometimes the breakfast-
bell found him at his desk.

Human nature could not long endure such abuse. His
eyes gave out, and for three months he sat day after day in a

dark room, his eyes heavily bandaged with wet linen cloths, and these covered by a black silk handkerchief. The rooms adjoining were kept perfectly dark, so that the opening of a door might not let in a ray of light to cause excruciating pain. Many of his lectures, when the pain became less intense, were delivered with his eyes thus bandaged. He was led to and from the halls and platforms leaning upon the arm of his friend Bronson Murray, a typical New York gentleman, tall, erect, elegant, and called the handsomest man in Illinois. Professor Turner, bowed with hard work and weary with opposition and cares, stumbled along in his blindness; but he was greeted everywhere by the masses with enthusiasm and listened to with profound attention. Many letters were daily received, of which the following extract is a sample:

LAFAYETTE, OREGON TERRITORY

Sir: June 1, 1856

I have read with interest your article, contained in the Patent Office Report for 1851, on the subject of industrial university. I have also conversed with many of the prominent men of our Territory on the subject, who generally seemed to regard the plan as one especially applicable to Oregon.

I have recently been appointed University Land Commissioner for this Territory, and have become painfully sensible, both from experience and observation, of the great want of agricultural knowledge among those who undertake to till the soil. My purpose in addressing you is to solicit such information as you are in possession of, that may be convenient to transmit, in regard to the practical working of such institutions. I am trying, and have been for some six years past, to farm in Oregon, but find that I am so ignorant, and the means of obtaining practical information so limited, that I am almost ready to give it up. . . .

From what I have learned of your character, I feel assured of your assistance in this work. Your interest is not circumscribed by the limits of your State boundaries, nor your expectations limited to the accomplishment of this object in your own State alone, but you will heartily respond to the call for help from the distant shores of the Pacific.

In the meantime, permit me to remain,

Yours, etc.,

AHIO S. WATT

More encouraging letters were received, one from Owen
P. Lovejoy, member of Congress from Illinois:

PRINCETON, ILLINOIS, June 2, 1856

PROFESSOR J. B. TURNER

My dear Sir:

I see by the papers that there is to be a meeting at Springfield
on the 8th, to secure, as I understand, the application of funds
in the hands of the State for the purpose of establishing an agricultural college or institution. First, I wish to express my entire
and hearty approbation of the object of the convention, namely,
to secure the funds alluded to for the education of the industrial
classes. If scattered among the existing institutions, it will, very
likely, be a bone of contention, and at best can do but little good
divided up into fragmentary portions; but, on the other hand,
if devoted to the object of agricultural education, it may at last
become the germ of something noble and useful. I hope, therefore, that the convention may be successful. I hope, too, that
they will feel they are acting for the future. Let every one of
the human family have a part of the great farm of the Heavenly
Father. It will make him loyal to his country, more able and
willing to sustain and protect her institutions, and a better man
in all relations of life.

Hoping and trusting that the convention will be governed by
the spirit of wisdom and beneficence, I am,

Very respectfully,

OWEN LOVEJOY

CHAPTER XVII

March 20, 1854
The Illinois Resolution Reaches Congress

The movement for national aid to industrial education, which Professor Turner had inaugurated and was working so hard to promote in Illinois, was already in 1853 making its influence felt throughout the country. How far it had gone is well shown by the comment of the Illinois *Journal*, published in Springfield, the capital of the State, on December 13, 1853:

A Washington letter says Caleb Lyon has prepared a bill, which will be presented soon, for the establishment of a scientific agricultural college somewhat after the plan of Georgians in France.

The first movement in regard to the establishment of such an institution in the United States was made in Illinois. But, while Illinois has faltered in carrying out the plan, New York has got up and endowed an agricultural and mechanical college which is fast becoming one of the most popular educational institutions in the State. The subject is agitated in other States, and we now see that one is sought to be established under the patronage of the government. We would much rather see Mr. Lyon engaged in seeking to obtain from Congress donations of land to enable each State to get up and sustain an agricultural college on their own account. Government has been liberal in regard to the encouragement of manufactures, by protective tariffs, but what has she hitherto done directly for agriculture?

The Ottawa *Free Trader* asserts that some person has been publishing a series of articles, upon the subject of establishing in western New York an agriculture college, in the Buffalo *Commercial*. These articles were entirely made up from Professor Turner's Granville plan, and in several instances the writer had taken from one to three pages verbatim from Professor Turner's plan. These articles were palmed off upon the people of western New York as wholly original, and so much delighted were they with this delightful conception that they forthwith put it into practical operation, while Illinois, where the plan originated, is lying upon her oars, and, instead of reaping the honors of her own invention, will probably be the last to adopt it. Still, let its friends keep its fire burning. Our Legislature will some day or other come to its senses. If we cannot be the first, let us be the second.

On March 20, 1854, the resolution passed by the Legislature of Illinois the year before reached Congress. The record of this appears in the *Congressional Globe* * as follows:

Mr. Washburne of Illinois, by unanimous consent, presented the joint resolutions of the State of Illinois relative to the establishment of industrial universities for the encouragement of practical and general education among the people in the several States of the Union, to coöperate with each other and the Smithsonian Institution at Washington.

It was presented in the Senate on the same day by James Shields, the junior Senator from Illinois.

The movement was making progress. Professor Turner was much encouraged, and records the development of the preceding two years in the following letter to his home paper, the *Morgan Journal* of Jacksonville, dated June 15, 1854:

---

* Vol. 28, Part I, page 678, First Session, Thirty-third Congress.

PRACTICAL EDUCATION IN ILLINOIS AND ELSEWHERE

MR. PAUL SELBY, *Editor:*

To bring this cause of industrial education and the "university plan" directly before the people, the Industrial League was organized. They have put laborers in the field, whose object has not been to solicit money, but opinion.

Instead of meeting with "disfavor from the people," we have abundant evidence that no educational movement, on its first being proposed, was ever investigated with so much interest, or ever received so general an approval in the popular mind, as this.

But this is not all. The movement has gained credit for the State abroad.

The New York papers yield to us the honor of having taken the first step in a cause worthy of the nation.

Horace Greely, in the issue of his paper, the New York *Tribune,* of February 26, 1853, has this remark, subjoined to the joint resolutions passed by our General Assembly relative to the establishment of industrial universities and for the encouragement of practical and general education among the people:

"Here is the principle contended for by the friends of practical education abundantly confirmed, with a plan for its immediate realization. And it is worthy of note, that one of the most extensive of public-land (or new) States proposes a magnificent donation of public lands to each of the States, in furtherance of this idea. Whether that precise form of aid to the project is most judicious and likely to be effective, we will not here consider.

"Suffice it that the Legislature of Illinois has taken a noble step forward, in a most liberal and patriotic spirit, for which its members will be heartily thanked by thousands throughout the Union. We feel that this step has materially hastened the coming of scientific and practical education for all who desire and are willing to work for it. It cannot come too soon."

And Congress has also already been touched, through the efforts of the Illinois Industrial League. Mr. Washburne has been complimented, in connection with his State, for the action taken, and other State Legislatures are imitating our good example.

The resolutions having been brought before Congress, it was now time for practical work toward securing congressional aid; and the Illinois members of Congress gave attention to the matter immediately. The following letter from Representative Richard Yates to Professor Turner discusses the situation as it was in the spring of 1854:

WASHINGTON, D. C., April 14, 1854

Dear Sir:

I received your letter by this morning's mail, and thank you for it. I am very glad to learn that my course on the Nebraska Bill has met with the approval of the people of my district. I took grounds against it before I heard from one of them.

Mr. Washburne has not introduced any bill on the subject of industrial universities. He presented the resolutions of the Legislature—that was all.

Will you please draw up a bill such as you think would accomplish the end desired, and forward it to me? *Question:* Is it best that these institutions should have any connection with the Smithsonian Institution? The officers of that institution have very ethereal notions about its objects, and, I believe, at one of the national agricultural conventions opposed its associations with the subject of agriculture, claiming that, as the bequest of Smithson was for the " *diffusion of useful knowledge*," it was to stand alone and separate from any *particular* institution.

Now, had the bill better not be so shaped as to avoid opposition from the strong influences which the officers of that institution might bring to bear? Would not an agricultural bureau be the proper head to which reports, etc., could be sent?

However, I have not studied this subject—you have. Therefore, send me at your earliest convenience a bill, and I will present it and do what I can to have it passed. In haste,

Very truly,

Your obedient servant,

RICHARD YATES

CHAPTER XVIII

July 2, 1862

The Morrill Bill, the First
Civil Bill Signed by President Lincoln

Professor Turner prepared a bill, as requested by Representative Yates, and forwarded it to Washington. It was not found wise to push the matter in that session, and the following fall Richard Yates was not re-elected to Congress, so the " Bill " was again delayed. Later a feeling of opposition was growing against land-grants, because of the over-lavish grants for various purposes in the early '50's; and the time was far from propitious. The situation was well explained in the following letter from Lyman Trumbull, then United States Senator from Illinois, written just before the opening of Congress in the winter of 1857-58.

ALTON, October 19, 1857

PROFESSOR J. B. TURNER

My dear Sir:

I thank you for your friendly letter of October 7. In my public course I have simply tried to discharge my duty, and it is a great satisfaction to feel that I have the approbation of those best capable of judging. Our free institutions are undergoing a fearful trial, nothing less, as I conceive, than a struggle with those now in power, who are attempting to subvert the very basis upon which they rest. Things are now being done in the name of the Constitution which the framers of that instrument took special pains to guard against, and which they did provide against as plainly as human language could do it. The recent use of the army in Kansas, to say nothing of the complicity of the administration with the frauds and outrages which have been committed in that Territory, presents as clear a case of usurpation as could well be imagined. Whether the people can be waked up to the change which this government is undergoing, in time to prevent it, is the question. I believe they can. I will not believe that the free people of this great country will quietly suffer this government, established for the protection of life and liberty, to be changed into a slave-holding oligarchy whose chief object is the spread and perpetuation of negro slavery and the degradation of free white labor.

Since the receipt of your letter I have re-read the pamphlet in regard to industrial universities. The idea is a grand one, if it could be carried out and made practical. I thought I saw in the last Congress an opposition springing up against any further grants of land in the States, but perhaps it was confined to those made to new States, and your project contemplating a grant to *all the States* might meet with more favor. Several large grants were made last year, but it was done grudgingly. For my own part I have ever been favorable to an early disposition of the public lands by the general government, and if they could only be secured to actual settlers, I would be glad to see it divested at once of this great source of patronage and corruption. If *some of the old States would take hold of the matter*, I think it not unlikely that a grant of lands might be obtained from Congress; but coming from the *new States*, which have already obtained such large grants for schools and other purposes, it would be likely to meet with *less favor*.

Objections to the feasibility of the plan will, of course, be urged; but no one can doubt that something, if not all that is expected, could be accomplished by institutions of the character proposed.

For the diploma you inclosed making me a member of the Industrial League, I desire to express my thanks.

Your sincere friend,
LYMAN TRUMBULL

Professor Turner had always planned to go to Washington with his bill himself, and watch its course; but it was
difficult for him to leave home. In December, 1855, a new
member entered the House of Representatives, to whom the
Illinois members, following the reasoning in Senator Trumbull's letter, felt the introduction of their bill could be
intrusted. This was Justin S. Morrill of Vermont. Mr.
Morrill reached Congress one year and a half after the resolution of Illinois had been introduced. But he was an able
man, of pleasing personality, and, best of all, a warm friend
of agriculture. And, after the receipt of Senator Trumbull's
letter, it was decided to send all documents, papers, and
pamphlets to Mr. Morrill, with the request that he introduce
a bill. This, at first, he was reluctant to do, but after much
persuasion he consented. The bill was introduced December
14, 1857, but was reported back unfavorably by the Committee on Public Lands. He submitted it again, omitting
the grant to the Territories (these were included later), in
a very able speech, April 20, 1858. I well remember my
father's intense anxiety for fear Mr. Morrill would give this
speech in a half-hearted way, and so the bill would fail to
pass. But I also well remember, when Mr. Morrill's speech
first reached the West, my father's great relief and great
delight. He was more than pleased, more than satisfied. It
did not pass the House, but it was introduced again the next
year. It then passed the House, but failed in the Senate.
Finally, in 1859, it was again introduced, and passed both
houses, but was vetoed by President Buchanan. Then, indeed,
were the hearts of its friends sad.

Before the campaign of 1860, when Mr. Lincoln was nominated, Professor Turner, talking with Mr. Lincoln at Decatur,
told him he would be nominated for President at the coming
convention and afterward elected. " If I am," replied Lincoln,
" I will sign your bill for State universities." A little later,
Stephen A. Douglas met Professor Turner on a train, as he
was going to Peoria, and assured him: " If I am elected I will
sign your bill." So, whichever way the country voted, for
Republican or Democrat, Professor Turner knew his labor

was at an end. After ten long years of arduous labor, the great plan for the education of the masses was an assured success.

In June, 1861, Senator Douglas wrote Professor Turner, requesting his plan for an industrial university and its history, as he wished to introduce it at the next session of Congress himself. Senator Douglas had declared long before this: " This educational scheme of Professor Turner's is the most democratic scheme of education ever proposed to the mind of man! " Professor Turner wrote, as requested, a full and complete account, and sent it to the post-office by his oldest son, Rhodolphus. To his surprise, his son returned with the letter, saying a telegram had just been received announcing the death of Senator Douglas in Chicago. In grief and disappointment, the letter was thrown into the waste-basket. Later Mr. Morrill again introduced the bill, and it passed both houses of Congress, and was the first civil bill signed by President Lincoln, July 2, 1862.

The text of the bill follows:

ILLINOIS INDUSTRIAL UNIVERSITY
LAWS OF CONGRESS

AN ACT DONATING PUBLIC LANDS TO THE SEVERAL STATES AND TERRITORIES WHICH MAY PROVIDE COLLEGES FOR THE BENEFIT OF AGRICULTURAL AND THE MECHANIC ARTS

Be it enacted by the Senate and House of Representatives of the United States of America, in Congress assembled, That there be granted to the several States, for the purpose hereinafter mentioned, an amount of public land, to be apportioned to each State, in quantity equal to 30,000 acres, for each Senator and Representative in Congress to which the States are respectfully entitled by the apportionment under the census of 1860; Provided, That no mineral lands shall be selected or purchased under the provisions of this act.

2. And be it further enacted, That the land aforesaid, after being surveyed, shall be apportioned to the several States in sections or subdivisions of sections not less than one quarter of a section; and wherever there are public lands in a State, subject to sale at private entry, at one dollar and twenty-five cents per

acre, the quantity to which said State shall be entitled shall be selected from such lands, within the limits of such State; and the Secretary of the Interior is hereby directed to issue to each of the States, in which there is not the quantity of public lands subject to sale at private entry, at one dollar and twenty-five cents per acre, to which said State may be entitled under the provisions of this act, land scrip to the amount in acres for the deficiency of its distributive share; said scrips to be sold by said States, and the proceeds thereof applied to the uses and purposes prescribed in this act, and for no other use or purpose whatsoever: Provided, That in no case shall any State, to which land scrip may thus be issued, be allowed to locate the same within the limits of any other State, or of any Territories of the United States; but their assignees may thus locate said land scrip upon any of the unappropriated lands of the United States, subject to sale at private entry, at one dollar and twenty-five cents an acre. And provided further, That not more than one million acres shall be located by such assignees in any one of the States. And provided further, That no such locations shall be made before one year from the passage of this act.

3. And be it further enacted, That all the expenses of management and superintendence and taxes from date of selection of said lands, previous to their sale, and all expenses incurred in the management and disbursement of the moneys, which may be received therefrom, shall be paid by the States to which they may belong, out of the treasury of said States, so that the entire proceeds of the sale of said lands shall be applied, without any diminution whatever, to the purpose hereinafter mentioned.

4. And be it further enacted, That all moneys derived from the sale of lands aforesaid, by the States to which the lands are apportioned, and from the sales of land scrip hereinbefore provided for, shall be invested in stocks of the United States, or of the States, or some other safe stocks, yielding not less than five per cent., upon the par value of said stock; and that the money so invested shall constitute a perpetual fund, the capital of which shall remain forever undiminished (except so far as may be provided in section fifth of this act), and the interest of which shall be inviolably appropriated by each State, which may take and claim the benefit of this act, to the endowment, support, and maintenance of, at least, one college where the leading object shall be, without excluding other scientific and classical studies,

and including military tactics, to teach such branches of learning as are related to agriculture and the mechanic arts, in such manner as the Legislatures of the States may respectively prescribe, in order to promote the liberal and practical education of the industrial classes in the several pursuits and professions in life.

5. And be it further enacted, That the grant of land and scrip hereby authorized, shall be made on the following conditions, to which, as to the provisions hereinbefore contained, the previous assent of the several States shall be signed by legislative acts:

First: If any portion of the fund invested, as provided by the foregoing section, or any portion of the interest thereon, shall, by any action, or contingency, be diminished or lost, it shall be replaced by the State to which it belongs, so that the capital of the fund shall remain forever undiminished; and the annual interest shall be regularly applied without diminution to the purposes mentioned in the fourth section of this act, except that a sum, not exceeding ten per centum upon the amount received by any State under the provisions of this act, may be expended for the purchase of lands for sites or experimental farms, whenever authorized by the respective Legislatures of said States.

Second: No portion of said fund, nor the interest thereon, shall be applied, directly or indirectly, under any pretense whatever, for the purchase, erection, preservation, or repair of any building or buildings.

Third: Any State which may take and claim the benefit of the provisions of this act, shall provide, within five years, at least not less than one college as prescribed in the fourth section of this act, or the grant to such State shall cease; and said State shall be bound to pay the United States the amount received of any lands previously sold, and that the title to purchasers under the State shall be valid.

Fourth: An annual report shall be made regarding the progress of each college, recording any improvements and experiments made, with their costs and results, and such other matters, including State industrial and economical statistics, as may be supposed useful; one copy of which shall be transmitted by mail, free, by each, to all the other colleges which may be endowed under the provisions of this act, and also one copy to the Secretary of the Interior.

Fifth: When lands shall be selected from those which have been raised to double the minimum price, in consequence of railroad grants, they shall be computed to the State at the maximum price, and the number of acres proportionately diminished.

Sixth: No State, while in a condition of rebellion or insurrection against the government of the United States, shall be entitled to the benefits of this act.

Seventh: No State shall be entitled to the benefits of this act, unless it shall express its acceptance thereof by its Legislature within two years from the date of approval by the President.

6. And be it further enacted, That land scrip issued under the provisions of this act, shall not be subject to location until after the first day of January, 1863.

7. And be it further enacted, That land offices shall receive the same fee for locating land scrip issued under the provisions of this act as is now allowed for the location of military bounty land warrants under existing laws: Provided, That maximum compensation shall not be thereby increased.

8. And be it further enacted, That the governors of the several States to which scrip shall be issued under this act, shall be required to report annually to Congress all sales made under such scrip until the whole shall be disposed of, the amount received for the same, and what appropriation has been made of the proceeds.

Approved, July 2, 1862.

Such was the first form of the Morrill Bill, known, naturally, ever since, by the name of its sponsor in Congress. It was the splendid result of the long fight started a dozen years before in Illinois. During all that time Professor Turner kept up his vigorous efforts in behalf of the measure, as is shown by the following letter written by Mr. Morrill shortly before the bill was passed:

HOUSE OF REPRESENTATIVES,
WASHINGTON, D. C., December 30, 1861

Dear Sir:

I was delighted to find your fire, by the letter of the 15th inst., had not all burned out. I presume I recognize Professor Turner, an old pioneer in the cause of agricultural education.

I have only to say that, amid the fire, smoke, and embers, I have faith that I shall get my bill into a law at this session.

I thank you for your continued interest, and am,

Very sincerely yours,

J. B. TURNER, Esq.,   JUSTIN S. MORRILL
Jacksonville, Ill.

CHAPTER XIX

Illinois Delays Acceptance: Extracts from Letters to the Honorable J. P. Reynolds

The Civil War had now become the one absorbing interest throughout the United States, and, therefore, many of the States were slow to avail themselves of the liberal provisions of the land-grant bill. Illinois was especially active in all duties relating to the war, and stood foremost in energy and patriotism. Her soldiers were most efficient, and more numerous, in proportion to her population, than in any other State in the Union. It was difficult to awaken interest in any subject outside of the terrible experiences and necessities of the fearful struggle through which the nation was passing. The extracts from letters written by Professor Turner to the Honorable John P. Reynolds, Secretary of the State Board of Agriculture of Illinois, printed in this chapter, give some idea of the arduous task that faced the friends of industrial education in their effort to secure the passage of a bill by the Illinois Legislature for a State Industrial University.

JACKSONVILLE, November 1, 1864

HON. J. P. REYNOLDS
Dear Sir:

Yours of October 17 is at hand, but my son William has been so desperately sick of typhoid fever that I have hardly had my clothes off for the last three weeks, and am, as usual, miserably behind in my correspondence.

I fully approve of your action in the matter on hand. Governor Yates, who is my personal friend, wrote me a letter appointing me on his committee. I wrote back to him that I considered such a committee an insult to the great industrial classes of the State, and that I could not serve on it; though I do not think he so intended it. But I am tired of seeing the great industrial representatives of this State ignored and trodden under foot by literary, professional, and political demagogues, and I won't coöperate with them, so help me God—Governor or no Governor, friends or no friends.

I do not intend to come to Springfield with any bill or measure whatever, cut and dried. I intend to come there open-handed and simple-hearted, to meet and hear the true friends of our cause. If they desire to hear from me, I will frankly express my views; but I am going with them, at any rate. "Where they go, I shall go; their people shall be my people, and their God shall be my God"; for I know they will design to do right. I have not the least ambition for any further leadership or control in this matter. I would prefer that it should move on to its destiny without even my help, but I am still willing to help, if our friends desire it, in any way I can.

I foresee we shall have trouble this winter; I shall endeavor to be on hand, as you desire.

Yours truly,

J. B. TURNER

The following letter somewhat modified Professor Turner's bitter disappointment in the appointments by his friend, Governor Yates.

STATE OF ILLINOIS EXECUTIVE DEPARTMENT

SPRINGFIELD, ILLINOIS, November 17, 1864

PROFESSOR J. B. TURNER
Dear Sir:

Enclosed I send you the Proceedings of the committee appointed by me in relation to the lands donated by Congress. Your letter was the first intimation that the State Agricultural Society had appointed a committee (my time having been so employed that I have not as yet been able to look over the Proceedings of that society). I regret that you should think I would insult that committee, or any one else. Perhaps I erred in naming the men who were to compose the committee, but it certainly was not with any design on my part to divert the fund from the original design of the donors. The committee was very hurriedly chosen, distributing them fairly over the State and selecting such men as I supposed were friendly to the cause of education. Some of the men are connected with colleges, but I believe not a majority. More of the committee who expressed their opinions at the late meeting were opposed to dividing the fund among the colleges—and certainly I never entertained any such desire, if plans similar to those you have in view can be adopted by the Legislature. The only object I had in view in yielding to the request of Colonel Eastman to appoint a committee was to have a preliminary investigation for the sake of presenting the subject to the Legislature, supposing that there would likely be minority and majority reports from the committee.

When I saw there was a disposition to prevent my well-meant efforts, and especially when I saw that the Agricultural Society had appointed a committee, and believing that was the best medium through which the Legislature could be reached, I determined to advise the disbanding the committee.

As I am soon to prepare my message, I would feel much obliged to you for a brief exposition of your views as to the best disposition of the trust.

I write you very hurriedly.

Your friend,

RICHARD YATES

The following letters from Professor Turner to the Honorable J. P. Reynolds were written in the latter part of 1864 and the early part of 1865.

JACKSONVILLE, ILLINOIS, November 19, 1864

HON. J. P. REYNOLDS

Dear Sir:

Yours of November 17th is at hand. I am sorry that the Governor's committee is defunct. It deranges all my plans. I intended to throw the laboring oar wholly into their hands, while we followed up with gunboats. By its dissolution we have lost that great advantage. Now they intend to make us row, while they fire upon us in the rear. I think that is plain from the wording of their resolutions. After a warfare of over twenty years, if I did not understand these old conservative interests and policies I should be a dull scholar indeed. The very wording of their resolutions show that they intend to insinuate and foster a difference of interests between the agricultural and mechanical interests, whereas you and I well know that there is no such difference, except what they ferment and foster. On this point they intend to divide and conquer. They think they can throw in an apple of discord which we can neither harmonize nor control. Look over these resolutions and you will see what they intend, and that we shall have now to provide against it with the great disadvantage of a fire in the rear and in the bushes. I intended to keep the Governor's committee square in front of us, and to have fought it to the bitter end; for I fear nothing that can be kept squarely before us. It is only these conservative bush-whackers that I fear, either in church or state or social affairs.

I wish you would get Mr. Bateman and Mr. Willard, and such other friends of education in Springfield as you can trust, together, and talk over the matter, and report to me their views. We have had several such talks here. Our educational and professional men now, thank God, are all right, to a man, on the general principles. President Sturtevant is all right; I advised him to stay on the committee as a safeguard, and to bring in a minority report if needed. Governor Yates' heart is with us, and always has been; but I felt bound to rap him over the knuckles, as an old maid does her favorite boy when he chances to hold his knife wrong at the table. I did not intend to rap hard enough to make him dissolve his committee. I did not intend to drive them into the bushes. It was bad generalship on my part, I confess; but I cannot help it now.

What shall we do now? Shall we meet on the 6th of December? Can you confer with your educational men and let me know the result? I have but little doubt in my own mind what ought to be done in the abstract; but what and how much of absolute truth and right we can, at the present juncture, command the men and the mind to execute, I have many doubts. In all these matters of practical policy, I feel that I am a mere child, though I can still fight well for a principle to the bitter end, if need be.

Please write me soon, if you have time.

Yours truly,

J. B. TURNER

P. S. My son Willie is worse this morning. He has been now for fifty days on the flat of his back of typhoid fever. I have watched with him until I am almost worn out. Nothing but his sickness or death, or my own, will prevent my answering promptly any demands upon my time at Springfield which you may think proper.   J. B. T.

December, 1864, Friday Morning

HON. J. P. REYNOLDS
Dear Sir:

Yours of Tuesday morning is but this morning at hand. I am pleased with its suggestions, and am fully sensible of the difficulties it suggests.

I agree with you that General Fuller ought to be the father of the bill; but he is a soldier and not a statesman, and probably cannot find time to look through this whole educational project, new as it is in many of its peculiar features, not only to us in the United States, but to the whole world of mankind, and see what *peculiar* powers the Board *may* need to use a hundred years hence, even though they might judge it inexpedient to use them at once. You must recollect that we wish now wisely to begin a peculiar university, which our posterity can erect into the strongest, broadest, and best university on the face of the earth. Nothing less will do at all for our gallant Illinois and the posterity of the heroes of a hundred battlefields. I fear, therefore, that General Fuller will be inclined to take a soldier's view of the case, and think that the shorter the charter the better, and the more easily it will go through the Legislature without friction. I agree with him perfectly in the idea that the hands of the trustees should not by any means be tied up, only so far as indispensable to safety. I would give them powers by the charter, and not restrict them, in most cases, by saying the trustees *may* instead of the trustees *shall*.

Our institution is wholly new, totally unlike the old-fogy concerns which have preceded it, and we want to let the people know in the outset something of what we wish and desire it to be in the future. We, therefore, want to put our finger-boards in the charter by showing what *may* be done if the people at any time should choose to have it done, or if they do not they can for the present leave it alone, or leave others who come after them to do what they are not ready to do.

The thoughts I have suggested for the charter in my letter are not simply my own. In every case I have consulted freely with the ablest educators and lawyers in this town, on every single point, who are old friends of the cause and have watched and studied it with much solicitude for years, and I ruled out every suggestion they did not approve. I did this because I wanted to know how it would be likely to strike other minds who have thought on the subject.

They all say, in general, " That is what our State will need at no distant day, and should go into the charter," independently of local issues or present policies. Even our professors now say that if such an institution can be endowed it will be the grandest university on the face of the earth; but they doubt if it will be possible to save the *fund* from division. I fully believe we *can* keep the *fund* together, and therefore *can* do it. Don't bring too many into your consultations; it will only breed discord. You, McConnell, General Fuller, and Bateman are enough. As I wrote you last evening, if you will send down the bill I can get Judge Dummer and Judge Berdan, and also some of the old friends of the cause, to look it over with me. A draft of it had better be made by General Fuller first, or at least submitted to him for his criticism. What he says about the practical difficulties is obviously true. Possibly you might name five commissioners on the bill, saying " these or such others as the Governor and Senate may appoint," and the same of trustees; but you ought to pick your men with great care. I have no further choice in regard to the men than what I expressed to you in my last, namely, that you shall be the commissioner for central Illinois, and that my name shall be left wholly out. *This much I shall insist upon,* for I am sure the good of the cause demands it. In writing the bill, a blank might be left for all names of persons, and the names written on another slip of paper, until after full consideration. The Regent of the University, as I understand it, will make up the odd member of the Board of Trustees. Sealed bids, I think, should first be received, and after that a careful personal examination made by the commission of all claims that can be supposed to stand at all as rivals.

Yours truly,

J. B. TURNER

JACKSONVILLE, ILLINOIS, July 23, 1865

HON. J. P. REYNOLDS

Dear Sir:

I thank you for the enclosed ticket. If I can do any good I will go; if not, I think it is doubtful, as I have no time to spend, at my age in life, for mere pleasure; though it would give me great pleasure to meet you there, and our other friends, it would hardly pay, unless some thing was to be done for the benefit of coming generations. I know that the Chicago folks will be there. Very well; if they have *justice* on their side, let them be there, and we will all hope that it will prevail. If they have not, the devil take the hindermost, Chicago and all—I will not concern myself about it.

My dear friend, after forty years of almost incessant effort in behalf of the true principles of freedom and education, I have settled down into the comfortable conclusion that if Almighty God, possessed of omnipotent power, don't care anything about them, I do not, and I am not going to run over the State any more, trying to raise them up, while He leaves the devil and the conservatives and the copperheads in solid phalanx to fight against me. Most true, I would like to see all our people educated for the highest ends and uses of humanity, and I would like to see our own State, Illinois, take a deserved lead in this great matter. But if neither the Lord nor the people care anything about it, who am I, that I should fight against God and the people too? Let Champaign and Chicago and the devil and "befooled Egypt" take the inside of the ring, if that be the Lord's will, although it is none of my will. For myself, I am conscious of only one great immaculate virtue in me: I bow submissively when I can't help it, and nowhere else.

But, more seriously, my dear friend, let us thank God and take courage, and still "keep our powder dry," in that the great State of New York has accepted the offer of Mr. Cornell of Ithaca of five hundred thousand dollars, and thus located its University there, with a fair start of a million and a half dollars. Let us labor and pray for its success. It is the first and the only tolerably fair start toward the right thing that I have seen in any of the States. We must help this matter along. I wish you would send to Mr. Cornell, of Ithaca, your last report, and whatever else you may have in your office of past or present reports that will tend to throw light on this matter. For a man who is willing to give a half million dollars to an enterprise is likely to have the brain to get it through, if he is properly protected. As to what should be published in our reports, I think that an article showing the real origin and general history of the matter in our State in brief would be very apposite. The whole matter was really begun and urged on to its present position by citizens in our own State, and not only so, but by the members and staunch friends of our State Agricultural Society. It is apposite, therefore, that the Society should note and chronicle, if it pleases, that fact; but I could not, of course, write the article. I have been personally too much mixed up with it; you had better do it yourself. . . .

We have had a thunder shower that lasted for about three weeks, and now it seems to have set in for a steady rain. We occasionally send out " a dove " in the shape of a corn-plow; but it soon returns to the ark again, loaded with mud and weeds, if not with olive branches. If it don't stop raining soon, there will be no use in executing " Jeff," for the hell-fires will all be squelched and he will have nowhere to go.

With love to all,

Yours truly,

J. B. Turner

Jacksonville, Illinois, August 13, 1865

Hon. J. P. Reynolds

My dear Friend:

Yours of July 31st is at hand. I thank you for it. " The world does move," as you say, " in spite of all our temporary discomforts." Our noble cause is advancing perhaps as rapidly as it is healthful that it should. I think this move of Mr. Cornell shows that we should not despair, but strive to get our State to follow with New York. She is equally able, and can just as well do the " clean thing," if we only get her started right. Indeed, Illinois can do a *better thing* at *real* education than any other State or nation in the civilized world, if she will only try. I want that she should try; so do you; so do we all. We will try and bring her up to her duty before God and man. Another thing shows me the truth of our ideas, and our certain success at last; I read lately, in some paper, an article in which even a conservative Englishman, in his report to Parliament, assails the great universities of Oxford and Cambridge as a humbug. If the slow-molded Englishmen begin to find out that they have been humbugged in that system of pretended education from which ours was copied, will not the lithe, agile, and wary Yankee find it out, too? I am still in good heart and hope, and all the better for the encouraging words in your last letter. I intend to write for papers after the hurry season is over. An American citizen needs to learn only three simple things: namely, when, where, and how to work, to fight, and to pray, to the best possible advantage. When he knows this he is well educated; he is fit to be a citizen of the great Republic.

The Chicago *Tribune* is now adopting our arguments for their own use and wielding them with power, just as we did, because they are true, but at the same time placing our plans at a disadvantage in discussion, and before the Legislature and the people, by making it seem that they understand the subject better than we do, and we, after all, will be obliged to adopt their ideas in order to succeed, and not they ours.

The *Tribune* is now stealing our thunder every week for this end. I have, therefore, sketched three articles which I think should at some place come explicitly into our charter. If you and Mr. McConnell think so, please devise the language to your liking, and put them into that part where they will best fit.

I think they should be very explicit and full, in order to furnish now and in all future times a just ground of appeal to silence all partizan or sectarian old-fogy professors. We only need say, " Gentlemen, if you do not like our teaching, endow your own professorships to suit yourselves; the institution is just as free and open to you as it is to us and all others, not only to learn, but also to teach." You will see the drift of the provisions in other regards.

Sketch of Articles

I. Any County Community Corporation or Association, Literary, Scientific, Secular, or Religious, may found and endow in this University any professorship of any science, art, or species of learning or knowledge which such endowment may desire to have taught in said University, by paying over to the Trustees such sums of money or property of other sort as the Trustees shall from time to time declare needful to a common endowment, and which shall not be less than is sufficient for the permanent support of such property or teacher. They shall have the right to choose their own name for such professorship, and also to choose the professor or teacher from time to time to fill the chair and prescribe his course of instruction according to his own views. Provided that no student of the University shall be obliged to attend the instruction or recitation of any instructor of course of study not previously elected by himself or by his parent or guardian.

II. The Trustees shall, as far as practicable, arrange all their regular and more important courses of study and lectures in the Institution so that the sons of farmers, merchants, and laboring men may pass through them during the six winter months, and leave them free to return to their several practical arts and industries at home during the six summer months of each year, or remain in the Institution and pursue such optional studies or such industrial avocations as they may elect, provided that no student shall be at any time allowed to remain in or around the Institution in idleness, or without full mental or industrial occupation suited to his ability.

III. The Trustees shall from time to time appoint such professors and instructors as the wants of the Institution may require and its means may allow; and they shall also appoint a *corresponding secretary*, whose duty it shall be to issue circulars, directions, and all other needful materials for conducting the proper experiments and eliciting instructive reports to the Institution from men in each county selected for the purpose and skilled in any branch of agricultural or mechanical and industrial art, and who may consent or desire to thus gratuitously promote the well being of the University and the people of the State. He shall receive and place on file in the Institution all such reports, and the Trustees may at any time direct and adopt such methods as they see fit for the appointment of such *county reporters* or *superintendents* of particular art or interest, and also direct the corresponding secretary as regards what particular experiments in the several counties they wish to have made, or what particular principle test or what particular information they desire to have elicited through these county reports touching any particular art or process or interest, so that the University may become in the highest practical degree a gleaner and elaborator, as well as a dispenser of knowledge to the people. And the Trustees may make such provision for the publication of parts, abstracts, or inferences from these reports, or other matters connected with the University, as they may judge the best interests of the people may require.

Yours truly,

J. B. TURNER

CHAPTER XX

The Farmers Ask for a Single University;
Industrial University Convention
Bloomington, Illinois
December 4, 1865

An industrial university convention was held at Bloomington, Illinois, December 4, 1865, at which a large representation of the agricultural, horticultural, and mechanical interests of the State came, in response to the call of the Executive Board of the State Agricultural Society, to discuss the great questions of what should be the character, and where the location, of the contemplated State Agricultural College. There were present the leading members and delegates from twenty-seven counties.

The following report of a committee having the matter in charge was laid before the convention:

To the Friends of Industrial Education in Illinois:

The undersigned, a committee appointed by the last of a series of mass conventions of farmers and mechanics, assembled during the State Fair at Decatur, in September, 1864, and especially charged with the duty of framing and urging the passage by the General Assembly of a bill for an act to organize, endow, and maintain an institution of learning in this State, in accordance with the terms and provisions of an act of Congress, approved July 2, 1862, donating lands to the several States for the benefit of agriculture and the mechanic arts, feel that their duty to you demands of them a brief report of progress.

We accept the trust with less reluctance than would otherwise have been felt, because, on all the main points and principles involved, the wishes of the great mass of our people, farmers, mechanics, and professional educators alike, as time and again expressed, were known to be in full harmony with the clear and explicit requirements of the fundamental act of Congress, both together forming a chart of instructions which could not be materially departed from by us.

That each of you may judge and decide for himself, we append to this report a copy of the act of Congress and of the matured bill which our friends in the General Assembly endeavored to pass; and also state some of the positions assumed by them and us in urging its passage:

I. The act of Congress contemplates a series of homogeneous institutions in the several States, *in every one of which* shall be taught the " branches of learning related to agriculture and the mechanic arts," and " military tactics," not excluding " other scientific and classical studies."

1. It was, therefore, insisted that any scheme which proposed to disrupt and dismember the institution, scattering its limbs hundreds of miles apart, would, if successful, violate the very law of its life, and, as an inevitable result, sooner or later produce its death.

2. It was also insisted that any scheme which provided merely for teaching practical art, either the art of agriculture or the mechanic arts or trades, one or all of them, would, if successful, utterly fail to comply with the spirit or letter of the act of Congress, which provides that " branches of learning *related* to agriculture and the mechanic arts " (not agriculture and the mechanic arts themselves) shall be taught; and thus recognizes the difference between a workshop or a potato-patch and a school of the highest possible grade. While making ample provision for the physical labor of the pupil, as will be observed by reference to the sixth section of the bill, we did not deem it necessary, or best, or possible under the law, to organize a university for teaching, exclusively, practical art, which every student may better and more profitably learn elsewhere, on the model farms

and in the model art departments which the Trustees were empowered to establish and conduct, or at home. While thus advocating the integrity of the institution itself, our friends no less strenuously urged:

II. The non-division of the fund and its appropriation to the endowment of a single university.

1. The bill is intended to become the organic act or charter of an institution to which, as its development progresses under a wise administration of its affairs, all the people of the State may confidingly look as the great fountain-head of popular in- a source of just pride to every Illinoisan; whose pupils shall come struction, the crowning glory of our common-school system and from it living Americans, sound in mind, sound in body, and thoroughly skilled in the practical sciences which underlie the industries of life; an institution soon to command the respect and cordial support of all, and become the favored legatee of the wealthy men of the State. If, therefore, this conception, this necessity, is to be realized (and anything else is unworthy of us), no meager sum will suffice to inaugurate it.

2. The amount to accrue from sale of the land-scrip in possession of the State is uncertain; if the whole were sold at present market price, say seventy cents per acre, and invested in five-percent. stocks, the annual income derived from it would be $16,800— a sum sufficient for the maintenance of any first-class university, with the addition of tuition fees; while, it is hoped the Trustees of this may be able, at an early day, to dispense with any considerable charge for instruction.

3. This is an experiment, at best, but is fraught with interests of such magnitude and enduring importance that no unnecessary risks should be assumed. If we can keep the people together, we are thus, and only thus, sure of adequate moral and financial support.

III. Its location in such manner and form as a due regard to honesty and fair dealing with the people of the various localities desiring it seems to require.

1. As an equivalent for the local benefits likely to flow from its being fixed at any point, the interest of the University demand, and the State is entitled to, not only a good bargain, but the best one obtainable; and that the greatest possible advantages, physical, financial, social, and educational, be secured.

2. If located in any manner which does not afford all portions of the State opportunity to make proposals, the sympathies and affections of the whole people cannot be expected to follow and bless it.

3. The precedents of this State were in favor of intervention of a commission of discreet persons, to be selected by the Governor and Senate, or appointed by vote of both houses of the General Assembly. There could be no appearance even of want of equity in submitting the matter to a commission; there were nearly two years and a half within which to secure the buildings; and our friends, therefore, adopted this mode.

On all minor points we were ready at all times to make concessions; but neither our friends in the General Assembly nor ourselves were willing to yield up any of these self-evidently just principles.

Even before the first day of the session, the advocates of a division of this fund among several of the existing literary institutions commenced pressing their peculiar views upon attention of members, but, soon becoming aware that success was not possible, abandoned that movement as hopeless.

Immediately on the presentation of the bill by our friends in the House, a copy of it was obtained by those representing an interest in Champaign County; the eleventh section, which provided for a commission to locate, stricken out; and a provision was inserted and introduced into the Senate, locating the proposed University between the towns of Urbana and Champaign, on condition of the transfer, for use of the University, of a certain edifice and grounds there situated.

The interests of the State demanded that competitive bids should be made by the different counties. The bill the Champaign County lobby had tried to force through the Legislature had contained one hundred and seventy acres less and $152,000 less than the law, afterward passed, required.

For reasons at once apparent, our friends could not give this scheme their support. The point of location was not in itself objected to, but to locate direct by law, without chance for competition, would be a breach of faith to the remainder of the State, and sacrifice, if not the life, at least the usefulness of the institution. This claim was, however, most persistently pressed, and, during the whole session, stood in the way of the passage of any other act upon the subject.

Near the close of the session, failing to bring the majority of both Houses, or of either House, to the support of their plan, a combination was formed and an amendment made to our bill in the House, providing for the location of the University proper in Champaign County, the creation of a school for the mechanic arts in Chicago, and a school for agriculture in southern Illinois, dividing the fund among them in no very definite manner, and thus practically dismembering the institution itself.

Aside from the mere fact of division, this scheme was objectionable because it provided for two schools of practical art only— a thing, as already stated, not contemplated by the act of Congress, and worse than useless anywhere. The bill, thus amended, passed the House, was sent to the Senate, and there sleeps—we trust, in death.

No law whatever on this subject was passed by the late General Assembly. The matter remains just as it was when your committee was appointed, except that the leading points and principles involved in it have been very generally and beneficially discussed. The enterprise was a new one; few members of the General Assembly had given it the study and thought its magnitude demanded before they could act intelligently upon it. Some of them, however, had comprehended it in all its great and enduring relations to the educational, industrial, and social interests of the State, and such battled manfully for the right. They are entitled to our lasting remembrance.

We do not care, in this report, to give the yeas and nays taken during the progress of the bills. Each constituency may ascertain for themselves how their immediate representatives voted; and, if not in accordance with their views, the corrective is with themselves.

The bill we presented was, at one time or another, except the eleventh section, voted for, and advocated by almost every member of both Houses, and, but for causes mentioned, would undoubtedly have become a law without serious opposition.

Its most radical features—those which embody the greatest innovations upon the forms observed in the old established universities—meet the enthusiastic support of many of our most eminent practical educators. Further thought and discussion will suggest valuable amendments, so that the compulsory delay of two years will not be wholly lost. Two years, or ten years, are as nothing in the life of an institution such as this, compared with the importance of giving it a substantial basis and right direction. It is for you to see that your representatives, when next they are called to act upon the organization of the Illinois Industrial University, fully understand your wishes, and do them.

Respectfully,

WM. H. VAN EPPS
J. B. TURNER
A. B. McCONNELL
B. G. ROOTS
JOHN P. REYNOLDS
Committee

The action of the convention is given in a contemporary report as follows:

On motion of O. B. Galusha, a committee of five was appointed to draft resolutions for the consideration of the convention. The committee consists of Messrs. J. B. Turner, O. B. Galusha, G. W. Minier, Henry Tubbs, A. R. McMasters.

The committee appointed for that purpose presented the following resolutions:

" *Resolved*, That whereas the true principles of education, like the true principles of civil government, everywhere require the greatest practicable union, coöperation, and concentration in all its highest department, combined with the utmost practicable diffusion in the lower departments;

" Therefore, *Resolved*, That the State of Illinois should at present, attempt to build only one University of the highest order, and that the energies and resources of our people should now be directed to that one end, and the undivided funds of our congressional grant be appropriated thereto.

" *Resolved*, That we approve of the principles of location adopted by former State conventions and presented to the State Legislature at its last session by the committee of the State Agricultural Society.

" *Resolved*, That we approve of the general principles adopted and approved by all parties at the last session of the Legislature, that in preparing the charter for the University all mere details of organization and government should be left to the future necessities of the institution, the board of the people, and the existing Board of Trustees, and that the charter of the University should limit their freedom only on those points indispensable to a fundamental law.

"*Resolved*, That a committee be appointed to urge these views upon the next Legislature.

"*Resolved*, That we urge upon the people the necessity of keeping the principles embodied in these resolutions before aspirants to office, and that they emphatically reprobate any man as a candidate for the Legislature who is unfavorable to these views.

"*Resolved*, That we request the Chicago and Springfield papers, and all others in the state, to publish the Proceedings of the Convention."

Adjourned till 1:30 P.M.

AFTERNOON SESSION

Professor Turner, in presenting the above resolutions, explained them at considerable length. He stated that the committee emphatically indorsed the action taken by the Agricultural Committee last winter, and the bill which they presented for the action of the Legislature, but which was defeated by combinations which are familiar to the readers of the *Tribune*, because they were fully discussed in its columns at that time.

He explained the Congressional grant, and said in fixing the charter the committee adopted the language of the grant. He explained that agricultural experiments could be made by individuals on small tracts of land without expense to the University. They would make their reports to the institution and through the press, and thus information would be conveyed to the people. He was opposed to the institution running into a dead literature, but, at the same time, was unwilling to tie down the institution to a strict code of procedure. He would have no red tape about the institution, except to make sure that there could be no possibility of the misapplication of its funds. Give a proper discretion to the managers in range of studies, and then hold them to a strict accountability.

It was not the intent of the managers to select the richest soil, but the soil best adapted for experimental farming. He also explained that there was nothing in the bill making the college a free institution, but only free to a single scholar from each county. He wanted it understood that these resolutions indorsed no details, but simply the leading features of the bill.

Professor Turner opposed the suggestion of Mr. Sanford that the session of the College should be held in summer instead of winter. He insisted that the human mind was more active and in a better condition to receive new ideas in winter than in summer; besides, parents want their sons to work on the farm during the summer, when they can get practical ideas in their studies of the farm. The moment the birds begin to sing, the boys are outdoors and will not study with a zest.

The Committee on Resolutions reported the following:

" *Resolved,* That the committee who have presented the report now before this meeting shall constitute the committee contemplated in the resolutions, and that we instruct them to secure the revision of the bill presented to the Legislature of this State at its last session by a committee appointed by a convention of the people of this State, and cause one thousand copies of the bill to be printed; also, that they be instructed to secure the appointment of sub-committees in each of the representative and senatorial districts of this State, whose duty it shall be to present a copy of said bill to each and every person whose name shall be before the people as a candidate for nomination to the offices of Representative and Senator to the General Assembly of this State, and shall receive the public pledges of such candidates for nomination that they will use all laudable endeavors, if nominated and elected, to secure the passage of said bill; and that, in case any candidate shall refuse or neglect to give such pledge, such sub-committee shall publish the fact of such refusal throughout the district in which such candidate resides through the newspapers published therein."

The resolution was adopted.

Convention adjourned, *sine die.*

CHAPTER XXI

The Progress in 1866; a Letter from Ezra Cornell

The Illinois Legislature, in the session of 1866, following this appeal from the farmers, favored their idea of keeping the Industrial University fund for one institution. The progress of the year 1866 may be shown by extracts from Professor Turner's correspondents, the most interesting of which was a long letter from Ezra Cornell, who was then engaged in getting under way the great University that bears his name.

Professor Turner, at the request of the friends of the House Bill, gave a lecture, on December 20, 1865, in the House of Representatives. His explanation of all the leading features was full and satisfactory.

In the *Illinois State Journal*, a few days later, Professor Turner made this reply to some criticisms of the bill providing for the organization, endowment, and maintenance of the Illinois Industrial University made in the Chicago *Tribune* on December 17, 1865:

Editor State Journal:

Some of those various Solomons, who have written for the Chicago *Tribune* on the subject, have at last discovered that the bill before the House is full of all sorts of " crudities."

The writer cannot conceive of what use a corresponding secretary can be to such an institution, and at the very name of one he seems to smell some sort of a " mice." I wonder if any one of the various writers of the conflicting editorials in that paper have ever read the act of Congress which conferred the grant? If so, how do they expect its terms to be complied with, without such an officer, call him what name you will? Will some of these discordant savants please to point us out the true way? The community does not know yet what the *Tribune* is really for, or what it is against. One week it seems to be for the measures of one party or interest, and another week for those of the opposite one. In the last strictures on the bill now pending before the House—which was prepared and concurred in by all the men who were appointed to represent the agricultural and mechanical interests of the State, by all our leading practical teachers and professors to whom it has been submitted, as well as by the old original advocates of the grant, some of whom have made that a matter of study, both theoretically and practically, for the past ten or twenty years—the *Tribune* has settled down to a very comfortable opposition, not only to the main features of this bill, but to the express terms of the act of Congress that gave us the grant. Very well; I admire heroism, even if it comes rather late in the day and somewhat mixed with crudities.

The writer has never heard, it would seem, that some of our oldest and most successful classical colleges are preparing to adopt, and some actually have adopted, a six months' regular course and a six months' optional course of study, in precise accordance with the proposed features of this bill. It will be news to these venerable professors and teachers to learn that the adopting of a course of optional study, for a part of the year, really implies, as this savant seems to suppose, that the students are to " hang around the institution " and do just what they please, provided they are doing something. Pray, send to each of these institutions a copy of the *Tribune*, and let them know the dangers they are incurring.

This writer cannot see what an agricultural institution can do with an experimental farm, unless the boys are actually kept on it all summer to look at it and work it with their own hands, and he thinks it is an exceedingly crude and absurd idea to imagine that any one else can see. Of course, if the writer cannot see through the millstone, who can? It is sufficient to say that all men of all classes, who know anything at all about the subject, can see so clearly that they need no instruction on that point.

This writer really fears that one hundred and two honorary scholarships, appointed on the same general principle with the appointees of our State Normal School,—a provision which is particularly approved and is particularly dear to all our most sagacious teachers, and which was first suggested from their ranks, as a powerful means for elevating all our common schools,—will produce a deluge of students that will overwhelm and sink the University. He also deems it an outrage to give English certificates of scholarships, instead of Latin and Greek diplomas. He is not aware of the fact that there is not, and never was, a scientific Institution on the Continent that does or can give anything but such certificates of scholarships as is proposed, and that none but classical schools have either any moral or legal right to issue diplomas and degrees in the usual form.

But the *Tribune* approves of the equal and democratic mode of deciding upon the location of the University, which the bill proposes, and which the people had been led to expect would be adopted.

All the old friends of the grant, and all the constructive and appointed representatives of the industrial classes, the officers of their societies, the representatives of the teachers in the State, and the committee who drew the House Bill, are opposed, to a man, as far as I know, to this whole proceeding. We think, by pushing this purely local interest so impetuously, its originators only stand in their own light; that they injure their own real interests, as well as all the best interests of the University and the State.

I know of no man who is opposed to the location of the University in Champaign if, after a full and a fair examination of the matter, and close examination of the officers of the best communities, it should be found the best place. But it is this attempt to take a " snap judgment," as it is called, on the whole thing, before other communities can be apprised of what is going on,— this pertinacious pushing of an obviously merely personal and local interest in such hot haste over all the other great interests of the State,—of which we complain. We regard the effort thus to commit in advance, before any proper deliberation or discussion has been had, individual members of the Senate and House, some of whom, as their public remarks show, have never yet intelligently read the enabling act of Congress, while others in the Senate seem really to suppose that the Champaign bill, about which they are talking, is the bill of the Agricultural Society, or that of the committee, to which it is diametrically opposed—we regard this effort as indecorous and injurious. I hope those gentlemen of the Senate will find out what the enabling act of Congress enjoins and requires, and what bill and whose bill they are really advocating, before they proceed to locate the institution. For the information of all who are in doubt, I will suggest that the House Bill is the bill prepared by this committee appointed by the agriculturalists and the people, while the Senate Bill is the bill in the Champaign interest.

J. B. TURNER

The friendly letter from Senator Ezra Cornell, following the action of the Illinois Legislature, is given below:

STATE OF NEW YORK, SENATE CHAMBER
ALBANY, February 19, 1866

My dear Sir:

Your favor of the 10th, addressed to me at Ithaca, has just reached me here, and I thank you for letting me know of the progress you are making in Illinois in this great American movement of education.

I am glad also to learn, as I infer from the documents you inclose, that your Legislature has decided not to waste your land grant by dividing it among such institutions now in existence as may attach an agricultural or mechanical department to their present schools. We were in great danger at one time of falling into that fatal error, but happily avoided it, and are now, I trust, standing on firm and substantial ground.

We are not, however, past all danger of making mistakes. I anticipate the making of mistakes; I do not possess wisdom enough to avoid all errors, and I fear the united wisdom of our directors may not be adequate to secure absolutely right action in all things. I hope, however, to secure such solidity of basis that our errors will not prove fatal, or even very disastrous.

We, therefore, start out upon the plan of funding our capital and living on our income, and financially we stand thus.

We have a farm of 200 acres and $500,000 cash, donated by Ezra Cornell. The former, valued at $50,000, we shall locate the

University upon. The latter is securely invested at seven per cent., bringing an income of $35,000 per annum, and constitutes our only building fund, and will be used for building purposes as long as required. The Congressional land grant to this State amounted to 990,000 acres. The State gives us the income of the fund realized from the sale of this scrip. Prior to the passage of the act creating the " Cornell University," the Comptroller of our State sold 90,000 acres of the scrip, from which he realized $62,000, which is invested at seven per cent., and last fall I purchased of the Comptroller 100,000 of the land-scrip for the University, paying therefor $50,000, which is also invested at seven per cent., making, with some accrued interest, $120,000 invested by the State, the income of which, $8,400, goes to the institution annually. This leaves 800,000 acres of land yet to dispose of.

The 100,000 of scrip that I purchased I am now locating in Wisconsin and Minnesota, and the remaining 800,000 in scrip I hope to purchase and locate for the University, and think I shall succeed in my plans to that effect, if Congress will exempt the land entered by such scrip from taxation while held by the University. I trust that your institution will also be able to purchase and locate the scrip, and thus become interested with us in asking Congress to exempt the lands from taxation. I will inclose you a copy of an act for that purpose, which I have drawn to forward to Congress.

We are maturing the plans for our buildings, and expect to begin their erection in the spring. Our plan of studies, the selection of professors, etc., etc., our trustees have not decided upon yet.

We shall have a meeting of trustees of the University at Albany early in March, say two or three weeks hence. If you will do us the favor to attend that meeting, I will forward you a notice of the time when fixed.

We shall be glad to coöperate with our great agricultural sister, Illinois, in this great enterprise, which must have a mighty power in the development of the intellectual and physical resources of this great nation.

I think, if you could make it convenient to attend our meeting, it would be to the benefit of both institutions, yours and ours.

Thank you for the membership to your " Industrial League." I am a practical mechanic and workingman.

Yours respectfully,

J. B. TURNER, Esq.   E. CORNELL

Later in this year of 1866 Professor Turner wrote the following letter, defining his idea of American education, to Colonel Smith, editor of the Jacksonville *Journal*, who has always been his faithful ally.

JACKSONVILLE, ILLINOIS, 1866

COLONEL SMITH, Editor of the *Journal*

Dear Sir:

You have grasped the idea of this scheme of American education, and present it with great force and clearness. I am ever glad when the cause finds able and competent advocates. I have for many years looked at this scheme of education as at once an inevitable and indispensable outgrowth of our American free institutions. It must necessarily develop out of them, and finally react and sustain them, if they continue to exist, and the question of the final existence of such institutions is only a question of time, for it would inevitably produce them, sooner or later—no shadow of doubt on that point, even in the darkest hours, has ever crossed my mind. Hence, in all conflicts and disasters, my only reply to my friends was, " Come they will, for come they must, whoever may oppose." And if all the funds now given should be sunk in the ocean, or wasted or squandered in any other inconceivable way, I should be of the same opinion still; my faith in this view of the case would not be in the least shaken; for America cannot exist without a distinctively American system of education; like the other lands, it must work out that destiny for itself, or perish from off the earth.

I thank you for your earnest and eloquent advocacy of the same great common cause.

Yours truly,

J. B. TURNER

CHAPTER XXII

College Presidents Organize
in Opposition

Although the Illinois Legislature of 1865 decided not to dissipate the Industrial University fund by dividing it among the various existing colleges of the State, the movement was still in danger. The time allowed the States for acceptance of the land grants had nearly expired, and Illinois, the originator of the movement, had not taken the practical steps necessary to secure the grant of land for her own university. The danger was finally averted by an act of Congress, approved July 23, 1866, extending the time limit of acceptance five years. After the passage of this act the advocates of the existing colleges continued their campaign to secure the advantages of the grant for their institutions, and their movement culminated in a meeting of college presidents, in the last of October, 1866, to form a permanent organization, one of whose chief objects would be to work to secure the land grant. This meeting was held in Chicago, and the Rev. Dr. A. G. Wallace, president of Monmouth College, was its chairman.

The Chicago *Tribune* of October 31, 1866, reported the convention, in part, as follows:

The Committee on Permanent Organization recommended that all the colleges of our State be invited to unite in a permanent association of fraternity, of which all of the several faculties shall be members, and in which each college shall have one vote. The anual meetings of the Association to be either during the Christmas holidays or during the long vacation of the summer. Carried. The committee further recommended a committee be appointed to draft a constitution, and the following gentlemen were appointed: Rev. J. Blanchard, D. D., Rev. R. Allyn, D. D., Rev. W. S. Curtis, D. D. Letters were read from several presidents, all of whom indorsed the meeting, except one (J. M. Sturtevant). His dissension was explained, by gentlemen present, to arise from his close proximity to and interest in the appropriation made by the Legislature for a separate Agricultural College. All letters were ordered to be placed on file. The Committee on Legislative Aid reported as follows:

" That the entire Educational Fund of the State amounts to between five and six millions of dollars; yet the colleges of the State which furnish, and which *will* furnish, a vast numerical proportion of the teachers, have, as yet, received from the State nothing but the naked donation of their charters.

" The original School Fund of the State, created by act of Congress, was three per cent. of the net proceeds of the sales of public lands in the State, less one sixth of the whole amount of said School Fund, and called the ' College or University Fund.' There was never a doubt raised or uttered about the intention of the law creating this College Fund, first borrowed by and afterward devoted to the common schools of this State, in the ' Normal University,' first, because, through trustees and officers of the colleges, they were and are, also, first of all, friends of our common schools, and wished, and still wish, all to be done for them which money can do. No meetings were held, and no attempts were made by the friends of the colleges to prevent this diversion of the College Fund from its original intent. And we, presidents of existing colleges, do not now propose to complain of or disturb this diversion. We simply allude to it to show that the colleges of this State are the natural and actual friends and mothers of popular education; and, instead of grasping at funds not properly their own, as some ignorant persons have been wont to insinuate, the colleges have seen their own fund diverted to the uses of common schools without murmur or remonstrance.

" Your committee further submit that in the breaking out of the late slavery rebellion our colleges were nearly depleted of our able-bodied young men, because our colleges were convenient recruiting-places and their officers and pupils were patriots. A remnant of our former students have come back to us, and with them a multitude of their comrades, whom the war has left alive. One of our colleges has given receipted bills to returned soldiers already amounting to some $2,000. Others may have done more; and none of us wish to charge these State troops with tuition bills. We think, therefore, that the members of our forthcoming Legislature will count it a pleasure to allow us something for the education of our State troops. And your committee respectfully recommends this body to petition the Legislature so to do.

" Your committee further submit that: July 2, 1862, the Congress of the United States had passed, and the president on that day approved, a bill donating public lands amounting to 30,000 acres for each Senator and Representative to each of all loyal States, for agricultural and mechanical colleges. Our share of this fund is 480,000 acres.

" And your committee further recommends that application be also made to our State Legislature for aid to our colleges, simply because they *are* colleges, after the example of Massachusetts, Maine, New York, Michigan, and other States; and that the time and mode of such application be re-referred to a special committee.

" The law provided that no buildings shall be paid for out of the fund that, with a slight exception, the principal shall be intact forever, and only the income expended, in the words of the law, for ' the endowment, support, and maintenance of at least one college where the leading object shall be, without excluding other scientific and classical studies, and including military tactics, to teach such branches of learning as are related to agriculture and the mechanic arts, in such manner as the Legislatures of the States may respectively prescribe.'

" The idea of the law is plainly that, though Rhode Island may need but one college, the large States may need more. Hence the phrase ' at least one college.'

" Under this law, Massachusetts has connected its share of this fund with Amherst; Rhode Island with Brown; New Hampshire its share with Dartmouth; and Connecticut with Yale; and, besides that, those Legislatures doubtless understand the law. There seems to your committee no difference in principle between connecting this fund with a college or colleges already built, and connecting it with a new college after it shall be built.

"Now, your committee are not in favor of connecting this vast fund with one college in one locality, for many reasons.

"1. Such single college and its model farm can only represent the soil, crops, seasons, atmospheric changes, etc., of one spot in a State running through five and a half degrees of latitude on our globe.

"2. Such single college will teach only some three or four farmers' sons in each of our counties, if it teaches even one to a county.

"3. Such single college must either exclude Christianity entirely, and so be either atheist or pagan, or, if it admits Christianity at all, it must support that form of Christianity which it admits, with our State fund, and so be a cause of jealousy and wrangling among sects and political parties.

"Your committee, therefore, think that our State Legislature should by this fund, and a small additional appropriation if needed, boldly attempt to teach agriculture and mechanics in every considerable college in this State, instead of teaching all the various branches of a college education in one college.

"Some of our reasons are:

"1. The fund is adequate, or nearly so. Two thousand dollars a year, fifteen hundred for the professor and five hundred for his books and tools, would respectably support an agricultural department in a college.

"2. By establishing a central board, or college, with branches, the Legislature, without meddling with the religions of the existing colleges, could forever retain control of the agricultural fund, and drop at will any branch, in any institution, which should be found unworthy or incompetent.

"3. And then such a diffused college, with branches, set in the different colleges throughout the State, would teach agriculture or mechanics, one or both, to all our youth, male and female, who in coming generations shall frequent these colleges, and thus agriculturize the education and educationize the agriculture of the State, which was and is the object of the bill creating this fund.

"4. And, finally, by a small model farm connected with each college, for trees and flowers, with a few acres for experiments in soils and crops, which farms, like public parks, will be places of popular resort, the art of agriculture will be placed, as it ought, in the forefront of the actual educational forces of the

whole State. Each religious denomination, satisfied with its just
and equal treatment by the State, will have no motive to plot
or wrangle; a wholesome rivalry, without the possibility of conflict, will incite each to excel the other in carrying out the objects
of the fund, and courtesy and kindness to the intercourse of
annual meetings will perpetually soften denominational pecu-
liarities without weakening denominational attachment to the
truth as each conceives it. The meeting of college officers with
the farmers at our State fairs, in connection with which the Agricultural College should meet, will give each the benefit of the
other, scholarship or strong sense, and thus make us one homogeneous, intelligent people, and so, more than any other agency
or institution, contribute to the true greatness and glory of our
State."

President Wallace took an optimistic view of the state of affairs.
He knew of many in his own institution who first chose the
scientific course, but soon inquired how they might enter into
the classical department. College men were not doing much,
and the youth were noticing it. "It is our own fault," he said,
"that there exists a hostility, and now we must change our own
course."

The report of the Committee on Legislative Aid was an
able article, and was in some parts difficult for those who
advocated the use of the land-grant funds for a central State
college to controvert in the public mind at that critical period.
The habit of trusting and believing what the prominent educational men of the State advocated, especially presidents of
colleges, as well as old customs and inherited views, lent
weight to the utterances of this committee. But at this late
day, with the proof of the fallacy of all these arguments and
our great State universities fulfilling their mission as an ever-
present object-lesson, it is amusing, to say the least, to read
the reasons given for dividing the "fund." One reason given
was that the fund was ample to give two thousand dollars to
each college, fifteen hundred dollars for a professor, leaving
five hundred dollars for his books and tools, which would
respectably support an agricultural department in a college.

A few weeks after the convention of college presidents,
President Blanchard began a series of articles in the news-

papers to prove that the State University must necessarily seem infidel, if it was not, because it would be under no denominational guidance. Professor Turner had these articles in mind when he spoke before the State Teachers' Association, December 31, 1866. Extracts from a newspaper report of this extemporaneous address show well the spirit in which he conceived the educational movement which he had led:

Professor Turner remarked that he agreed with the views given by the president of the convention in his opening address in regard to this university, and then continued:

" We have," he said, " from the start aimed to build a system of industrial universities in each State, covering the continent, and not a mere local State College. Such was the spirit and aim of our first petition to Congress, years ago, as the express wording of that petition plainly shows. Such is the explicit aim of the grant from Congress. But, somehow, the strange idea has got abroad that political States cannot successfully build universities. While the fact is that no university and no institution that has the least hope of ever becoming a university, in any proper sense of that term, was ever built on this continent or any other without the direct patronage and control of the political State to a greater or less extent."

He instanced the past and present history of Harvard, Yale, and Union colleges, the universities in Virginia, Kentucky, Missouri, and Michigan.

" So far, then, from its being true that political States cannot safely be trusted to build universities, it is strictly true that no other power is or ever has been adequate to the task; and if Illinois, or any other State, is ever to have a university worthy of the name, the State unquestionably must build it. But what is the State, and who rules it, on this continent, that we should be so anxiously cautioned to distrust it? Under our institutions the State is simply the people, neither more nor less. And who and what are the people of Illinois, and of this Union, that they should be told to their faces that they are unfit to be trusted to plan and build institutions for the education of their own children?

" Mr. President, this people has just returned from a great funeral, in which, for the love of God and Christ, for human justice and human rights, they have, most sadly, it is true, but still cheerfully, buried a quarter of a million of their sons and brothers on the field of battle, and wiped the great disgrace of the age from the realm. And is this people to be thus ruthlessly told, with these tears still upon their cheeks, that they have not sense, and piety, and self-devotion, and patriotism enough to plan and build the needful institutions for the proper education of their surviving sons, and daughters, and friends? And that the result of their efforts will be 'pagan or atheistic'? Is this common-school convention pagan or atheistic because we, for the time being, suppress our peculiar denominational or individual views in deference to the great common claims of a higher Christian humanity? And do you, my friends, necessarily turn more atheistic and pagan while here to discuss the great practical interests of the proper education of the children of the millions of families in the land, and to prepare them for the destinies of this world and the world to come, or do you feel less love to God, or to Christ, or to men, than you would if you were met to wrangle over some dry ecclesiastical dogma which no man of sense on earth ever did believe or ever will believe?

"Mr. President, I am sick and tired and disgusted with hearing about a Christianity that can only be kept in the world in a bandbox or in the care of a dry-nurse. And I wish here to affirm that wherever freedom is, there Christianity *must* be; and wherever Christ is, there freedom *must* and *shall* be. For this is the everlasting decree of the Infinite and Eternal God; and man can neither revoke nor resist it. You have asked how you could get Christianity into our schools. I ask you, in turn, how will you get it out of them? And I defy you to do it so long as God lives and freedom exists.

"Men will still say and do foolish things about it, as heretofore, and perhaps it is the only thing on this earth which even its friends cannot kill. With such a people, and such a Gospel, and such a God, we do not need ecclesiastical supervisors and guardians to climb up and bore gimlet-holes in the sky to let the light of heaven down into our schools and hearts. All we need is simply to sweep away the absurd fixtures and customs and usages which have ever only obstructed its light, and its wide and broad day beams will stream in from all sides upon us, of course; and all these unseemly and untoward words and influences will no more disturb the solid basis of its being than the ripples and spray on the ocean beach will wash down the far-off mountain heights in the serene bosom of the continual lands beyond. I wish that some of these good, anxious, and fidgety souls could ever be persuaded that Almighty God did not send them into the world to act as the dry-nurses of Christianity; on the other hand, He sent Christianity into the world to nurse and take care of them. But we must allow good men sometimes to mistake their calling; and on this point I have prayed for years that ' Otello's occupation ' might be gone. After all the effort to breed distrust of the capacity of the State and the people to manage public institutions with Christian wisdom and beneficence, I here and now undertake to say that there is not on this broad earth a system of institutions that have been generally better managed than the State institutions of this same people of Illinois, including the Normal University at Bloomington and the several institutions in this town. And so it will be in the history of that great system of national universities which they are about to found, till, ere long, we, here in Illinois, so recently the home of the prairie-wolf and the panther, shall have a complete system of beneficent, humane, literary, scientific, and professional institutions, unsurpassed by any in their practical benignity, efficacy, and power over all our interests, by any beneath the circuit of the sun. And, my friends, it is in your power, in the power of those now in this town and in this room, to do in the few short weeks to come more to further this glorious result than it ordinarily falls to the lot of man to do in a lifetime."

Then he clearly pointed out the necessary connection between the proposed university and the common schools.

The following note from Professor Turner was printed in the *Tribune* following its report of his address:

Mr. Editor:

Should any deem my remarks inapposite in the Teachers' Convention on the inevitable perpetuity of Christianity in all our schools on this continent, I beg leave to suggest, in further illustration of the subject, that we have already tried the experiment of attempting its extermination on over four millions of colored slaves on a great scale.

We shut them out from all light from the Bible, and from all our schools and literatures; we hemmed them in with fugitive-slave laws, and employed the whole force of our courts, our army and navy, to crush out all the Christianity that was in them, and keep out all that might by any possibility get into them; we leveled against them almost the entire force of our arms, our votes, our schools, our literature, our pulpits, and our prayers; we called on our doctors of divinity, with their " Onesimuses," their " Hams," their " Hagars," devil and all, to try to physic it out of them; we even, at last, forced our brave boys in blue to stand guard over " this kind of property " and keep Christianity out of them at the point of the bayonet. But, after all, it turned out, at last, that the negroes had got more Christianity than all the rest of us, simply because the good Lord would keep pouring it into their hearts in spite of us. With this ever memorable experiment before us, I think we may safely conclude that the Lord has determined that this shall be a Christian continent. At any rate, we are no more competent to take care of Christianity than we are the solar system or the laws of nature.

Yours truly,

J. B. TURNER

This encouraging letter from Julian M. Sturtevant, president of Illinois College, was written December 24, 1866:

PROFESSOR J. B. TURNER

Dear Sir:

Yours is received and read.

You are not to infer that the action of the trustees of Illinois College will not be all which we desire in respect to our present plans.

For myself, nothing can be added to the intensity of my desire for the success of our plans, or my dread of a failure. I agree with you that " concentration " we must have. There is nothing noble, generous, great, or good which the spirit of sect is not reducing to weakness. May the spirit of the living God descend on us and upon the people in this crisis.

Yours truly,

J. M. STURTEVANT

CHAPTER XXIII

The Choice of Champaign

The efforts of the presidents of existing colleges to prevent the foundation of a single new industrial university were unsuccessful. The Illinois Legislature of 1867 not only held to this policy, but definitely located the new institution on its present site in Champaign.

Champaign County had put forth efforts earlier than any other section of the State to secure the new University. It placed its claims before the Legislature of 1866. But the State agricultural, horticultural, and educational societies proposed that the various sections of the State be allowed to bid for the right to secure the new institution, and the Legislature of 1867 adopted this plan. In the meanwhile, the advocates of Champaign appeared again to renew their fight at the opening of the session of 1867. The following letter from Professor Turner to an Illinois paper shows the situation at that time:

Mr. Editor:

I am not a little surprised at the ground taken by your paper upon this question. I am not aware that any one wishes to disparage or undervalue the noble efforts and generous offers of the citizens of Champaign. But their agents have broken away from the fair and equal democratic rule of free and open competition among all the counties, which was proposed by all the State agricultural, horticultural, and educational societies, and urged by their authorized committees through the last session, and at the same time with the bill offered by General Fuller in the State yesterday. They insist on the direct isolated claims of Champaign against all other competitors. Had they not persisted in this unwise course at the last session, there can be but little doubt that the institution would have been running in Champaign County to-day.

The friends of free competition have now again revived that same bill. They not only ask, but they demand, its immediate passage. Give the counties the forcible power of legal action before you taunt them with indifference and voluntary inaction. Let the Legislature first untie the hands of the counties, and in some way open this great interest to free legal competition, and then, if they remain inactive, let them locate the institution at once at Champaign or wherever they think best.

Yours truly,

J. B. TURNER

On January 25, 1867, the Illinois Legislature, following the general idea of those interested in the movement, passed an act, in relation to the location of the University, which permitted all towns, cities, and corporations to bid for it. Champaign, Logan, McLean, and Morgan Counties were the most active bidders, offering bonds and money and fine tracts of land.

Champaign County, which was very enthusiastic, had sent a committee to Springfield to make its bid and watch the Legislature. Bidding was strong and spirited; each advance made by one county was met by a greater from another county, except in the case of Champaign, which was content simply to increase the value of what had been already offered, thus constantly keeping in the lead with little effort and no extra expense.

After the passage of the law allowing competitive bidding, the friends of the movement in Morgan County were spurred to greater effort. A committee was appointed, consisting of J. B. Turner, Joseph Morton, and Judge William Brown, to find out the wishes of the people. Circular letters were printed, precinct and town meetings were held, and the greatest enthusiasm prevailed. The people at first planned to raise Morgan County's bid by taxation. A vote was taken, the ballots counted, and the project reported to be carried by a large majority. Great was the rejoicing. But, alas! a later and official count revealed that it had not carried by the *legal* majority. Not dismayed in the least, it was decided to raise the amount by private subscription. Professor Turner was naturally interested in securing the University for his own county, and, with his friend Mr. Ralph Reynolds and others, worked untiringly to raise this fund, with the result that $521,000, in land and cash, was offered. This was reduced to $491,000 in value by the legislative committee that had the matter in charge; yet this reduced sum exceeded the next highest by $21,000, and the Champaign County bid by $216,000—being almost double, as can be seen by the official report below. The legislative committee in charge of the location was, in the meanwhile, touring the State to examine into the claims of the various sections. The following note gives an interesting glimpse into its visit at Champaign:

SPRINGFIELD, ILLINOIS, February 10, 1867

PROFESSOR J. B. TURNER, Jacksonville, Ill.

My very dear Sir:

I've been to Champaign and seen the "Elephant."

I can't give any opinion as to where it may go, but I don't believe that any power short of Omnipotence can take it to Champaign. We leave here to-morrow for Bloomington, and can't reach your place before Tuesday "nohow."

Our Champaign friends made two mistakes. One was, they had not made all their titles undoubted. Don't make such a mistake at Jacksonville. The other mistake you may guess at from the following enigma. If it becomes necessary to make anybody drunk (?), for God's sake don't have it on the day the committee visits you.

Yours for the University, G. W. MINIER

P. S. Show this to Goltra.

The final report of the Joint Legislative Committee on the Industrial University follows:

The joint committee, appointed in compliance with a concurrent resolution of the Senate and House of Representatives, beg leave to report: That they have endeavored to discharge the duties assigned to them by said resolutions, in visiting the counties of Champaign, McLean, Logan, and Morgan, and, as fully as possible in the limited time allowed them, have examined the propositions of each of said counties in relation to the location of the proposed Industrial University, and find the same to be as follows:

Champaign County

The County of Champaign proposes to donate the Champaign and Urbana University, a new brick building with stone foundation; the main part 125 feet front and 40 deep, five stories high, and a wing in the rear 70 by 44 feet and four stories high, containing 181 rooms, having cost $120,000. Said building is nearly ready for occupancy. We estimate its cash value at $75,500. Also, 10 acres of land, in the center of which the said University stands, being about equi-distant between and within one mile of the depot of the Illinois Central Railroad, in the city of Champaign, and the courthouse in the city of Urbana. We estimate the cash value of said land at $2,500. Also, $160\frac{1}{2}$ acres of well-cultivated farm-land within one half mile of said University and adjoining the city of Champaign, through which runs a stream of ever-living water—the cash value of which land we estimate at $20,000. The average assessed value thereof is $20 per acre. Also, 410 acres of like farm-land adjoining thereto, with orchard, farm-house, and barn—the estimated cash value of which is $30,000. Its averaged value, by the last assessment, was $15 per acre. Also, 400 acres of like farm-land within about two miles of said University—the cash value of which is estimated at $20,000. The average value of the same, by the last assessment, is $15 per acre. The entire amount of land offered by Champaign County is 980 acres. Also, $2,000 worth of shade, ornamental, and fruit trees, at catalogue rates—to be delivered from the neighboring nursery of M. L. Dunlap, Esq. Also, $100,000 in Champaign County ten-per-cent. twenty-year bonds—the cash value of which is estimated at $100,000. Also, $50,000 in freight on the Illinois Central Railroad, for the said Industrial University—the estimated cash value of which is $35,000.

The total offers of Champaign County are estimated, in cash, at $285,000.

McLean County

The County of McLean proposes to donate $200,000 in McLean County ten-per-cent. twenty-year bonds—the estimated cash value whereof is $200,000. Also, $100,000 city of Bloomington ten-per-cent. twenty-year bonds—the estimated cash value of which is $100,000. Also, $50,000 in freight on the Chicago, Alton, & St. Louis Railroad, for the proposed University—valued at cash at $35,000. Also 43½ acres of land, for the proposed University site adjoining the Normal University, through which runs a stream of water. The estimated value of this tract is $15,000. The average of last assessment was $18 per acre. Also, 100 acres of land, adjacent to the Normal University, and now held in trust by the trustees of said Normal University—the estimated cash value of which is $20,000.

The total offers of McLean County are estimated, in cash, at $470,000. McLean County offers, in lieu of the said lands, at the option of the State, other lands equally valuable. All the foregoing offers of McLean County are guaranteed by a bond, signed by its citizens, who are represented to be good and fully responsible for the entire amount.

Logan County

Logan County proposes to donate $300,000 in Logan County ten-per-cent. ten-year bonds—the estimated value of which, in cash, is $300,000. Also, $50,000 in city of Lincoln ten-per-cent. five-year bonds—the cash value of which is estimated at $50,000. Also, $50,000 in freight on the Chicago, Alton & St. Louis Railroad, for said University, which is guaranteed by the citizens of Lincoln, and valued, in cash, at $35,000.

Logan offers, in lieu of $46,000 of said city bonds, 355 acres of highly cultivated farm-land, adjoining city of Lincoln, averaging, by the last assessment, $10 per acre, or 640 acres of like land, also adjoining said city—the last average assessment of which is $14.25 per acre; or, 420 acres of like land, also adjoining said city—the last averaging assessment of which is $15 per acre. A stream of water runs through each of the said tracts, and each is estimated to be worth, in cash, from $40,000 to $50,000.

The total offers of Logan County are estimated, in cash, at $385,000.

Morgan County

Morgan County proposes to donate $200,000 in Morgan County ten-per-cent. ten-year bonds, whose estimated value in cash is $200,000. Also, $50,000 in city of Jacksonville ten-per-cent. ten-year bonds, whose estimated cash value is $50,000. Also, 200 acres of highly improved farm-land south of and adjoining the State Hospital for the Insane farm, the estimated cash value of which is $40,000—the average of which by the last assessment was $55 per acre. Also, the Berean College building, in the city of Jacksonville, whose estimated cash value is $12,000. Also, about 6 acres of land in the center of which the said college stands—the estimated value of which, in cash, is $13,000. The above offers are estimated, in cash, at $315,000. Morgan also offers to put in the Illinois College building, whose estimated cash value is $21,000. Also, 31 acres of beautiful land, in the center of which said buildings stand, estimated, in cash, $60,000. Also a library and apparatus, estimated as worth, in cash, $5,000. Also, the college endowment fund—estimated, in cash, at $90,000. Said Illinois College property is, in all, estimated, in cash, at $176,000. Said Illinois College property is under the control of its trustees, who propose to merge it into said Industrial University, as far as they can under their powers, but will be bound, under the terms of their charter and the conditions of the endowment to said college, to continue the organization of said board of trustees, and see that their trusts are fully executed and the funds and endowments are not diverted from their original purpose.

The total offers of Morgan County are estimated, in cash, at $491,000.

All the lands offered by each county are eligibly situated, of the best quality, and well adapted for the purposes of model and experimental farming or pasturage. The titles to the lands are all good, or can be made good upon the acceptance by the State. The abstracts of title, together with the plats of the lands, are now in the hands of the committee.

All of which is respectfully submitted.

A. I. ENOCH, *Chairman of Joint Committee*
SPRINGFIELD, ILLINOIS, February 16, 1867

In spite of the relative values of the bids shown in this report, the Legislature located the new University at Champaign. Professor Turner, whose heart was strongly enlisted in the claim of Morgan County, the highest bidder, wrote the following comment on the result to the Chicago *Tribune:*

This is the first time in my life I ever saw or knew a valuable piece of property to be knocked down to the lowest bidder.

Through all the years of arduous work in establishing this Industrial University, I never saw my father discouraged or disheartened until this decision of the Illinois Legislature to locate the State University at Champaign. Whether true or not, he believed that it had been placed in the hands of those who cared to use it only for their own selfish purposes, with no consideration of the great blessing it was intended to be, or appreciation of the thought and labor bestowed upon its conception and birth; and when the board of trustees nominated Dr. Gregory to be its first president, his cup of sorrow was full to overflowing. With a groan of anguish, I heard him exclaim, as he head the news, " O Lord, how long, how long! An ex-superintendent of public instruction, and a Baptist minister! Could anything be worse? " Not that he had any prejudice against ex-superintendents and Baptist ministers, but he believed that class of men to be wholly unfitted to lead in a movement so new and untried. Besides, Dr. Gregory was from another State, knew nothing of the condition of things in Illinois, and was wholly ignorant of the whole movement. He had had no part in the great work, and was entitled to no consideration, for that reason, if for no other. But, wisely and heroically, Professor Turner cast aside all personal feeling, and aided the new president in every way. He counseled, encouraged, and helped him to rectify mistakes, and stood shoulder to shoulder with him in the bitter fight that later was waged against the University and its administration.

Dr. Gregory found his duties in the untried field most perplexing, and his path strewn with everything except roses. Two causes of anxiety weighed heavily upon him—the attacks of jealous presidents of other universities, and the fear of repudiation of the Champaign County bonds pledged by her

supervisors. People who had anticipated a rich harvest from
the many diversified interests that were expected to cluster
around the University, which had been pictured in such
glowing colors, found, instead, only hard work and many
debts at the beginning. As the years passed on, and experiment and inexperience gave place to broader views and
greater ambition, it grew into the grand University that is
now the pride and honor of Illinois. This experience was
true of all the State universities at first: the way was new and
unmarked, and gropings and blunders were in evidence
everywhere. Massachusetts had her trials, as the following
extract will show:

Massachusetts Agricultural Colleges

Judge Henry F. French, who was elected president, has written
a letter to his trustees, tendering his resignation, and assigning
his reasons therefor. The following are the most important:

1. Because the unwieldly organization of the board of trustees,
which consists of eighteen persons, residing in different sections
of the State, each absorbed in his own business, has rendered
this work of organizing the school almost impracticable. The
act of incorporation requires that the plan of organization, government, and course of study prescribed for said college shall be
subject to the approval of the Governor and Council, and that
the Board of Agriculture, with indefinite powers and duties, are
made overseers of the college.

2. The value of the coöperation of the Governor and Council
in advancing the enterprise, unanimously adopted by your board
and submitted to the Executive on the 23d of January, 1866,
never received approval until the 31st of August, 1866, and then
the approval was accompanied with a condition, which at the
next meeting of the board you voted to be entirely inadmissible.

3. After a year's delay, since your committee was stopped in
its works, you have adopted no plan whatever of the grounds;
the site of your single building is not fixed; you have no plan
for farm buildings; you do not propose to complete any building
for more than a year; and, although you have employed the best
talent in the country, you have rejected all its advice, and I, as
your representative, am held responsible for the delay.

4. I have encountered persistent opposition at every point.

This opposition has been made secretly. The scheme at the bottom of the opposition is that the college shall be placed on a military basis, that the students shall be kept in barracks on the farm, as at West Point, that they shall be marched to and from their work at the tap of the drum, and that they shall daily be marched in military order to Amherst College, more than a mile, to the lecture and recitation rooms there. This is impracticable, contrary to the wishes of the farmers of the State, and utterly subversive of the whole idea of an agricultural college. I know you do not intend to make this institution a mere appendage to Amherst College, nor do you mean to commit the commonwealth, without its consent, to a scheme involving extravagant expenditure; but to one or the other you are surely drifting.

Illinois was perhaps a little slower than the others to attain preëminence. Many pitfalls beset her way. In later years the College of Agriculture, the one great object of our State Industrial University organization, drooped and withered until life had almost departed. Repeated warnings were received from the Department of Agriculture at Washington that a new leaf must be turned, and turned quickly, or the experiment station, in which so many hopes were centered, would be taken from them. Humble apologies begging for a little more time, most earnest pleadings and most anxious fears on the part of those in charge of the College of Agriculture, were the only reward during years of battling with seemingly insurmountable difficulties. Finally, those for whom the College of Agriculture was intended—presidents, officers, and friends of all the Illinois associations of labor— arose in their indignation and might and demanded their rights. To-day the College of Agriculture of Illinois is the equal of any and the superior of many.* Providence overrules all things for good. The location of the University in Champaign County has proved most advantageous to the State and to the people. Logan, McLean, and Morgan

---

* The following quotation from Professor Turner's speech at the first State Fair held in Springfield, Illinois, October, 1853, greets the visitor as he approaches the building: " Industrial education prepares the way for the Millennium of Labor.—J. B. Turner."

Counties each have State interests in their midst. Morgan had then large institutions. It was wise and just that other parts of the State should be recognized and great public trusts confided to their keeping. It was not the location that the friends of the University movement feared, but the spirit in which it was sought and won; for this reason they secured, after a bitter fight, the following legislation:

An act supplemental to an act entitled " An act to provide for the organization, endowment, and maintenance of the Illinois Industrial University."

Section 1. Be it enacted by the people of the State of Illinois, represented in the General Assembly, That if the legal authorities of the County of Champaign shall not, by or before the first day of June, 1867, convey or cause to be conveyed to the board of trustees of the Illinois Industrial University a good and unencumbered title, in fee simple, all the real estate mentioned and contained in the propositions of said county, and which real estate is described and set out in the act to which this act is supplemental, amounting to 980 acres of land; and if said county shall not also pay over and deliver to said trustees, by said day, all the bonds and other property offered by said county mentioned in said act: then said board of trustees, or a majority of them, shall proceed without delay to permanently locate and establish said Industrial University in McLean, Logan, or Morgan County. Such county so selected shall in like manner be required in all things to fulfill and comply with the conditions and provisions of the offer heretofore made by such county as an inducement for the location of said University in such county.

Section 2. This act shall be deemed a public act, and be in force from and after its approval.

Approved March 8, 1867.

United States of America, ⎱ ss.   Office of Secretary
State of Illinois.   ⎰

I, Sharon Tyndale, Secretary of the State of Illinois, do hereby certify that the foregoing are true copies of enrolled laws now on file in this office. In witness whereof I hereto set my hand and affix the great seal of State, at the city of Springfield, this twelfth day of March, A. D. 1867.

SHARON TYNDALE,
Secretary of State

CHAPTER XXIV

Address at the Laying of the Corner-Stone

Professor Turner accepted the invitation to deliver the address at the laying of the corner-stone of the first University building, but he steadfastly refused to hold any office, either as trustee, professor, or lecturer—though his friends urged, and the opposition had tried to bribe him with the offer of the presidency.

In the beginning they had openly charged that he was seeking a university to preside over and replenish his depleted purse; this made him very sensitive and all the more unwilling to accept any position. He delivered the commencement address in 1878, and again in 1892, when he was eighty-seven years of age. This last address, a short one, was read by Dr. Burill, while Professor Turner sat upon the platform. When his daughter, in 1896, was the second woman to be elected upon the board of trustees, he was greatly pleased.

In his address at the laying of the corner-stone of the University, on September 13, 1871, Professor Turner showed how his forebodings had already changed to an appreciation of the great career upon which the University was already launched. He said:

Fellow Citizens: It gives me joy to meet you on this interesting occasion. For more than twenty years a little band of brothers in this State labored as well and as faithfully as we could for the promotion of industrial education in this great Republic of ours. In this labor no one of my comrades ever received one cent of public funds, in payment for either time or expenses, which was not at once appropriated to the advancement of the general cause. We sought and accepted no offices or perquisites whatever in connection with the enterprise; and not one single man of that original band of brothers holds any such relation to-day, or ever has held it, or, to my knowledge, sought to hold it. If, then, our hands are not clean, let those whose hands are clean wash us and make us clean.

At one time, as you all know, the whole enterprise seemed to us to stumble and fall—to come to naught, so far as our day and generation was concerned. I say, it so seemed to us; and, however mistaken, we were honest in it. It was a dark day to us—to me one of the saddest and darkest days of my life. But we all decided not to attack the institution, but to let it live amid its new surroundings, if it could, even though we had no faith that it could. Then came the criticisms of its friends who were supposed to know of its condition, deepening both our gloom and our despair, and intensifying all our natural prepossessions, prejudices, and fears. We shut our mouths and bit our lips, and bitterly hoped for some better resurrection of our idolized principles after we were in our graves. But all this is now changed; and it is not only our duty, but our great joy, to change to meet the new conditions.

For the first time I came to this University last winter to see it for myself. I did not find any one of its professors or its teachers either omniscient or omnipotent; nor yet angels walking the earth in sublime grandeur, with wings at their shoulders, all plumed and ready for the skies. From the newspaper accounts I had previously read of them, I hardly expected this. But I found (or, at least, I fancied that I found) good, honest-hearted, intelligent men, prosecuting a great, arduous, and difficult public work new in its ends and aims, and untried in its modes and methods, with a patience, a zeal, and a self-devotion worthy of their great cause; and when I have said that I have said enough in praise of any set of mortal men that ever lived.

They frankly told me (what it is easy to see in any similar institution under the sun) that they had made mistakes, and were striving to correct them, and expected to make more, and to correct them, too. What more or better did any man expect who knew anything about the newness, the difficulties, and the natural and artificial obstacles of the great enterprise in which they are engaged? It will probably take a thousand years for a single one of these great free States to learn to endow and manage these industrial universities in the best possible manner. But what of that? Shall we never attempt to learn the greatest of all possible arts—the preparing of our American youth for a true American life—because our art is difficult and our lesson a long one? I shall soon die; you will soon die; we shall all soon die: but these institutions will live—still live to learn their art and their duty, and to help the race, long after the oaks have grown, and fallen again, and rotted over our graves. Here, then, is my triple joy. I come here again to-day to cast off and abjure all my former prejudices and prepossessions,—if prejudices and prepossessions they were,—and to bury them beneath the corner-stone of this new and beautiful edifice now rising to our view. And what greater joy can any man have than when he finds things better even than he had dared to hope? In this case, a resurrection a half century sooner than I, for one, dared to hope for it, only a few short years ago. Why, then, should I not this day rejoice?

This institution will need in the future, as in the past, a magnanimous patience within and a magnanimous forbearance from without its walls. A little censorious criticism can neither destroy nor aid it. Thank God, it has already become too big for any such result. It must now live; it ought to live; and it will live. The fly that annoys the elephant cannot devour him, even though he may continue to keep him in an unseemly wagging of his tail. Do the best it can, this institution will not, and can not, do all we desire, for at least a round hundred years to come; though it may, and it can and will, do a good work to-day and to-morrow and forever.

Some lament because that only a small per cent. of the youth educated in our agricultural colleges remain in after life in industrial pursuits, and, therefore, deem these institutions a failure.

Now, several if not most of our older colleges were founded for the special and avowed purpose of training up the youth for the ministry of the gospel; and yet, it is doubtful whether five per cent. of the graduates ever, in fact, enter the ministry at all. But do we hear their trustees and graduates and patrons talk of abandoning these colleges because such is the result? Not at all. They well know a student will and must, to a greater or less extent, imbibe their spirit, become possessed of their animus, and tend to diffuse it over the whole surface of human society, in whatever profession he may be engaged. Verily, the children of the world are, in their generation, wiser than the children of light.

If, then, these sons of our farmers and our friends are educated in institutions which are in no sense conventional, partizan, or sectarian, but in all their methods, ends, and aims truly, grandly, and fondly industrial, natural, scientific, and American, and therefore Christian, I care not into what particular professions they may choose to go in after life. This is a free country, and they have a right to go where they please; but, wherever they may go or in whatever they may engage, they must and they will carry the broad scientific, catholic, and truly American Christian spirit of their alma mater along with them, instead of the narrow and scholastic spirit of caste and sect. We may treat them, then, as our men, true sons of the Republic and true sons of God, whatever they may do, wherever they may rest, or wherever they may roam the whole world around.

It is said that there is also, in our State, a small class of seven-by-nine politicians who occasionally sneer at the great cause of industrial education, and begrudge it the crumbs it gathers. Let them sneer. To all such in this State, and in all States, I have but one answer to make in behalf of the farmers and working-men of the Republic: We intend to keep on asking for endowments for each and all of these institutions throughout the land, until we have made each one of them, in some degree, in all needful buildings, apparatus, perquisites, and endowments, what they ought to be; and when they shed the full radiance of their united glory and light over every State and every hamlet on this continent, from sea to sea, we intend to point to them and say to these grafters: " These are all our stealings from the treasuries of the Republic; we obtained every dollar of them by the honest vote of a proud, a patriotic, and a grateful people. And now, where are yours? Can you, dare you, show them to us? "

The mass of our people pay the taxes and fight the battles of the country; and, whichever party is in power, they do *none* of the stealing out of the public treasury. I, for one, am tired of the groaning and whining of a few who do it all, whenever these masses ask for a few dollars, out of the general or State treasury, for some great agricultural or industrial interest of their own. I have no doubt that the majority of our people, and of the Legislature, who are not thieves, will continue to give us all we may need in this regard, and that, in spite of all these croakers, these institutions will at last achieve a great and glorious success.

Let, then, these beautiful walls rise as the monument of our past endeavor and the memorial of our plighted faith—if not *where* we preferred, still to become *what* we preferred. Let them rise till the myriads who dwell upon the rich plains shall throng around to uphold, to endow, and to bless them; till their rising light shall shine far abroad over this great green sea of prairie-land, with its woodland isles and ravines, to gladden and bless every farm and enlighten and exalt every soul—till ministering angels shall come to greet and bless their inmates with every morning sun, and bid them rest and sleep in peace with every evening shade.

CHAPTER XXV

An Address of Dr. Newton Bateman and a Letter from J. M. Gregory

At the inauguration of Dr. John M. Gregory, first president of the University, which took place at Champaign, Illinois, Dr. Newton Bateman, State Superintendent of Public Instruction, delivered the address, a few extracts of which follow:

But the era of great combined movements, in this country, in behalf of the better education of the masses for the manual industries of life, may be said to have commenced about twenty years ago. And, whether considered in the light of the magnitude of the interests involved, the millions of people concerned in the issue, and the grandeur of the thoughts and the conception advanced, the number, eminence, and power of the men engaged, or the undaunted persistency and faith with which the contest has been carried on—whether viewed in one or all of these aspects, this era of effort and conflict for industrial education deserves to be called sublime.

Convention after convention was held; league after league was formed; society after society was organized; pamphlets, appeals, and addresses were written and published by tens of thousands of copies; petitions and memorials went up, from the lakes to the sea; the law-making power was involved, and earnest, determined men thundered again and again at the doors of the general assemblies and congressional halls, demanding to be heard on

this great question. At times, in some of the States, the issue went
to the hustings, and even the tumultuous roar of political parties
was awed and hushed for a time by the great voice of the tolling
masses, demanding an education suited to their needs. Repeated
disappointments and defeats only resulted in fresh combinations,
more determined efforts, and large accessions of strength. Able
and gifted men from every pursuit in life, from every class of
society, and from every quarter of the Union poured into the
swelling tide the contributions of their learning, experience, and
genius.

In the West, the man whose voice rang out the earliest, loudest,
and clearest in this great movement—whose words pealed and
thundered through the minds and hearts of the people, and the
round shot of whose tremendous broadside of irrefragable facts
and logic, and fiery rhetoric, plowed and plunged and ricochetted
through these prairies with an energy and vehemence that no
bulwarks of ignorance or apathy could withstand, and which
brought nearly every farmer and artisan hurrying to his standard,
from far and near, and put in motion the imperial columns of
our free-born yeomanry—the man who threw into the struggle not
only the best energies of his mind, but the unwavering faith of
his soul and the deepest longings of his heart, and who pleaded
for the uplifting and regeneration of the masses and for the
" millennium of labor," as the patriot pleads for his country and
the Christian for the salvation of God—the man whose able
reports, instructive addresses, and thrillingly eloquent speeches
were caught up and reëchoed by the enlightened press of the
whole country, without regard to sect or party, and which furnished at once the material and the inspiration of auxiliary and
coöperative movements and organizations in many other States—
and the man who, as I believe, through all these multiplied and
overwhelming labors, was animated not by considerations of
self-aggrandizement or sordid gain, but by the loftier purposes
of serving his race and honoring God by uplifting and blessing
the toiling millions of His children—that man was Jonathan
Baldwin Turner, of Illinois.

This is not blind adulation nor fulsome eulogy. I know
whereof I affirm; I am familiar with the procession of events to
which I have referred, and the connection of that great and good
man therewith; and I could not suffer this glad day to pass
without a few words in vindication of the truth of history and
the promptings of my own feelings and judgment. No other

person is in any manner responsible for what I have said, or may say, in this regard.

And if I speak warmly of Professor Turner as a man, it is because I have known him over thirty years, during twenty of which he was my near neighbor, during four of which he was my teacher, and during all of which he has been my friend, ever kind and true. If his right to the pace to which I have assigned him as the Western pioneer and leader in this great educational movement is challenged, I refer to the printed records and documentary history of the whole agitation, from the convention at Granville, in November, 1851, down to the passage of the bill creating this institution, on February 25, 1867. Through all those sixteen years of struggle and effort, you will find him towering up as the central figure, the very Ajax of the fight, closely identified with every phase of the controversy, and with all its vicissitudes of fortune. His reports, addresses, memorials, and other papers are scattered through all the earlier published Transactions of the State Agricultural Society. The record of his personal labors is, in fact, in epitome, a record of the whole movement.

But I have also referred to the commanding ability and power with which he led the forces of the people *and championed their cause in the great march to the gates of Washington*, and the final achievement of the supreme purpose—national recognition and aid by acts of Congress. None who have heard him will dissent; let those who have not, read his ringing oration on the " Millennium of Labor," delivered in 1853; or the " Plea in Behalf of Industrial Universities " for his people, published in 1854; or his " Essay on Industrial University Education," prepared by special request of the Commissioner of the National Bureau of Agriculture; and scores of other papers written and published during that period. The recognition, too, of the signal energy and grasp with which he handled the profound themes involved in the discussion was general and hearty, not only from the rural and metropolitan press of the country, both East and West, but also from the solid columns of some of the oldest and stateliest reviews, and even from presidents and faculties of existing colleges and universities, although utterly dissenting from and vehemently protesting against his views and opinions upon many points.

But then, Professor Turner does not expect anybody to think and believe and act precisely as he does—he would rather they would not; it would savor too much of a blind faith, which is the especial horror of his soul. He would a thousand times rather a man would fight him from honest conviction than indorse him from stupid servility. I think that, upon the whole, he rather relished the criticism of the man who, after listening to an address from him on a certain occasion, remarked: " That was a magnificent thing, but I don't believe a word of it." He cares nothing for the *ipsissima verba* in speaking or writing. So that he can get his harpoon well into the heart of the ugly whales of error that prowl God's great ocean of truth, he is not particular how it is done, or who drags the dead monsters to the shore. So that he effectually breaches the walls behind which cheats and humbugs are intrenched, he cares little what people think of his engineering. When pitted against an antagonist, his sole purpose is to knock him down in the speediest and most effectual manner possible, and so that everybody can see that he is down, regardless of the rules of pugilistic science.

A sample or two best illustrate his way of " moving upon the enemy's work."

Speaking of the causes of failure in previous attempts to establish industrial colleges, he pulverizes one of them in the following style:

" One capital and fatal error has been the idea that we should send a boy to school to learn to work, and not simply to learn to think; thus absurdly attempting to teach, by public endowment and munificence, the little arts of personal manipulation, instead of the magnificent science of universal success. Nothing could be more fatal. When I have taught a boy merely how to hold a plow, I have only taught him to be a two-legged jackass, twin brother to the four-legged team in front of him. But when I have taught him, truly and scientifically, all the mighty mysteries of the seas, stars, oceans, lands, and ages that are concerned in that act of plowing, I have made a man of him—had we not better say an angel? Art, in the sense of mere labor, mere servile imitation alone, is only animal—the common property of asses, dogs, and monkeys. But true labor, inspired by universal science and intelligence, is not only characteristically human, but also divine. What could be more absurd than to take a hundred boys, in their teens, away from their parents, the year round, and set them to dabbling with a hundred teams for a few hours per diem, half of which break their traces and run away the first hour, under the absurd pretext of teaching these boys how to plow? When Almighty God created the heavens and the earth, and ordered man to eat his bread by the sweat of the brow, He created, and most likely endowed, the best possible university for learning all such mere manual arts; and if we expect to supersede Omnipotence by grants of land for endowments, it will prove worse than a Bull Run defeat; for no institution for teaching the arts and the habits of bare manipulation and industrial skill can ever be endowed at all comparable with those which the great Father of all has most munificently spread abroad over every household, every shop, and every field, throughout the civilized globe. The principles of science, therefore, and not the bare manipulations of art, should form the sole end of industrial universities."

So wrote Professor Turner four years ago, demolishing a great fallacy and enunciating a great truth in a manner not to be resisted or forgotten, whatever may be said of his zoölogical illustrations.

The first term of the new University began on March 11, 1868. Professor Turner followed the early work of the institution carefully, and soon came into sympathy with its management, and with President Gregory, whose selection he had at first so deplored. The relations established between the two men is well shown by the following letter from President Gregory:

CHAMPAIGN, February 4, 1871

PROFESSOR J. B. TURNER
Dear Sir:

Your very kind and cheering note came to hand last evening.

Your visit to us will be long remembered both by the faculty and by my family. I think you did us much good in every way and your friendly efforts with the Legislature place the University under new obligations.

I ought to express the personal gratification your visit gave myself. If we had been misrepresented to you, you had been equally misrepresented to us, by men who are too bigoted and ignorant to understand you. Your bold rejection of their little theological dogmas seems to them infidel, and they cannot comprehend the sublime and large faith you avow. I have not met any one for years whose views more harmonized with my own.

Our prospect of legislative aid seems good. God grant, for the sake of Illinois and our common humanity, it may come. We have no light struggle before us, and we want to be put on vantage-ground to meet it successively. If we fail, the cause of industrial education receives a severe check; but if we succeed, the days of fogyism are nearly numbered for our colleges.

Again let me thank you heartly for your visit and good service, and invite you to come often among us. My doors will be always open to you.

Yours for God's truth in church and schools,

J. M. GREGORY

CHAPTER XXVI

A Petition to the Constitutional Convention

The plan along which the development of the new University was begun produced more or less criticism among the farmers of the State. Just what this criticism was is shown by the following contemporary report of the meeting of the Northern Illinois Horticultural Society, which was held at Bloomington on Wednesday, March 2, 1870, and which resulted in a petition, in December, 1870, to the Illinois Constitutional Convention, to enlarge the scope and resources of the institution:

Pursuant to call of committee, the delegates from the Northern Illinois Horticultural Society, and also delegates from some of the county agricultural and mechanical associations in the State, met at the court-house in this city.

The object of the meeting, as stated in the call, is " to express the opinion of the industrial classes in regard to the reforms needed (if any) in the management of the Industrial University, as may be deemed proper."

J. H. Bryant was elected permanent President, and H. D. Emery Secretary.

President Gregory invited the convention to adjourn and meet at Champaign, offering the members free transportation by railroad. He urged their acceptance of his invitation.

He said that if there were objections to the management of the University, those objections could be better ascertained by being on the ground. That the buildings, the grounds, and every department were open to inspection and criticism, and he thought that where a statement of proceedings were to go to the public, it was due to the institution, to the people, and to the State, that they should adopt the best means of knowing the fact whereon to base their actions. He thought that this city, being fifty miles away, was not the proper place to pass judgment upon such a matter.

Mr. Periam replied that he thought it was especially right and proper that this convention should sit here, away from the influence and seductions which sometimes are found in the purlieus of large institutions.

Mr. Ellsworth said this meeting was called here with regard to convenience of access. He did not come here to sit in judgment upon the University; he came to join with others in ascertaining from the official reports, from the facts as known to members, whether the institution was fulfilling in its general scope the results contemplated by the law of Congress and the intention of the Legislature.

Mr. Harmon said: "If this body wants to do the fair thing, and not prejudge the case, they will visit the institution. They cannot judge otherwise."

Professor Turner said that, for himself, he should accept the invitation, and would also like this body to visit the University. But, as he understood the object of this meeting, it was to discuss the scope of the organization, and not to speak of its management in detail. We must not do the wrong of passing judgment upon the detail of the management, but we have the perfect right, and it is our duty to ourselves and the people, to see if the wise design of its founders is carried out in the general results obtained, and in the organization of the institution. For this purpose we could sit as well here as there.

President Gregory again urged at length that the convention adjourn to Champaign, claiming that it was not safe to either censure or approve until they could see for themselves.

Mr. Shepherd said we had here the published official report of the trustees, and upon that evidence, which showed clearly what the plan and effect of the organization was, we could learn whether this was an industrial university or not; whether the law had been complied with or not. He wished to find out, not if this was a good school or college, but if it was an agricultural or industrial university.

Professor Turner suggested that we take up simply the organization and discuss that.

"But one institution that I know in the United States is organized to teach absolute science, to teach the realities of human life, the manual, the intellectual, the physical, the mental, in their natural relations as applied to the mind of the growing youth. That is Cornell University of New York. I want to see in this State somewhere an institution that approaches the field of absolute science, that will teach something better than words and mere technology.

"It belongs to us of Illinois, the Empire State of the Mississippi Valley, to battle with the effete idea of feudalism in education, and to build up the American idea of real science.

"Our Champaign friends have not accomplished impossibilities. They have not the means to rise above the other colleges which follow the feudal idea and build up a human monument or elaborate metaphysical nonsense. We must extend their facilities and give them more means, so that they can give us what they so earnestly desire. Champaign University ought to have $100,000 per annum forever, and by so expanding its means of usefulness the wants of industrial classes could be met."

Professor Turner then offered the following resolutions:

"*Resolved:* 1. That it is the sense of this convention, judging from the annual report of the trustees of the Illinois Industrial University, that the course of studies at the University of Illinois Industrial University is not in accordance with the design of the originators of the scheme of industrial education in the United States, or with the act of Congress, or with the charter establishing the institution.

"2. That, in our opinion, the ancient languages should not be made prominent, or taught as an independent course, in the Industrial University, but only in connection with an agricultural and mechanical education.

"3. That we claim the right, as citizens of Illinois, to criticize freely the doings of our State institutions, so far as the same is made public in their published reports.

"4. That a committee of five be appointed by the chair, in compliance with the invitation of the Regent of the Industrial University, to examine into the management of the same, and make such report as circumstances shall seem to justify to a future meeting to be called by said committee."

On motion to adopt the resolutions, Professor Turner was called on to address the convention. He read from the official report the course of study at Champaign, which showed that it was so arranged that the languages were the last requirements of the curriculum, which was as it should be. He held, however, that the feudal theory of curriculum was too closely followed in its course; that scholarship was not the chief end of life; that elevated upright manhood was the great end of life.

" The greatest curse impending over the American people is the fatal mistake of confounding schooling with education. Our theory of education does not develop the muscle, does not strengthen the nerves, does not give breadth to the imagination or depth to thought. It is words, words. It teaches to avoid labor, to avoid solitude, and to evade the responsibility of actual life.

" We have too much intellectual education, creating the crowd who throng our cities, who hang out their shingles on every street, who want to be supervisors, governors, congressmen, or presidents. We are growing into a nation of intellect to the default of will, energy, muscle, and power. We are growing fast toward becoming a nation of supervisors and officials. We are growing out of the age of physical and intellectual development properly allied and combined into an age of brain-work. Never was a more fatal error.

" Champaign University fails because it makes scholarship the chief end of the student. It doesn't allow a boy to go there and study such agricultural or mechanical branch as he may choose without taking everything else in the curriculum. If a man has peculiar faculties for blacksmithing, in God's name, let him be a blacksmith. Metaphysics, what is it? Ten pages will contain the substance of the labors of all the metaphysical fools from Aristotle down. All the new theories are simply changes of words.

" Professor Baker, of the Industrial University, gave a history of the present condition and past progress of this institution.

" After more discussion, Professor Turner offered the following resolution, which was adopted:

" WHEREAS, The time has come that the State of Illinois should assume her true position before the American people on the great subject of education; therefore,

" *Resolved,* That it is the unanimous desire of the members of this convention that the convention now assembled to revise the Constitution of the State should make some appropriate provision for that end."

To secure this result the following appeal was made to that convention:

To the Members of the Illinois Constitutional Convention
Gentlemen:

A number of citizens from various parts of the State, and of both political parties, having felt a deep interest in the subject discussed below, came together a few days since at the city of Springfield, to consider the best mode of presenting the matter to the consideration of your honorable body; and after free consultation it was decided to request Professor J. B. Turner, of Jacksonville, to prepare a paper which should embody their views; and, having carefully considered the paper, respectfully present it for the consideration of the convention. The paper is as follows, in part:

" In the practical prosecution of this work our power and our inspiration must here, as everywhere else, flow from above downwards and not from beneath upwards; the greater and the stronger must uphold and inspire the less and the weaker, and not the reverse. That order of intelligence by which the university, so-called, derives its knowledge fresh from the hand of nature and nature's God above it, and showers it down upon all the colleges and academies and schools of all sorts below, can no more be reversed or dispensed with by us than can the fixed order of the solar system.

" Eclipse the sun, and you at once darken all the planets around it.

" The extent to which all our colleges and academies and common schools are to-day suffering for this new inspiration and new life, to be poured down from above through them and around them, to save them from the dead logomachies of a dead and buried age, in which they are to so great an extent still compelled to dribble and to drizzle, to launch them upon a new career of life and of power, is known to all who have given special attention to the subject. It is true, much, especially in the realm of pure physics, has already been done; but much more even here still remains to be done. We stand on the threshold of a new order of things; the old order of things, whether for good or evil, has passed forever away—it can never be recalled. The grand sum total of our maxims, our laws, our faiths, our philosophies, our schools, our industries, and our arts need a reëxamination, and a readjustment to the new order of life which we have now entered.

" For the present purposes, all mere intellectual education may be considered as consisting of two parts:

" 1. Technology, or a knowledge of the uses and power of words.

" 2. Science, or a knowledge of the uses and power of beings and things.

" We have ample means of instruction in the former in all our district, graded, high, and normal schools, academies and colleges. Fortunately, the means of instruction here are very simple and very cheap, as books are the only thing for most part studied; a few cheap books, with perhaps a very little apparatus of some sort, and a competent teacher, are the only things wanted.

" But the moment we step out of the school-room, up into the university, to study the actual facts of science, the uses and powers, not of words or of books, but of living beings and of actual things, we must have the objects of our study before us and around us, and the whole process becomes at once immensely complicated, wide-reaching, and expensive. So much so that all the cabinets and apparatus of all the colleges, and all of the high schools and academies west of the mountains, would not make even a respectable outfit for one single first-class university.

" To develop and put in successful operation such institutions, with their needful libraries, apparatus, cabinets, museums, etc., demands heavy disbursements of money, such as no neighborhood, and few States, have the ability to command; and, if not achieved by the combined resources of some great State like New York or Illinois, it can never, in fact, be achieved at all.

" Another obstacle in sustaining any great number of such universities results from the want of men capable of instructing, controlling, and directing them toward their proper ends.

" No State and no nation can, in the present age of the world, furnish but very few such men.

" What this convention can most wisely do with great confidence we leave for them to determine.

" The war has closed; the land is at peace; new people and nations, not yet too much enlightened, are already knocking at our doors for admittance. They ask for light; let us give it to them. They want fraternity; let us proffer them a brotherhood and a civilization worthy of their acceptance. Our own State is now nearly out of debt, and already begins to pant for her full share in the great and good enterprises of the Republic. She was no laggard in the war. She stands, at least respectably, in the forum. Only give her young men half a chance, and they will stand as well in all the arts and industries, the intelligences and illuminations, of that era of peace that is soon to irradiate and bless and gladden the land and the race.

" Whether these proposed endowments should be conferred on any institution now existing, to enable it to assume the full responsibilities of this new position, or whether some entirely new institute should be endowed for the purpose, I leave for others to determine. Certain it is, however, that first-class men in science can never be rallied around universities whose endowments and means of progress are unsatisfactory or uncertain.

" I am aware that our States in all such enterprises are still unschooled and inapt. I am aware that they may make many mistakes, and waste very considerable sums of money, before they finally succeed; but when I consider that they are really pledged before God and man, in their own fundamental laws, to do this work, to give a genuine liberty, and a genuine and not a sham intelligence as its basis, to all the people; when I consider the vast good to our industries and our arts that would accrue from gathering our finest State professors of geology, entomology, and natural science, and others like them, from all parts of the Union, into one school, where, by social converse and use of abundant means and apparatus, all the narrowness of the specialist would be worn away and the breadth of the true philosopher imbibed by each one of them; when I reflect upon the probable benefits that would result from their sharp and trained eyes, and the eyes of hundreds of students under their care, being constantly thrown over the myriads of insects, and blights, and diseases that now ravage and destroy our crops and our herds to the amount of tens of millions of dollars annually; when I look at the civil, social, and moral prestige such an institution would give Illinois over her sister States, throwing abroad annually, all over the Union, hundreds of well-trained young men into all departments of life, imbued with her own sentiments, feelings, interests, and impulses, and annually gathering in an equal number for new schooling and new impressions—when I consider these and similar things, I am fully prepared to say, and to maintain, that if Illinois should sink millions of money in vain effort at success to assume this high position, and should then at last succeed, her success would even then be cheaply bought. Does any intelligent man really dispute it? Why, then, should we hesitate? We need not fail for one single year.

" Respectfully submitted,

" J. B. TURNER "

CHAPTER XXVII

The Hospital for the Insane

During the twenty years devoted to his great agitation for industrial education, Professor Turner engaged energetically in the many other important movements of that important period of the nation's history. He was a participant at Jacksonville, in the summer of 1853, in the first meeting in Illinois of the organization that later became the Republican party. Nine citizens met in the room over the store of J. O. King, located on the north side of the public square. The meaning was organized by the election of Elihu Wollcott, chairman, and J. O. King, secretary. The following names were enrolled as members of the Republican party, and were the first persons in Illinois so to announce their political preference for the party that was then in a most embryonic condition: Elihu Wollcott, J. O. King, Anderson Foreman, John Mathews, William Harrison, Charles Chappel, James Johnson, William Barcroft, and J. B. Turner.

One of the prime objects of the organization was declared to be " the use of all honorable means to prevent the extension of African slavery into the States and Territories known as free States and Territories."

Another great movement with which Professor Turner was connected from the first was the treatment and care of the insane.

In 1846 Miss Dorothy L. Dix came to Jacksonville with a

letter of introduction to Mr. J. O. King, in order to investigate the condition of the insane in that part of Illinois. Mr. Reynolds King, Mr. J. O. King's brother, drove her in a buggy over the State. At the next session of the Legislature, she went before that body and told of the cases she had seen with her own eyes, and the necessity of an appropriation for an asylum for the insane in Illinois. She had seen one man, who was violent and dangerous, buried up to his neck in the ground, with only a log shanty over his head.

As a result of Miss Dix's appeal, supported by many private citizens, the Legislature awoke to existing conditions, and on March 1, 1847, an appropriation was made for the founding of a State insane asylum. Plans were adopted for the erection of the first buildings, and this proved to be the beginning of an institution at Jacksonville which now accommodates sixteen hundred patients. On February 24, 1851, Professor Turner was appointed upon the board of trustees, consisting of nine members. The institution was opened for the admission of patients in November of that year, with Dr. J. M. Higgins as its first superintendent. By this time a sharp contest had developed between members of the board, which was about equally divided, in reference to the management of the institution. J. T. Holmes, Joseph Morton, and Aquilla Becraft were Professor Turner's personal friends and earnest allies on the board. Mr. Becraft was a Kentuckian by birth, and a Democrat—honest, brave, and determined, and all the more pronounced in his attitude toward other members who were of his own party and, as he believed, untrue to their trust. These four stood shoulder to shoulder, and finally succeeded in establishing a record for honesty and honor in the management of State funds for the benefit of the State's unfortunate wards. The laws enacted and put in practice during their incumbency and through their influence gave to Illinois a prestige in the management of State institutions, and her laws were copied by other States. The attitude of Governor French, who, as State Executive at this time, exercised the appointive power, is indicated in the following personal letter addressed to Professor Turner:

SPRINGFIELD, May 2, 1851

PROFESSOR J. B. TURNER

My dear Sir

It seems to be the general wish here—besides, it is thought to be the best—that yourself, Mr. Morton, and Mr. Becraft shall take seats in the board and unite in organizing. After you have organized it may appear that you can count upon a majority to carry out your wishes.

The above is but a charity object, and may require a few sacrifices of feeling; upon the whole, I am inclined to think there will be very little difficulty in the board hereafter. But, if it shall appear it is impossible to get along, why, then you can take such course as you think best. This letter is equally for yourself, Mr. Morton, and Mr. Becraft, and besides these altogether private.

Yours truly,

AUG. C. FRENCH

As a result of the change of administration on the retirement of Governor French in 1853,—when Joel A. Matteson assumed the governorship,—there came a change of policy in the management of the State charitable institutions. Governor Matteson fell under the influence of what was known as the " clique," whose highest ambition was to manage the affairs of the institutions for the pecuniary benefit of themselves and their friends. A sharp controversy soon followed, which finally found its way into the columns of the local press. Some people thought, and said: " Professor Turner is always fighting for something. What does it matter if some of the money does stick to their fingers? They draw no salary; they ought to have some compensation," etc., etc. But the foundation established for just and honest management of all State funds, during these years of strife, placed Illinois in the front rank, and contributed not a little to her future years of usefulness and honor. Yet the feeling at the time was very bitter.

In the summer of 1853 Professor Turner had been invited to deliver an address, on October 14, in Springfield at the first State Fair ever held in Illinois. The night before the lecture was to be given, while he was in Springfield, his barn in Jacksonville was set on fire in three different places, while a high northwest wind was blowing, the incendiary hoping to have him called home and so prevent him from making his address. The fire spread to a long shed and a conservatory, just finished, partly filled with fruits and vegetables. All the animals, vehicles, and farm machinery, with grain and provender, were burned. Had it not been for the heroic efforts of friends and neighbors, the house south of these buildings would have burned also.

The wife and mother, awakened at midnight by the light of the flames and the cries of the tortured animals, gathered her little children around her, saved what she could, and the next morning sent a telegram to her husband; to which he replied by telegraph:

" As I see you and the children are safe, will return *after* my lecture."

A little later Mr. Becraft came to Professor Turner on the fair grounds in Springfield and said: " Do you know what absurd rumors are spreading over these grounds? They say your buildings were burned last night." In reply, Professor Turner took the message from his pocket and handed it to his friend, who exclaimed: " You call me friend and keep such a thing as this from me? " " Go over the fair grounds," Professor Turner replied, "and see who are most active in spreading the news; but tell them, every one, the lecture will be given this afternoon at three o'clock." Soon the friend returned and said: " You are right; ' an enemy has done this.' "

From this lecture, on " The Millennium of Labor," a few extracts will serve to illustrate the enthusiasm in behalf of the laboring-man by which Professor Turner was inspired:

There is a good time coming. Poets have sung of their golden era. The devout of all ages have clung to this hope, and their sages and prophets, in the hour of their darkest gloom, have ever fixed their eye upon the future risings of this millennial dawn. . . .

This millennium of labor is fast coming. I see it in its errand boys born from the thunder-cloud, outracing the sun; in its horses and chariots of fire and steel, that dart with lightning speed across every continent and over every mountain height. . . . I see it in the crystal palaces and in the world's fairs of either hemisphere; in the pride, the prowess, the chivalry, the glory, and even in the sovereigns and monarchs of earth, as they congregate to bow the knee and pay their homage to the rising greatness of this overmastering, all-conquering power. . . .

Whenever the time comes that the real farmer gets abroad in the world, he will exhibit a loftier character than any other living man—man fully restored from the fall—and herald a brighter day then even when his antiquated progenitor, the schoolmaster, came. The same in substance, too, may be said of the true mechanic. In that day all the humbuggery and the cant that now reign in the books and the schools, about these schools being unfavorable to the development of the very highest order of intellectual and moral power, will vanish away; for the living man will be there to give the lie to it all, and the whole world will find out, at last, that intelligent labor is the friend, not the foe, of mind, and that Almighty God was not mistaken when he put the first man in the garden instead of the academy, and made his own son a carpenter instead of a rabbi. . . .

Shall not the millions of free laborers that are, in all coming time, to throng and till the vast plains of our great Western green ocean home, rise up hereafter and, over your prairie graves, pronounce your names blessed and your very dust sacred and hallowed, for one more act of imperishable beneficence done so them and to theirs? In your hearts let this, this day, be decided, and, at your homes and at the polls, let it be enacted, and posterity shall declare you worthy of the name you have assumed for yourselves and your State—Illinois—the men—the men———

After the address, which was most enthusiastically endorsed by the people, Dr. John A. Kennicott, of Chicago, corresponding secretary of the State Agricultural Society, stepped to the front of the platform and told the people at what loss the address had been given, and announced that a little box had been nailed up at the entrance gate, so that any who so wished might contribute toward making good this loss. When the box was opened, over five hundred dollars were turned into Professor Turner's hands—a large sum for him in those days, though small in comparison with the four thousand dollars lost in the fire.

Nine months later the following offer of reward was published in the *Morgan Journal:*

$1,000 REWARD

Will be paid by the corporation and responsible citizens of Jacksonville, in Morgan County, for the detection and conviction in court of the principal, or any one of the accomplices, in the crime of firing the plant houses and other buildings of Professor J. B. Turner, on the night of the 13th of October last, during his absence at the State fair. The above reward was voted and subscribed immediately after the commission of the crime, but its publication deferred from considerations of expediency.

STEPHEN SUTTON,
President Board of Trustees

J. B. TURNER,
In behalf of the citizens

W. MATHEWS, *Clerk*
June 18, 1854

But no one was arrested. To prove the incendiary in court would have been a difficult thing.

On December 29, 1869, Professor Turner was again appointed a trustee of the Hospital for the Insane, holding this position for another two years. It was during this period that Dr. Andrew McFarland, who had held the office of superintendent for sixteen years, tendered his resignation, and Dr. H. F. Carriel, of the State Lunatic Asylum of Trenton, New Jersey, was appointed his successor.

On July 1, 1870, Dr. Carriel arrived in Jacksonville with his wife and two little boys, and began a most successful and admirable administration. The sum of seven thousand dollars had been appropriated by the Legislature for improving the ventilation of the buildings, and a plan for constructing ventilating-flues had been adopted and workmen engaged to do the work. Dr. Carriel advised delay, and decided to examine the old walls carefully before proceeding with the work. He found that flues had been constructed in nearly all of the walls, and, with very little expense, a system of ventilation was established which proved a great success.

Professor Turner was greatly interested in Dr. Carriel's work, and greatly admired his energy and executive ability. System, organization, and classification of the patients soon changed the asylum into a place of quiet and comfort. So quickly and so perfectly was this accomplished that the Board of Charities became alarmed, believing that Dr. Carriel was using chloral—an anaesthetic recently discovered and placed upon the market. However, before resorting to a public investigation, they decided to investigate more closely themselves. They discovered that patients, carefully classified, and when comfortable and free from exciting causes, were inclined to be quiet rather than noisy.

The intimacy that began so pleasantly between the trustee and the superintendent was strengthened into a stronger tie when, some years later, Dr. Carriel, after having been a widower for some time, married Professor Turner's only daughter. This companionship lasted through many years; and when the doctor and his family came to live with Professor Turner after his son Fred's death, it was Dr. Carriel who cheered and solaced his declining years.

In April, 1871, Professor Turner, for a third time, was appointed a trustee of the Hospital for the Insane, and served until 1873. During these six years Professor Turned labored unselfishly and devotedly for the benefit of this dependent class.

CHAPTER XXVIII

An Attack on Corporation Abuses

In August, 1873, Governor Oglesby appointed Professor Turner for his fourth term as trustee of the Illinois Central Hospital for the Insane, subject to the approval of the Senate at the next session of the Legislature. A short time before this, Professor Turner had delivered an address upon the railroads and other corporate interests, which was nicknamed the "Heathen Chinee." It greatly angered these corporations, and the lobbyists who were at work for them, as well as members of the Legislature identified with them. He was most unjustly attacked and misrepresented. The question of his fitness for the position of trustee, which he had held for so many years with credit to himself and to the State, and to the help of the institution and its inmates, was entirely lost sight of in their anger and spirit of revenge. He was ably defended by Senator Whiting and others, but the majority refused to confirm his appointment.

A correspondent of the *Nation* attacked the address. The following article will give Professor Turner's opinion of the correspondent's criticism and its editorial:

January 22, 1874

JACKSONVILLE JOURNAL

Mr. Editor:

I am glad you called my attention, this morning, to the criticism in the *Nation* and his frightened correspondent; I had not noticed it. I am glad I have stirred up the old setting hens about the *Nation*. They set very kindly, and even ably, on their stone eggs; but if anything under them begins to hatch and crack the shell, they are frightened quite out of their usual propriety.

It was so with them through the whole slavery contest. That small and scholastic world which takes its minutest look, and squint, and method from the *Nation* is all right. All the rest of us expect to go to the bad anyhow, whether in Congress or out of it, in the Cabinet or out of it; so we go on in our own way.

I understand popular agitation as well as the *Nation* does. I have some faith in it; the *Nation* has none at all. I think it is now needful.

The *Nation* has been reading homilies to us, on the decorum of discussion and debate, for years. Meantime, no paper that comes West vents more spiteful personalities against all men, in high places and low places, who do not take their cue and their methods precisely from it.

The *Nation* selects a few paragraphs, designed for mere agitation and excitement of popular thought and interest, as specimens of the whole discussion; but neither he nor his correspondent has attempted to turn to the right or the left any fact I allege or any position I take. Nor can they do it, if fairly construed and used only for the ends I use it.

Yours truly,

J. B. Turner

This address, which he named " Railroad Corporations, or the Natural *versus* the Artificial Man: Our Little Heathen Chinese," well illustrated, in its keen sarcasm, Professor Turner's method, at times, of dealing with what he regarded as serious evils in public affairs, as well as his foresight in regard to some abuses of the present day. It was, in part, as follows:

I have often thought, and sometimes said, that I can see no way by which the farmers of the West can get rid of the evils that now oppress them until we can contrive to get up several thousand first-class funerals of old judges, legislators, lawyers, editors, etc., etc., with a sprinkling of divines sent along with them to act as chaplains.

We hear much said against our railroad men on all sides. I have not a single word to say against them, except that they are, as a body of men, precisely like all the rest of us, neither particularly better nor worse. Personally, I have never met one single railroad man who was not courteous, gentlemanly, and just toward me, under the known rule of the law, which is equally obligatory on us both. In pressing their legal claims and interests up to the full extent of the law, they do nothing more than most other men do, and always will do. Nay, it is best, in the long run for the public good, that they should do so; for the only rule of financial interests we can at present adopt is the rule of the civil law; and, as General Grant once most wisely said, the best if not the only way practically to get rid of an unwise or unjust law is " to execute it."

If either the laws or the lawyers or lawmakers desire the voluntary respect of mankind, they must first, like other people, continue to be respectable in fact as well as in mere pretense.

But, till we can in some way get rid of those old judges of the law, lawyers, legislators, and their abettors, who are so thoroughly steeped with the antiquated lies and quibbles of the law-books that there is no room for common sense in their heads or common justice in their hearts, I, for one, can see no relief. The infamy of our present laws has been both thoroughly executed over us, and thoroughly apparent, for years past.

I am neither treating our laws nor the decisions of our courts with undue disrespect. An unjust law, or court decree, deserves no respect from any freeman; and it shall have none from me.

I wish it borne in mind that I most fully admit, in the outset, all the moral, social, and financial benefits of all our corporations, and railroad and other companies, that any one, however sanguine, chooses to ascribe to them; while still their pretended vested rights to steal by law, or to get hold of other people's property without their consent and without a just equivalent, call it what you will, has in no respect whatever increased their usefulness or their power for good, but ever has been, and now is, an unspeakable damage and curse, both to them and to the whole country alike.

Some years ago, one of these old grannies of the courts and the law-books decided that a black man, in this free and Christian land of ours, " had no rights which any white man was bound to respect." There was not a man, woman, or child on the whole

continent that did not know that that decision was a lie, as soon
as it was uttered. Yet it was law—*Supreme Court law!* Well, we
soon took our bayonets and pushed that lie into a bloody grave;
threw in on top of it a quarter of a million of better men than
old Judge Taney ever was, to hold it down; and expended about
ten thousand millions of money in covering it up and in erecting
over it a suitable monument of warning to coming generations,
inscribed:

" JUDGE TANEY'S LIE."

Now, the whole of our present most appalling financial troubles
arise from two simple causes.

First: Our Legislatures have given to certain " bodies corporate," so called, a vested right to steal.

Second: The courts and lawyers have agreed to lie them
through in the theft; and not a few of our newspaper men and
editors, for a small share in the spoils, hold the lantern to help
them while they are setting their traps, and keep a dogged silence
after they have sprung them.

The law compels you and me to go into court, either as juryman or witness, and leave our business and family and hang
around it through the whole term, for one or two dollars per day,
whether you are willing or not; or it arrests you and forces you
into court, wholly without pay, and compels you to employ and
pay your counsel, on a suit that proves wholly unfounded and
unjust; and you are obliged, in self-defense, not only to lose your
own time and trouble, but to pay your lawyer all the money he
pleases to screw out of you—it may be five hundred or a thousand
dollars for one or two hours' work in court and a few hours of
preparation. This is custom. Is it right? I deny it. So far as
any man is compelled to come into court to seek justice, all
service pertaining to that justice ought to be as much fixed by
law as is the salary of the judge or the fee of the witness or
juryman.

The way the law makes these big men is this. It has a certain
set of molds called " acts of incorporation." It takes one of these
legislative molds and puts a dozen or two, more or less, of the
little men whom God has made into it, and by due process of
law out pops one of these huge men whom the law makes, having
great and signal advantages over all us little folk in many most
important respects, some of which I will enumerate. God has
never yet learned the knack of making a human " body cor-

porate " without putting a soul and a conscience into each and every one of them. The consequence is that all we little folk are, all the way through life, in all possible financial operations more or less burdened and annoyed, restrained and plagued, by a soul and a conscience, while the body corporate is not; for how can men give up the ghost who have no souls out of which to make a ghost?

One of the greatest of English jurisprudents has laid it down as a proper rule of law that it should everywhere protect the " *party taken at a disadvantage* " against the " *party that holds the advantage,*" a rule that would seem sufficiently self-evident to any civilization, and one which is everywhere applied to us little folk, but never to " bodies corporate."

Paul of old knew of only two classes of men—natural men and spiritual men; but we, in this age of improvements, have three classes to deal with: natural men, whose souls are not yet spiritually alive; spiritual men, whose souls are spiritually alive; and law-made artificial men, who never had any souls at all, either dead or alive—" bodies corporate," mere financial corpses in deed and in truth. So it turns out that when this whole artificial man, this body corporate, lies or cheats or swindles or robs or steals, even by the million, no crime is committed; for how can a corpse commit a crime? Or, if it did, how would you punish it? All you can do is simply to strip it of its trinkets, if it has any.

Let us, then, look at some of the legal and artificial advantages which these big people have over us little ones. One great legal advantage which these law-made fellows have over all us little folks is that we have no vested rights to steal according to law, while they have any amount of them. So we have to do all our little stealings against the law and in full view of jail and penitentiary.

For example: I have contracted with my fellow to steal for him one hundred horses. I want to be able, according to law, as a simple business transaction, to steal these hundred horses and sell them to him at fifty dollars per head. I want to be able to have a vested right to hire any one of my neighbors, who make it a business to carry lanterns, to go with me from stable to stable, for a small pittance of the profits, and hold the light, and help reconnoiter and lay plans, and then say no more about it; and, if interfered with by the State courts, I wish to show that I am

acting "*under contract*" and the Constitution of the United
States prohibits the State courts from interfering with contracts.
And if opposing counsel object that a contract to steal horses is
not a legal contract, I wish the court to be compelled to hear to
law and reason, and admit that my contract to steal horses is
every whit as moral and as legal as any contract can be which
takes away from me, against my will, a strip of my land for railroads, solely for "*public use and the public good*," and then, by
any process whatever, transfers it to sharpers for their own private
use, so that, in the end, I am swindled out of both all private
and public use and benefit of my land, which I have purchased
of " Uncle Sam " and he confirms and ratifies and certifies to the
contract, not on paper, but to make the evidence as complete and
durable as possible on the best and stiffest of parchment.

Say anything to any old granny of a judge or legislator or
lawyer about this whole matter, and he will at once roll up his
eyes, look wiser than forty full-feathered owls, and very patroni-
zingly tap you on the shoulder and tell you that " you are getting
into waters quite too deep for you "—that "*you* do *not* know
the law." Now, just tell the darned fool, as politely as you can,
that you do know the law, and that is exactly what troubles you
and what you are complaining about. " But these are simply
pure business transactions, and in a free country you cannot embarrass business." We know it, my dear sir; we by no means ask
it. Do we wish business facilities enlarged so that we, all these
millions of little fellows whom God made, can steal by law
too? . . .

No; we do not complain of these privileges because they are
not equally open to all who are willing to avail themselves of
them, but because they are not fit to be granted to any man,
and ought not to be. We ask for no new privileges, for no mere
law, common or uncommon; Heaven knows, we have had enough
of it already. But we ask for justice, for equal rights before the
law, where we now stand, as individual men, without the necessity of going into a corporation of any sort to get them, and we
intend to have it. It may cost time and labor—it may even cost
blood; but come it will, sooner or later, either by fair means
or foul.

What fool, outside of our courts, does not know that a mutual
contract, defining unfulfilled conditions by both parties, must be
signed by both parties alike, or it is good for nothing and binding

on neither party? Are our railroad charters so signed, by both parties alike? They have, from beginning to end, not even the form or the semblance of a written contract between two parties legally empowered to contract. They are, in form and intent and spirit, a mere conditional gift, a mere franchise, good only as long as the conditions are truly and fully complied with; and on that point the donor, who alone made the gift or grant and signed the contract, alone has the right to judge. At least, and at worst, has he not as good a right as the receiver has? Did this one or two or half dozen men at first appear before the Legislature, to even propose to make a contract with the State in behalf of their fellows? Nay, verily; they came there to simply ask a *privilege on conditions of promoting the public good.*

Without this primal plea and promise of securing the public good, the Legislature had no more right to listen to them, for a moment, than they have to steal my horses. This pledge of the public good, therefore, becomes vital to the franchise from its incipiency. They came to ask, as individuals, that they and their fellows might in that privilege be legally empowered to make contracts, " to sue and be sued." Until that power was granted, until that franchise was given, they had no more legal power to make a contract with anybody on earth than so many horses or wheelbarrows have. They well knew this; the legislators all knew it. How, then, could a party make a legal contract, while still totally incapable in law of doing it? Either with the Legislature or with any other party on earth? And while the very thing they are seeking is the power to make contracts, to " sue and be sued " ?

As things now are, the " Heathen Chinee," either directly or indirectly, makes nearly all our laws, fixes all our tariffs and taxes, and controls all our commerce. He can by an easy combination anywhere pay twenty or thirty or one hundred thousand dollars to elect any senator or representative. He can " do vast good " with all sorts of " Crédit Mobilier " stock: He can pass word to his thousands of employees, mercenaries, and dependents to vote for this man or that. He can, in fact, bribe all the principal attorneys to silence, in any town or city where he is likely to have a suit in court, by paying them what is called a " retainer." In court and in Congress he can get his own men in place where he wants them, and get all ours out of place and out of the way, and deal obstructions called law, which are not likely to run afoot and alone, either in court or Congress, without some one to uphold and guide them. The paper rescript is mighty nice—most admirable; but the devil is in the practical outcome of it. He alone can see clearly through all the fogs of " tariffs," of " taxes," of " commerce," of the " laws of business and trade," because he alone hearkens solely to the " voice of the prophets," which, to economize ink and letters, he always spells p-r-o-f-i-t-s. Smart fellow, this Heathen Chinee! And it will cost us more to release his grip from the throat of the public than it did to unclasp that of his first cousins, the old slave-holders. . . .

" Oh, but the law comes down from England." No doubt; but it never came down from heaven, or any other place where even any pretense of truth or of justice reigned. Who is so stupid as not to know that English common law was made first, from top to bottom, to wring poor men's noses and put money into rich men's pockets?

The first thing we need to do is to abate some of our stupid reverence for the law *as it is*, and begin really to inquire after the law as it *ought to be*. It cannot be doubted that our people have been robbed and plundered of more money within twenty-five years, through the ignorance, negligence, and depravity of those who have pretended to administer the law over them, than all the single-handed knaves have taken from them since the continent was first settled; yes, many thousands more—all done by due process of law.

Professor Turner's nomination as trustee of the Illinois Central Hospital for the Insane was not confirmed by the Illinois Senate principally because of the stand he had taken in this speech. More than one State senator was publicly condemned for his negative vote by his constituents, and Professor Turner was invited by the Farmers' Legislative Club of Illinois to deliver an address in the Representative Hall at Springfield, in reply to the attacks made by the New York *Nation* and the Illinois State Senate. This address, which was frequently interrupted by applause, was to the point, and at its close Senator Whiting, after a brilliant eulogy of Professor Turner, offered the following resolutions, which were adopted:

Resolved, That the speech of Professor J. B. Turner, to which we have just listened, in reply to the assaults of the *Nation* (a newspaper published in New York City) and of other parties, in defense of the position assumed by him in his essay entitled " Railroad Corporations: the Natural *versus* the Artificial Man," embodied in the tenth volume of the Transactions of the State Board of Agriculture, be published in the agricultural journals, and, as far as practicable, be distributed to the farmers' clubs and granges of this country.

Resolved, That Professor J. B. Turner, for his long and useful labors in the cause of education and industry, of equal rights and human progress; for his heroic and disinterested labors for reform; for his self-sacrificing labors for the elevation of the masses and a nobler and better civilization, is entitled to our profound respect and warmest gratitude; and we greet him as a leader among the noblest champions of labor, and are proud our own State can claim him among her distinguished citizens; and we fondly cherish the conviction that the name of Jonathan B. Turner will go down the ages, adding honor and luster to the history of our State.

CHAPTER XXIX

As Author and Lecturer

Professor Turner's book entitled "Mormonism in All Ages," published in New York City and London, England, in 1842, was quoted, not only in this country, but in Europe, as the most logical and accurate exposition of the causes and trend of Mormonism ever published. Many years after it was out of print, he often received letters asking for copies. The motive for its publication may be seen in the following extract from its Introduction:

The Mormons boast of one hundred thousand adherents in this country, and more than ten thousand in Great Britain, where their faith is making rapid progress. This may be an exaggeration, but at all events, it is time the absurdities of their scheme were exposed. . . . It ever has been true that they have made one hundred infidels to every dozen converts. There is much reason to believe that many of their popular leaders are, at heart, infidels. In their public addresses they defend the "Book of Mormon" by attacking and ridiculing the Bible. They are, in truth, the most dangerous and virulent enemies to our political and religious purity and our social and civil peace that now exist in the Union—not so much, however, on the ground of their direct as of their indirect influence.

Professor Turner carried on a correspondence with neighbors of Joseph Smith in New York, Pennsylvania, Ohio,

Illinois, and Missouri. These letters, with the sworn affidavits accompanying them, were the evidence by which he showed that the manuscript of a novel written by the Rev. Solomon Spaulding, and stolen from his publishers in Pittsburgh, Pennsylvania, in 1812, was the original of the " Book of Mormon," published by Smith in 1830. (See the American Encyclopedia under " Mormonism.")

Nearly forty years after his book was published, Professor Turner received the following letter from a former member of the Mormon Church:

OFFICE OF KIMBALL & LAWRENCE

SALT LAKE CITY, UTAH, February 6, 1881

PROFESSOR J. B. TURNER
JACKSONVILLE, ILLINOIS
Dear Sir:

Your letter of the 29th came duly to hand, which I am pleased to receive, and very much regret that your work, " Mormonism in All Ages," is not still in print. I believe a great many of the books could be sold if another edition could be got out, but it would be rather expensive to get them printed here in this Territory. There is one copy of your book in the Masonic Library here, and it is being read by a number of our citizens. I formerly belonged to the Mormon Church, and was with the Mormons at Nauvoo, Illinois, being then quite young and living with my mother. We came to Utah in 1850 and I have lived here since. In the year 1869 I left the Mormon Church in company with a number of other friends, and since that time we have been doing what we could to bring the Mormon people around in harmony with the laws and sentiments of our country, but it has been slow work. Priesthoods are the same in all ages— never learn anything, until they are forced to. The great advantage Mormonism has had for the past thirty years has been their isolation from the rest of the world, and their local political control of Utah Territory. When this political power is taken from the Mormon priesthood and its adherents, then they will give up their assumptions and submit to the government which has been so lenient to them in the past. I must say to you now that I am not a member of any church, and believe in no creed but that of Humanity, and if your new matter, that you call

"Christ's Creed," is broad enough to save all the human family, instead of a few favored people that may be inclosed within a certain creed or fenced off by themselves, then, in that event, your Christ's Creed would suit me. I am a believer in the Christ spirit and his teachings, but not in the atonement doctrine or his immaculate conception. If you get out a new edition of your book I will take one hundred copies.

Yours very truly,

H. W. LAWRENCE

In later years Professor Turner was much opposed to the admission of Utah into Statehood upon any of the terms proposed. As to this he wrote:

I have seen the Mormon people about their homes and shops, in their temples and churches; and I know very many of them to be an industrious, hard-working, and worthy people, well worthy of the best nurture and care of the Republic, but a people most woefully priest-ridden, tax-ridden, befooled and enslaved by their priesthoods. From this enslavement the government should deliver them instead of enacting constitutional laws like this, which, on the face of it, consigns them to that slavery forever.

In 1842 Professor Turner published a pamphlet on the "Philosophy of Money and Bank," which Daniel Webster, when he was Secretary of State, said was the ablest exposition on that subject that he had ever read. In the '50's was published his book upon "The Great Races"; in 1891, "Universal Law and Its Opposites"; in 1892, "Our Republic"; in 1894, "The New American Church"; and in 1895, "The Christ Word *versus* the Church Word." In 1847 a little book was published entitled "The Kingdom of Heaven, or Christ's Chartered Church *versus* Hierarchies and Sects."

Although this was prepared at the request of the editor of one of the leading quarterlies, the peculiar handling of the subject prevented its acceptance. It had been taken to New York by Mr. George C. Noyes, afterward so well known and beloved as the pastor of an Evanston, Illinois, church. He was an alumnus of Illinois College, and took the manuscript with him when he went to New York to attend the Union Theological Seminary. But he searched the city in vain for a publisher. It was then sent to New Haven to David Hale, editor of the New York *Journal of Commerce*, one of the most able defenders of genuine Protestant Christian freedom, who consented to honor the essay with an introductory notice. A short extract will show the spirit of the little book, and also explain why it was considered objectionable, if we will bear in mind the doctrines of the church in that day.

Men talk, forsooth, about whom it is proper to invite to the Lord's table. But they have no authority to invite to it or to invite away from it: it is the Lord's; and when they have declared who, in their opinion, the Lord invites they have done their whole duty. And if the members of their church need discipline, let them attend to that, too, in accordance with the law of Christ's house at some other time, and in its own appropriate place and mode. Here let them obey the Scriptures, and simply "examine themselves," and not other people. But the habits of the church are sometimes so unscriptural and degenerate on this point that the most worldly, ill-tempered, and un-Christian professors are so puffed up with sanctimonious conceit and spiritual pride that they will not commune because some one against whom they have a grudge is allowed to partake. Are these people so much holier and purer than Jesus Christ? He could commune with Judas himself without offense, without a murmur, without even an unkind word, or look, or thought. Such people surely must be quite too pure for Christ's church.

The following notice of a lecture delivered before the Young Men's Christian Association of Peoria, on February 2, 1854, is taken from a newspaper of that city:

The text of Professor Turner's lecture last evening was the story of Diogenes, who, on being asked why he lit a candle at noonday, replied, "I seek a man." The lecturer took this candle and searched, with keen scrutiny, for true manhood in the various walks of life, holding his light so close to the pretensions and deceits of men as to reveal a great absence of that which the old cynic philosopher sought. The Professor is a very solid reasoner, and advances his conclusions with a confidence which evinces that he knows how he arrived at them. He spares no theory or creed which he thinks wrong, and hesitates not to uphold any that he thinks right. We believe all, whether they agree or disagree with his views, will admire him for his independence.

On June 30, 1858, was organized, in the city of Bloomington, the Illinois State Natural History Society, with Professor Turner as its first president. This society later received an appropriation from the State Legislature, and made considerable progress in the collection of a library and museum, which were furnished quarters in the State Normal University building. In 1871 the museum and other property of the society were transferred to the State Board of Education, but later received the name of the State Laboratory of Natural History, and in 1884 was transferred from the State Normal University at Normal to the University of Illinois.

Professor Turner delivered an address before the original society on June 24, 1862, on the subject "The Oceanic Avalanche and Its Counter-Currents." While treating of the differences in temperature, density, and depth of the waters of the ocean, the discourse described the consequent effect of ocean currents (as exhibited in the Gulf Stream) upon climate, soil, and natural production.

In 1868 he delivered a lecture, in St. Louis, Missouri, on "A New Route to the Ocean," from which the following extracts are quoted:

If we look to the northwest of us, to the country lying about the head-waters of the Missouri River, we find the finest natural wheat-fields in the known world,—larger in extent than the whole of the States of Illinois, Indiana, Ohio, Virginia, Pennsylvania, and New York combined,—as yet all undeveloped and scarcely rippled by the plowshare of the pioneers, who are flowing in upon it at the rate of more than a quarter of a million per annum. Immediately west of us lies a natural corn and stock field, scarcely less in magnitude and importance.

This immense trade naturally flows to St. Louis; put this grain into gum-elastic bags and throw it into the rivers, and it will go there itself, a thousand miles, right through the heart of this great wheat-field, without the aid of steam or men.

The Ohio River is already navigable, for the greater part of the year, from its mouth at Cairo as far as Charleston, Virginia, on the Kanawha Canal. Both of these waterways were in operation before the war, one to the vicinity of Lynchburg, the other to Covington, through one ridge of mountains and almost up to the base of the other ridge on the west side of the Shenandoah Valley.

Practical engineers have examined this route to the ocean and report it wholly feasible, at small expense; that the maximum grade on the Green River is only twenty feet per mile, less than we frequently encounter here on our prairies; while the general elevation to be overcome is nearly eleven thousand feet less than the most favorable present route from east to west.

Norfolk is two hundred miles nearer to St. Louis and Cincinnati than New York. By this route grain and produce would go, neither imperiled by heat nor blocked up half the year by ice, up the Ohio and Kanawha by only a single reshipment, out to the ocean at Norfolk, and on to New York and Liverpool, at less than half the cost it now requires through any more northern route. Unlike railroads, to every man or boy in the land who can steer a boat or barge, it proffers free trade and transit over a great democratic highway thousands of miles in extent, with full room for elevators and storage at any point along the banks of these rivers, admitting of no possibility of combinations for unjust monopolies either in transportation or storage. Washington and Jefferson both predicted that some day this route would be opened; but Virginia did what southern Illinois is now doing: she went to sleep, and dozed over politics and partizan triumphs, office-seeking and President-making, and discussed all imaginable two-penny issues on the stump, until her more adroit rival, New York, ran away with the trade of the world.

Professor Turner strongly advocated the removal of the capital from Washington, D. C., to St. Louis, Missouri, or some place more central than Washington, claiming that a capital at the extreme border of so large a Republic could not have an equal interest in all the remoter parts. The greater influence of the people nearer—working for the especial needs and advantages of their own States—must at least be stronger and more continuously exerted.

On the same occasion he pointed out the advantages of San Diego, California, as a port on the Pacific coast one thousand miles nearer Canton, China, than San Francisco. As evidence of his foresight regarding important issues of a later day, he advocated the construction of a deeper waterway, by way of the Illinois and Mississippi rivers, between the Great Lakes and the Gulf of Mexico; and in 1882 he delivered a lecture advocating the preservation of natural forests, and became an active member of the Forestry Congress organized at that time.

Letters had come to him, at intervals during many years, urging Professor Turner to become a candidate for Superintendent of Public Instruction, Attorney-General, member of Congress, and Governor. In later years he was persuaded to run for Congress—with no expectation of winning, as the district was strongly Democratic. The campaign, however, was interesting and gratifying.

He was foremost in every movement for the advancement of the working-people in the State; was president of the State Natural History Society, president of the State Horticultural Society, and for many years of the Jacksonville Horticultural Society. He was identified always with the Illinois State Agricultural Society, by lectures and contributions on practical subjects, and was always a leader in the advancement of education.

But after the passage by Congress of the University Land-Grant Bill and the location and development of the State University, he turned his attention to the one subject which all his life had been most interesting to him—the teachings of Christ. In religion, as in all other subjects, he was fifty years in advance of his time. In the evening of his life, one day his daughter said to him:

" It has been such a pleasure to us all, Father, that you have lived to see the thoughts you uttered in your early life, which were so ridiculed then, become the accepted belief of mankind in later years; and especially that the land-grant universities, for which you worked so many long years, are an enduring monument of which any man and his family may well be proud."

"Yes," he replied; "it is, of course, gratifying to me. But my religious writings will be my monument by which I will be longest remembered and most beloved." A prophecy that is beginning to come true. Christ and his Word is now the text of almost all religious teaching. No longer is it Paul, the heroes of the Old Testament, but Christ, the bread of life.

The union of all sects was an ever-present hope with him. Would that he could have lived to see this day, when it is common for ministers of almost every denomination to exchange pulpits with each other!

While Professor Turner was preparing for publication his book, "Christ's Words," he received the following letter:

STATE OF ILLINOIS
DEPARTMENT OF PUBLIC INSTRUCTION

SPRINGFIELD, February 16, 1874

My dear Friend:

I have just received your letter of the 13th inst., and have read it with great care and deep interest. And I must frankly say that your reasons for declining to entertain the proposition of your friends to make you Governor of Illinois commend themselves to my judgment. You are probably right about it. At all events, I can truly say, for myself, that if your acceptance of that or any other office would seriously interfere with, if not wholly prevent, the accomplishment of the good work you have in hand, then I shall willingly see you remain in private life the rest of your days. It matters little who is Governor of Illinois for four years, but it is of infinite concern that the human race be not in spiritual bondage to doubt and fear and superstition for all time.

Very truly yours,

NEWTON BATEMAN

The following extracts from the Preface to Professor Turner's book entitled "Christ's Words" give some idea of his belief and teachings:

The leading chapters in this book were written many years since, but incessant calls in other directions have delayed their publication; their main principles, however, I have maintained for the last half century. Many books written on the evidences of Christianity are evasive and unsatisfactory; their writers seldom think, but simply reiterate; their only legitimate effect is to transform all simpletons into bigots and all wise men into doubters.

Such books and such modes of professed reasoning are the natural heritage of that ecclesiastical despotism which for fifteen centuries stood wrangling over the mere outer form and drapery and symbolism of Christ's religion, until it had well-nigh driven its *essential spirit* and its peculiar power from the face of the earth.

Through all these dreary and disastrous centuries Christ's gospel was officially interpreted only in the interest of some *despotism*, either of state, church, or sect.

Would it not be well for us, who have the needful freedom and capacity, to commence our new national century by simply endeavoring to read the gospel, as in fact it is, as the sole logical cause and basis of all the *true freedom* there has ever been on earth, and the only " divine power from on high " through which it can be perpetuated?

It is said that this is an age of mental imbecility, which craves only stories and concrete ideas well suited to overgrown children, and rejects all professed theological or philosophical discussion. May it not be that the age has already outgrown our hereditary theologies and philosophies, and mentally pronounced them both false and delusive? Is it not rather an age of strength than of weakness? The religion of any age cannot long afford to outrage the intelligence of its most able and thoughtful men.

It is impossible in a preface to outline the course of thought in this book, for the book itself, at best, is but a preface to the subjects of which it treats.

It is impossible to conceive of a true religion and a true science or philosophy that do not harmonize together; they are and must be a unit, unless it is possible that God can be divided against himself. The modern scientist presents to us his wholly unverified dogmas as the voice of science and the voice of nature; the antiquated ecclesiast presents us his as the voice of God. But, quite unfortunately for us, these teachers make God and nature tell us more monstrous and utterly unbelievable lies than all other talkers put together.

As a man's habitual selfish spirit, mode of life, and action at last arms against him all men, so the opposite unselfish and self-sacrificing spirit and mode of life draws all men unto him. Gravity does not rule in physics more certainly than does this eternal law of all living mortals. Every child knows it in principle before he knows that twice two are four.

This selfish mode of spirit and life Christ symbolizes as eternal or perpetual moral and spiritual death; its opposite as eternal or perpetual moral and spiritual life. This one is hell, and creates hell in whatever being or world it rules; the other is heaven, and makes heaven in whatever beings or worlds it exists.

Everything else in Christ's teachings, revelations, life, death, and resurrection is only motive power, gift, symbol, or incident to this one most philosophical and sublime end—the mere divine power and moral mechanism that eternally lifts all beings up toward God and heaven.

Where, then, is the difficulty in verifying Christ's real religion? It is exactly the same as the difficulty in verifying sunlight. All that we can see or know confirms it.

J. B. TURNER

JACKSONVILLE, ILLINOIS

The book, which was read by Professor Turner's friends and by people interested in such critical works, brought its author many letters, which varied widely in commendation or opposition. Some of these letters are quoted below. The first two are from an alumnus of Illinois College, the Rev. Thomas K. Beecher, who was for many years pastor of the Congregational Church at Elmira, New York.

ELMIRA, NEW YORK, January 27, 1878

PROFESSOR J. B. TURNER

My dear Sir:

Send on that book. Of course I will read it, and of course I will tell you what I think of it, and thus have my revenge on you, who, thirty or forty years ago, used to make me read my compositions to you and tell me what you thought of them. Turn about is fair play.

Yours truly,

THOMAS K. BEECHER

ELMIRA, NEW YORK, April 19, 1878

My dear Old Friend and Teacher:

Your book came this morning, and I have gone through seventy pages or so—marveling.

Scarcely a sentence that does not astound me into silence. You see, I assume you to be an intelligent, honest and observant man. I claim for myself no more. Before us both have lain open the same books—history, experience, science, and human nature. We have each done our own thinking, and, lo, what astounding diversity! If I were able, I'd "go for you" as you do for the insolent ecclesiastics. But no man ever found the truth by pounding fools. To show up men's folly is a far easier task than to build "upon a rock" the house of wisdom.

Ah, me, dear old Hercules, the wrath of man never works the rightness of God.

This much for a first instalment of frankness—based on the first reading of the first few pages. I note here and there a choice sentence. Possibly I may annotate the book and send it back. But never can I enjoy a book, by whomsoever written, that is so largely destructive as yours.

Cut it down four fifths. Cut out the polemics, the negations, the invective. Set up the fair fame of God's truth as revealed in Christ Jesus holding forth the Word of life. And so, fare you well; and may you be taught in meekness to oppose—if God peradventure may give repentance to the acknowledging of the truth.

Yours lovingly and in a hurry,

THOMAS K. BEECHER

It is interesting to note how two men having such opposite opinions on religious subjects could be such warm friends. Mr. Beecher must have been sorely tried, for in one place in the book he annotated: "Stop your scoldings; go on with your interpretations." At another place: "Insufferable repetition. You have stated this five times already." But frequently we read in the margin: "Good. Very good. True—profitable and true. This is gospel." And in one place: "This is good enough to redeem the chaff and bran of the whole volume."

A letter from the Rev. William Allen, another old friend, indicates a quite opposite opinion:

GENESEE, ILLINOIS, January 22, 1879

My dear Friend:

I have read about two thirds of your book (" Christ's Words "). There is enough in it to require a good deal of thought, and I have read it thus far with some care and much attention.

Your iconoclasms and denunciations of priestcraft and tyranny are grand. I glory in your freedom of thought and plainness of speech, and I rejoice greatly in your optimism in the general view you take of the divine government. It gives the soul rest—it satisfies the ineffable yearning of a thinking mind.

Yours truly,

WILLIAM ALLEN

A letter from another alumnus of Illinois College reads:

CHANDLERSVILLE, May 12, 1884

PROFESSOR TURNER
Jacksonville, Illinois

Dear Sir:

I have just reread your article in the *American Monthly*— " Christ's Words." I want to thank you for it. I suppose it will receive abuse. It ought to—for it is true, and the truth always is abused.

You have done a good thing. Hearts will gain courage for the fight against wrong when they see success has its rewards in this life and on this planet, and are not confined to the attainment of bliss in some more or less fanciful future which men call heaven.

If I were rich enough, I would like to print and distribute more copies of your article than the Anti-Tract Society published pages.

Very respectfully yours,

C. E. LIPPINCOTT

In 1891 Professor Turner published " The Only Thing in All the World," basing his title upon Professor Drummond's discourse on " The Greatest Thing in the World," giving the

emotive side of Christ's gospel, while Professor Turner continues the subject of Christ's gospel on its logical side—the
central idea being that Christ came into the world and died,
not instead of or in any possible way as an atonement for
men, but for their good, as a teacher of eternal truth, whose
teaching was emphasized, for all time, by the tragedy of his
life and death.

CHAPTER XXX

Spiritualism and Mental Telepathy

My father had some very interesting views on spiritualism and mental telepathy, which were founded upon personal experiences so remarkable that I feel they ought to be preserved. In this chapter, therefore, I have put down his opinions and experiences as he many times expressed them to me.

I was always a firm believer in what is now known as mental telegraphy, the science of which has never been understood, much less written. Spiritualism is based upon this unknown science, but oftentimes used to deceive and defraud. Many of my best friends were spiritualists, and many discussions we held upon the subject. I often attended meetings with them, and, as was my custom, never spoke slightingly of any one's convictions, and especially their religious belief; yet I never assented to this belief. The last meeting that I attended, when I was old and blind, was at the home of a friend, Mr. Eben Peck, whose sister had long been a medium in Jacksonville.

Maude Lorne, then the most celebrated of mediums in this country, had consented to stop here, on her way from California to New York, and give a séance. The many friends were assembled and sitting in a circle in total darkness. All were required to sing—to join with the heavenly voices of father, husband, child, or friend who had been called home. I did not sing, and, when remonstrated with, said I never sang in my life, and could not sing a note. Then it was announced that all who could not sing should hum. I again demurred, and, after a good deal of discussion, I, on account of my blindness and age, was permitted to remain silent. I became convinced that Maude Lorne was the spirit in the centre of the circle, and that she had a small music-box, such as my grandchildren played with, which was playing the same airs that were being sung by the company, and that she darted hither and thither, waving it above the heads of the seated guests. The last time it came near me, I made a grab and snatched it from her hand. I put it in my coat pocket, intending to lay it down somewhere when the opportunity offered, but forgot it and brought it home. Soon the singing ceased, and it was announced that the spirits had departed because some unfriendly influence was present. Great was the astonishment and disappointment. What or who could it be? Many were grieved—one especially, a young lady, who had heard the voice of her father singing as distinctly as she had ever heard it when, a little child, she had been sung to sleep in her father's arms. Many had been enjoying the voice of a noted singer, Mr. Josiah Day, who had recently been called home. With sad hearts the company dispersed. The next morning I took the music-box back and gave it to the hostess, telling her I had found it in my pocket and thought it must belong to some of her guests.

At the time my buildings were set on fire and burned, in October, 1853, I was in Springfield. A clairvoyant was at the hotel, and some of my friends urged me to consult her. It was not necessary, for I knew perfectly well who had instigated the crime, if they did not do it with their own hands. It was before the days of daily papers and Associated Press despatches, so, outside of the parties interested, the matter was not known. When I entered the room and asked her to tell me something of my past and future life, she closed her eyes and exclaimed:

" I see a man setting fire to the corner of a large building, the wind blowing hard from that direction. I see a big fire—two large buildings and a long shed connecting them in flames. I hear the cry of animals tortured by the flames. I see wagons, carriages, cultivators, and implements, machines new to me burning. I see many people running. I see a mother gather her little children around her; and as you go out of this room you will meet the man who set your buildings on fire coming up the stairs."

I thought some one had told her about it; but when I started down the stairs, and saw the man who I believed had done it—or had hired it done—start to come up, look up, and, upon seeing me, turn very red in the face and then turn and run down the stairs rather than face me, I wondered if it could be that she had unusual powers.

In August, 1856, I was invited to deliver an address in Detroit, Michigan. My wife and little children were nervous about my leaving home, especially since the burning of my buildings and the bitter fight that had attended the building and organizing of the Hospital for the Insane. I had refused many invitations to lecture, but this one I was anxious to accept; so, promising to return immediately after the lecture, I left them, with much anxiety and many regrets. In those days the trip would take a week at least. After the lecture I rushed to the depot. Two trains were standing on the track, one facing east and the other facing west. Thoroughly despising myself, I took the one that faced east. With the tearful faces of my wife and children ever before me, I persisted in going directly away from my home, to which I had promised to return as quickly as possible. When I entered my childhood's home in northern Massachusetts, and heard my father's voice from his bedroom moaning, " If I could only see Jonathan before I die! If I could only see Jonathan before I die! " and found my mother and sisters gathered around my father, who was propped up in bed, sick unto death, and longing for me—I came to believe in mental telegraphy.

CHAPTER XXXI

With President Lincoln in 1862

One day in August, 1862, a few weeks after the passage of the University Bill, while Professor Turner was working in his hedge-plant nursery, a telegram came to him from Washington: "Charles very sick, typhoid fever. Come immediately." Signed, "George Bibb." Turner's son Charles, then a student at Illinois College, had enlisted in the Sixty-eighth Regiment of Illinois Volunteers, under a three months' call, in Captain John W. King's company of students, and had been sent to Washington, D. C.

Professor Turner hurried to the house, and, handing the telegram to his wife, said: "I am going. I have only time to catch the train. Good-by." And, without stopping for baggage or even to wash his hands, he ran all the way to the depot, and just caught the last car as the train pulled out. It was fortunate that he had acted so quickly, for that was the last train through for several weeks, owing to the Confederates' raid through Maryland and Pennsylvania. He reached Washington just in time, for his boy had been laid aside with the dead and dying. That morning the doctor had said to the nurse: "Poor boy! Give him plenty of brandy and let him go off easy." But the soldier, conscious for the first time in days, heard, and determined that he would not touch the brandy if he could help it. If he had to die, he would die conscious. He was lying as if dead, when his father entered and laid his hand on his forehead. He opened his eyes, and, with a feeble cry, " Father! Father! I'll get well, now that you have come! " he dozed off into a peaceful sleep. When he awoke the crisis was past, though a very long and tedious convalescence was before him. For weeks he had been delirious. He would crawl out of bed at all hours, when he appeared too weak even to move, and, crying out, " I'm going home," would escape from the ward.

Extracts from Professor Turner's letters home at this time relate some of his experiences during his stay in Washington:

STONE HOSPITAL, WASHINGTON, D. C.

September 2, 1862

My dear Wife and Children:

It is after three o'clock, and I have not eaten anything since six this morning, and have been constantly on the tramp over the hot pavements. I don't believe I have slept six hours since I left home. Charley! Charley! was in my mind all the time, and to-day I confidently expected he would be dead before I should see him; but I can not, and will not try, to express my gratitude to Almighty God and the kind friends He has raised up around him, for the unexpectedly comfortable condition in which I find him.

We ought to thank God and bless His holy name for His signal goodness to us.

Yours truly,

J. B. TURNER

P. S. At the depot I could find no omnibus or carriages, as they are all off the street to make room for the immense throng of army-wagons, cavalry, and infantry, which, as secretly as possible, are passing up to the rear of the rebels in Maryland. That is, so I judge. Not a word of it is allowed to be printed in the papers. But what I see I can see without a newspaper. I hope they will nab them. The country generally has no idea of what an enormous force we now have about Washington; nor is it best they should. General Burnside left the grounds this morning with an enormous force, and his cavalry is still pouring down the hills, toward the northwest, I presume, to cut off the retreat of the rebels, who, some forty thousand strong, have crossed over into Maryland, as rumor says. I hope they will take them now, for, if they do not, I see not how Washington can be defended, as it it has no defenses on the north but living men. If the rebels shoot up toward Harrisburg or Baltimore, they will be able to do much damage before our men can overtake them. True, it may all be a false alarm, and most of the people are persuaded it is so; but the army seems to be upon a sudden and desperate move, for some reason.

Yours truly,
J. B. TURNER

STONE HOSPITAL, Washington, D. C.
Tuesday, September 9, 1862

My dear Wife:

Charlie is about the same. Troops still pour in and out, and more than fifty buildings right around here are full of sick and wounded, besides some in tents and in other parts of the city; and the multitudes sent away testify of the horrors of war. I can give you no idea of what I see and hear here.

Yours truly,
J. B. TURNER

STONE HOSPITAL, 17th Street, Washington, D. C.
September 12, 1862, Friday evening

My dear Wife:

I have written you every day and telegraphed you once since I came. Charley continues to improve.

Fitz-John Porter's division of some thirty thousand men passed the hospital to-day to reinforce McClellan, near Frederick, where a battle is already expected, some ten or twelve miles more or less north of town. All the hospitals have been cleared of wounded soldiers who could be moved to make room for others from the expected battles near by.

I met some twenty-five or thirty wagons full of shot and wounded in all sorts of ways going to Oakes Hospital, down the Potomac, to-day. So common is the marching of troops that the passing of Porter's thirty thousand, which filled the streets full for some miles, did not excite a passing remark; and I should not have seen them if I had not happened to go downstairs, as my room is on the other side of the street. Even the little children playing on the porch took no notice of them, and no one in the house either knew or cared where they were going. I went out and learned of the soldiers themselves. They're a fine body of men; but I have not the least faith in their commander. This is no place, I assure you, to get confidence in the generals that lead in this war. My hope is, God may deliver us. Charley sends love to all.

Yours truly,

J. B. TURNER

WASHINGTON, STONE HOSPITAL

September 19, 1862

My dear Wife:

I have just received the first line and the four drafts all right from you. I am not surprised that you failed to get the despatch and the first letter I wrote you within one hour after I succeeded in finding Charley. I thought perhaps they had been sent by the Baltimore road, and that the rebels had intercepted them; but there was no help for it. I could only write you again and again, which I did at first every day and since every other day, hoping some of my letters would reach and relieve you, and it is now a great relief to me to know that such has been the case.

Now that Charley is convalescent I find some relief from the harrowing scenes in the hospital by visiting various places of interest in the city, especially the contraband camp. I had a long talk with the President at the White House yesterday. He is confined to his room with a lame ankle. He told me he intended to issue a Proclamation of Emancipation, which he said had been prepared for weeks, awaiting the winning of a Union victory.

With sly humor, he also told of the visit of a delegation who claimed to have a message from God that the war would not be successful without the freeing of negroes; to whom he replied: " Is it not a little strange that the Lord should tell this to you, who have so little to do with it, and not tell it to me, who has a great deal to do with it? " And the sly old coon at that very moment had the proclamation in his breast coat pocket!

But I will write you about the contraband camp. There is as much real difference between the actual intelligence and civilization of these contraband negroes and our negroes in Jacksonville as there is between our negroes and our first-class citizens. The facts in the case at once amaze and appall me. The best of them are not even respectable grown-up children. They seem really alive to nothing but music and mere animal enjoyment. An armed guard, sword in hand, night and day is kept constantly around the camp. No military camp here is guarded with half the same rigor. At first I happened to walk in on the Sabbath day, by invitation of my host, while they were engaged in their religious meeting. I was at once noticed and arrested, my business, name, etc., required. When this was given, I was very politely introduced to the superintendent, who went with me the next day through the camp. Their worship, when left to themselves, is as truly heathen, both in spirit and in form, as ever it was in Africa.

I did not hear in that meeting a single prayer or hymn or exhortation of any sort, in our sense of the term, nor anything that in the remotest degree resembled it; nor did I hear one single intelligible, coherent idea of any sort uttered by leader or people, though I understood most of their words. They nearly all belong to the church; all deem themselves pious, and in the sight of God may be so; but it surely is not what we call Christian piety. Their religious devotions, instead of having any tendency whatever to check their licentiousness, are in fact as well adapted, whether intentionally so or not, to incite their lust as were the ancient orgies of Pan or Venus. Many of them are totally untrustworthy, even in the matter of their own most vital personal interests.

I have since attended religious meetings of these contrabands, and once addressed them myself on colonization. All the ringing of bells and the vociferous commands of the superintendent can not get them together; but the moment some few of their old leaders strike up one of their songs you will see them, big and little, male and female, at once trot up from all parts of the camp and join in. One song at least, therefore, is as indispensable to a negro meeting as an order to charge is to a battalion of cavalry. The day they were addressed by white preachers, they sat still and were decorous in the extreme. But the moment they were to themselves, they rushed into some form of their own bush meetings; and, however nonsensical their words, their gestures and tones were always musical, plaintive, and eloquent. Their pantomimic song, "Go and say unto Pharaoh, Let my people go," with slight revisions in its words would be one of the most thrilling and dramatic things in the English language.

Mr. Palmer, with whom I board, a civil officer of the city, a most violent pro-slavery man, begged me to go and hear them, and said he would rather hear it, as an amusement, than all the theatrical performances in the city. But the evening I talked to them about their home under the equator, they sat perfectly still; and as soon as I was through, they made no effort even to sing, but went at once to their quarters, saying one to another, " I will go; I will go."

I tried, while speaking, many times to get them to express their own minds by asking them questions which I was sure they did know, and tried to have them answer me to keep their attention and interest; but, from a seeming bashfulness, I could get no response, only a silent and deferential nod of assent from some of their leaders. At last this question was asked: " Do you know old John Brown?" "Yes, yes, Massa; we all know him." It was really affecting. No question touching their own vital personal interest of themselves and their children could break through their rigorous sense of deference to a white speaker whom they considered their friend; but old John Brown was quite too much for them. They could not remain silent under the resistless spell of that name.*

I now consider Charley's case entirely safe.

I spent the evening with President Lincoln at his country seat, three miles out of town, last night. Colonel Chester of Chicago † went out with me. General Hunter, from the South, and his wife were also there. He is a plain, sensible man, no contemptible upstart with epaulets, and a man, I think, of tolerable abilities. Mr. Lincoln took General Hunter and Mr. Chester

---

* We are prone to forget the marvelous progress these people have made since the days of slavery, simply because we wish to forget. No people in the history of the world ever made such rapid advance from ignorance and superstition. Even the children of Israel were obliged to wander forty years in the wilderness before they were deemed worthy to enter the promised land of freedom. No cloud by day nor pillar of fire by night have guided our freed negro slaves through their wilderness, and no miraculous showers have fed them. Today one of their number is shining in the halls of royalty with kings and queens for his companions, and many others are holding positions of honor and trust.

† Colonel Augustin Chester was one of the earliest residents of Kankakee, Illinois, where, about 1853, he built the first house and founded the first paper (the Kankakee *Gazette*). At that time he resided in Washington, D. C., and was an attorney practicing before the Supreme Court.

and myself out into the back parlor away from the ladies, and we had a most interesting talk about the war.

I can not write you what I heard last night at the President's, but will tell you when I see you, as I have this morning taken notes of it all and asked Colonel Chester to do the same, so that I might be sure to be accurate. The facts are more and more overwhelming.

I am already virtually the colonel of a regiment of cavalry left here. It happened in this way. Their colonel went a week ago with a brigade to Maryland, and was killed. Their chaplain went up to bury him. Their hospital of sick men is in this house. I became interested in them; went to the town and got them cots, sheets, shirts, food and jellies, wine, etc., which they needed. I took the poor fellows off the bare floor and made them comfortable, and, as they had no surgeon, I got our Stone Hospital surgeon to go over to them. For these slight acts of kindness, everything they have—their houses, teams, persons—are as fully at my command as though I owned them all. The under officers left in charge anticipate my smallest wishes. It affects me even to tears to see some of these rough and sometimes violent and profane men so easily and deeply moved to gratitude for even the slightest acts from an entire stranger. Their under officers are in the field or dead, while here they were a drunken, worthless set—would even take the brandy away from the sick in the hospitals and get drunk on it themselves; and everywhere treated them more like dogs than men, even after all their deadly experience in the Chickahominy swamps.

Colonel Chester has been here for some time, and, like me, has a son in the army. He confides all his thoughts to me, and I do mine to him. He has introduced me to many of his old friends and new acquaintances. Yesterday, when we went to the patent office, I noticed the men looked startled. Afterward they said I looked so much like old John Brown, they thought, when I came in the door, his ghost had come up from Harper's Ferry.

Apropos, Lincoln, the other day, alluded to Harper's Ferry while I was in his room, and showed me one of McClellan's private despatches to him which came in while the battle was still raging. When he ceased speaking, I said to him, " Don't you think, Mr. Lincoln, old John Brown's blood is getting pretty well washed out of Harper's Ferry? " His look and answer were eminently characteristic and significant. It was too good to lose.

He also told me his only instruction in the English language had been from me, through the Green brothers of Tellula, Illinois, while they were students of Illinois College and he was a hired hand working for their mother in the harvest-fields.

I have thus filled my letter with the gossip about myself because I wanted to write something to you; but those things I feel most deeply about I cannot write. You will all be humbugged enough by the newspapers. You cannot believe on their authority that there is any such place as Maryland or Washington City; or that there are either battles or rebellions, much less great victories. But if they tell you there is a constant and dreadful game going on here all the time, you may believe it, for it is so. I spent evening before last with Professor Ferguson, professor at the National Astronomical Conservatory, and had a most pleasant time talking over my heresies in natural science.

Yours truly,

J. B. TURNER

Dear Wife:

Colonel Chester and I walk out, in the evenings, three or four miles to Lincoln's summer home, and watch for him as he comes riding out on horseback or in his carriage, and then spend a delightful evening with him. Sometimes he is detained and cannot come. In talking with our friends from Illinois, it was decided that Colonel Chester and I ought to tell Mr. Lincoln what we had seen and heard in the city, and that we were convinced that there was a great conspiracy among all officers in command, more threatening to the Union than all the rebel soldiers in Southern camps. We feared he, in the center of all this whirl and turmoil, surrounded by such a vast multitude of people and care, could not see and realize as could an outsider, free to go and come.

To our amazement, he not only assented to what we had to say, but went on to tell facts far beyond anything we had ever dreamed of, much less seen or heard. When we criticized General McClellan, and said we did not believe him to be incompetent, but a traitor, Mr. Lincoln paced back and forth across the room, his hands behind his back, and in tones of deepest anguish replied: "I know it—I know it! But show me the man; show me the man. I am searching the country over. Show him to me; show me the man."

Colonel Chester had spoken of a brigade of stragglers. Mr. Lincoln interrupted him by saying: "It would be more proper

to say that McClellan's whole army is an army of stragglers."
And then, in the presence of General Hunter, who sat by and
assented, he went on to state in the most bold and unequivocal
terms, as though he desired the whole world to know it, that
" In McClellan's army on the peninsula he reported 91,000 men
fit for duty, and 55,000 men, or more than one third of his
whole, army unfit for duty; that for all the corps ordered under
Fitz-John Porter at the second battle at Manassas the United
States had actually to pay for 200,000 soldiers, and Porter should
have had 140,000 fit for duty, but, instead of that, all he could
muster in his report was 60,000 on hand out of the 200,000. The
rest were straggling behind in the forts, weeds, or hospitals."
The provost-marshal reported three hundred men found mur-
dered in the single town of Alexandria during the passage of
McClellan's army, though there was a strong guard of Illinois
volunteers stationed, night and day, at every corner of every
street, showing not only that his army was undisciplined, but
had become utterly frantic and infuriated. The causes of this
last I will not stop to discuss, though they are interesting and
sufficiently apparent.

Said the President, further: " We have got the best clothed,
the best equipped, and the best paid and the best cared for,
and the worst disciplined army the world ever saw. It takes
it the longest time to start, and the slowest after it is started."

I quote his exact words, taken down at the time both by
myself and Colonel Chester. As he was so bold and frank, I
ventured to say to him that " the Army of Maryland was beaten
in fact before it went out of the city, for I saw it with my own
eyes, and, though I pretended to know nothing about military
affairs, if he or his generals or any other set of men should strap
up and overclothe and overload a set of men for our Illinois
harvest-fields, for even a single week, as these generals compelled
their soldiers to march in the hot, dusty streets through whole
summer campaigns, I, for one, would turn out and help hang
them."

The President then added that " It took McClellan's corps
five days to go forty miles, while in urgent pursuit of an active
enemy; and Porter's corps had been ordered two whole days
before it began to start, and then would not have started if
Halleck had not told Porter that he would order his arrest if
he were not off in two hours. And all this when there was an

invading foe, holding in triumph Frederick and other towns in Maryland, forty miles distant, with which our army was even then fighting." And still the confounded fool, or traitor, managed, after all this, to take his whole army, baggage and all, away down to the Baltimore depot, and then march them back to the right street again, with all their baggage in the hot sun, and it was two o'clock before he fairly got out of town, and five whole long days before he got to Frederick, forty miles distant. Then McClellan posted the scramp as a reserve and left such men as Reno and Mansfield and Hooker to make his charges for him, and two of them perished in the contest. And so it seems to go all the time.

The President also said that "McClellan took sixty baggage-wagons for his own use, though any one could see in the patent office that the whole of General Washington's camp furniture, medicine-chest and all, could be carried on a strong man's back, and with ease in any light wheelbarrow. Thus we lost the whole campaign in Maryland because our army could not be got up there until the enemy had had time to collect their plunder and choose the position of their rear-guard, where we fought them at immense disadvantage, and no gain except to hurry them out of the State a little sooner than they otherwise would have gone, instead of bagging or destroying them as we should have done."

One cannot be in Washington without knowing that there is the most utter lack of all discipline, the most open and shameless system of knavery and thievery, going on all the time and reduced to a regular system in almost every department of the service. For example, oats, corn, hay, and so forth fall short of their marked weight almost habitually from twenty per cent. to thirty per cent. over and above all their defects in quality. More than three square miles of James River was completely covered with hay, bought and paid for by the government, and left uncovered to spoil and be thrown overboard into the river. Many boat-loads of soldiers' knapsacks, full of their clothing and little stores, delivered to the commissary for safe-keeping when they went up the peninsula, and to be returned to them, were left in the hold of the boat until they all rotted and were thrown out as so much manure. All this while the men went without their clothing and the horses were literally starving for hay. Almost all of those that lived were totally unfit for service. New ones had to be bought, and the cavalry troops had to lie around

Washington and wait for their horses while the battles were being fought in Maryland. In the harbor of the city itself there are ships now lying, at seventeen hundred dollars per day, and have been for months, with their cargoes undischarged.

I was quite surprised to learn that Mr. Lincoln was perfectly aware of this systematic knavery, but he said: "It cannot be helped. So far has this thing gone that it is scarcely possible for an honest man to get any contract by public bid under the government, in those departments where it is possible to steal; for these thieves will at once bid it down below actual first cost, and rely upon cheating and stealing for the whole of their profits."

Many years afterward, when Professor Turner was ninety years of age, in speaking of the notes that he and Colonel Chester so carefully wrote down while in Washington that evening, he said:

It was during one of the darkest periods in the second year of the war, when, after McClellan's long delay at Manassas, he had been defeated in his attempt to reach Richmond by the way of the Chickahominy, and the rebels, having crossed the Potomac, were threatening Washington itself. Everything was most doleful and discouraging. The whole city and country were sunk in the depths of gloom, if not in despair. All the public buildings, churches, and schoolhouses, and all the confiscated private dwellings were filled to overflowing with sick and wounded soldiers, and still, four miles out, where I found my son, were rows upon rows of sick and wounded as thick as they could lie on each side of the walk, on long stretches of tent-cloth. The city itself was full enough of rebels and spies to report everything they saw and heard.

One night, as we were looking for the approach of Mr. Lincoln on horseback or in his carriage, we saw in the distance a nice accoutered troop of cavalry riding on each side of the road in double file, and wondered what it meant. As the party came nearer, we discovered President Lincoln and General David Hunter, the latter being in command of the troops, riding between the lines, which appeared to constitute an escort.

We said to Mr. Lincoln, "We are glad you are learning to take care of yourself." "Yes," he replied. "My friend here,

General Hunter, and Secretary Stanton make such a fuss about my going without an escort that I have yielded to their entreaties." After salutation, the troops were placed in charge of a subordinate officer, and General Hunter and ourselves were invited into Mr. Lincoln's parlor.

I had known of Mr. Lincoln ever since, as a hired man or boy, he was employed to gather Mrs. Green's crop in Old Salem, before he had ever been in a law office. I had heard him make his most magnificent stump speeches, and had voted for him every time I could get a chance; I had been one of the first to assure him of the certainty of his nomination for the Presidency, and the first to warn him of his extreme danger after his election; but I confess that Abraham Lincoln himself never had stood out before me in such grand, overwhelming proportions as during that brief midnight interview. His almost boundless insight, foresight, and capacity, his matchless prudence, justice, and humanity toward all and over all with whom he came in contact, appeared in complete equilibrium in that one grand head of our warring and discordant Republic; the one who seemed to foresee and await the end in the only way it could be brought about with entire safety to the nation. In that darkest hour Colonel Chester and myself were entirely willing to trust the interests of the Republic wholly in his hands.

Now, mark the final issue of that meeting and all its accompaniments, as they have since become known, though not even thought of by Colonel Chester or myself at the time. More than thirty years after this meeting, I first learned, from the second Boston edition of the trial of Lincoln's murderers, and Father Chiniquy's book, "Fifty Years in the Church of Rome," that Booth and his comrades were, at the very time of the passing of this escort, hidden in a little thicket which Lincoln was compelled to pass on the road to his summer home (now the Soldier's Home). Had the guard been appointed one night later, Booth would have accomplished his murderous scheme three years earlier than he did. As it was, he went back to his rebel friends in the city, cursing his luck. Father Chiniquy often remonstrated with Lincoln for not providing himself with a suitable escort; but Lincoln's reply was always, in substance: "We must all be prepared to die for the Republic." It was as impossible for him to discharge his duty without exposure as it was for any private soldier to perform his free from danger.

In a letter to Professor Turner from Colonel Chester, under date of January 28, 1896, written by his wife, when the colonel was eighty years old and nearly blind, Colonel Chester said:

Yes, I do know Booth was lying in ambush in those bushes, having seen the article to which you refer. I shall always remember that twilight visit to our true friend, Abraham Lincoln, at the Soldiers' Home. How promptly he responded, after a moment's thought, to our errand! And how, when our errand was finished and we rose to leave, in that pleading voice he earnestly implored us: " Don't go. Don't go. I am lonesome and want some one to talk with." We resumed our seats, and soon after General Hunter came in; after that a number of others—a very interesting evening. Little were we aware of that conclave of bloodthirsty men outside. Then our walk to the city under the shade of forest trees, where wretches were plotting murder. I cannot at present enlarge upon my memory of that evening; I cannot forget.

CHAPTER XXXII

The Evening of Life

In 1879 Professor Turner's first great sorrow came to him. The mother, from whom was all physical comfort as well as loving companionship and counsel, was suddenly stricken and peacefully crossed to the shining shore. The husband and the youngest son, Frederick Clifford, were left alone; and dreary work it was, trying to reorganize the home without the wife and mother.

A few years later Fred married Elizabeth Alexander, and once more the old home was full of sunshine; and when, in 1888, a baby girl was born, Grandfather's cup of bliss was full to overflowing. A tender sympathy and strong chord of love bound the two together. He never wearied of her baby prattle, and when she was old enough to learn to read, Grandpa enjoyed with his little companion the wonderful stories of dog, cat, and fairy.

On December 18, 1880, Rhodolphus, Professor Turner's first-born, died, as had his mother, quickly and painlessly. A second son, William, died in September, 1886. But the great unexpected sorrow came in February, 1896. Fred, the mainstay of his old age, his youngest and his dearest, upon whom he had depended in his old age and blindness, died. Sorrow and bitter disappointment still awaited him. Fred's wife and child went to a sister for a home. My father's grief at giving up his little companion was pitiful to see. His children and grandchildren gathered around him, friends and neighbors all striving to comfort and to cheer.

Soon after this his daughter and her family came and made their home with him. After her mother's death, Fred's daughter, the little " companion," returned, and once again the old house was full to overflowing. The jokes and merry pranks of the young people again filled the house with laughter. The grandsons, named for his own sons, came and went at the ring of the college bell; the daily college life was brought near again.

Professor Turner's one long-continued and unabated literary pleasure was in " The Club." In 1860 Dr. David Hamilton, pastor of Westminster, and Professor William D. Sanders organized The Club, the first in the town, if not in the State. It was limited to twenty members, and was made up of literary, professional, and brainy men.

They met on alternate Monday evenings, at the home of the host, for supper, the literary program coming afterward. This was conducted by an appointed leader, each member taking his turn, who selected his own subject. After the reading of the paper, each member was expected to take part in the discussion that followed.

Every question of state, church, literature, or politics, home or foreign, was most ably presented and most warmly discussed: science, metaphysics—every subject that ever was presented to the human mind—making Jacksonville, as one pastor said, " a paradise for ministers."

The success and promise of each and all of his grandchildren was a great comfort. He took great pleasure in visiting " the farm," which he had given to his sons John and William, eleven hundred acres near Butler, Illinois, where the most delicious fruits and melons in their season were to be found, and where there were horses, sheep, and fine droves of Hereford cattle in the pastures.

But finest of all the products of the farm was the large family of children. John had two, and William eleven— sturdy, good-natured, industrious, and studious, always a comfort and never a care.

My father liked to report what the neighbors said; how they watched for the two-horse spring-wagon, full of boys and girls, always merry, punctual, and polite, as they drove the two and one half miles back and forth to school. He enjoyed a joke, and all the more if upon himself. When nearing his eighty-fourth birthday, he took a trip with his son Howard, his daughter, and her daughter to the Yellowstone Park; and although his eyesight was so poor that at times he could hardly distinguish light from shade, he learned more, with the aid of his finger-tips, of its geological and physical history than did most of those who could see, and appreciated more keenly the peculiar grandeur and weird beauty of cañon, geyser, and pool.

While the party was stopping at the Cañon Hotel, near the falls, there was a great deal of excitement over the forest fires, which were very near and very dangerous. Telephones rang constantly, and anxiety and fear were in evidence everywhere, in spite of the efforts of the proprietor and employees of the hotel to conceal it. Hoping that Professor Turner would not hear or notice this, his son Howard took him to his room, away from the noise and confusion, and, telling him that he wanted to make some arrangements for the morning, left him to go to bed. At midnight more hopeful news came; the wind had changed and the danger was lessened. The son returned to his father's room. What was his surprise to find him fully dressed and sitting on the side of his bed. " I heard the ringing of and the talking over the telephones," he said, " and thought, as I am so slow, I had better not undress, but be ready to start if necessary."

Howard saw how anxious he must have been, all alone, blind and helpless; but he was an inveterate joker, and liked best of all to get " one " on his father. He began to laugh, and answered: " The devil has been after you for a great many years. He has rejoiced over your heterodoxy and peculiar religious views. Now that he thinks he has cornered you, with the cañon one mile deep on one and the forest fires on the other, he is sure he has got you this time." His father laughed and began to undress, and was soon peacefully sleeping.

Professor Turner's brother-in-law, Mr. John Olmstead, a banker and manufacturer of Springfield, Massachusetts, was from early manhood one of his most congenial friends. He often came out to visit him. At the last visit Mr. Olmstead said:

" You are looking fine. I must have a photograph of you. This afternoon we will go to the photographer's."

While Mr. Olmstead was downtown in the morning, the daughter, in the pride of her woman's heart, prepared her father for the coming visit to the artist's gallery. She trimmed the straggly beard, cut the soft gray hair, and clipped close the shaggy eyebrows, brushed and dressed him until he looked like a tailor's mannikin. The surprise and disappointment depicted on her uncle's face when he returned she will never forget. She had destroyed all traces of that rugged, vigorous old age which he had expressed in the words, " looking so fine."

My father was very fond of nature in all its forms. Flowers, fruit, or tree, vine, grain, or grass—all were of equal beauty and interest. Bird, insect, or animal he studied, and knew them for themselves, and for their value or danger to mankind. The bee, as long as he had his sight, was the object of his greatest care and pleasure. He was one of the first in Illinois to import an Italian queen bee. The avenue of her hives in the back yard was his recreation ground. Nothing made him more indignant than to hear the complaints that the bees were destroying the fruit. Over and over again he would explain how it was utterly impossible for a bee to bite anything even so soft and thin as a ripe peach or a grape skin. They could only suck the juice after the skin had been broken by a bird or an insect.

His son William, when a boy at home, brought from their nest in the woods, before their eyes were opened, two gray squirrels, which proved most interesting pets. They were never kept in a cage, but were given the freedom of the place, going away every fall and returning every spring for several years. They would come from the top of the highest trees, at a call and oftentimes without a call, alighting on a shoulder or head, and then scrambling for a pocket where nuts were to be found, or begging for them if they were not. Often, when at a neighbor's or downtown on business, Professor Turner would find one fast asleep in his coat pocket.

In later years his favorite pet, and the favorite of his " little companion," was the dog, who had loyally followed the vicissitudes of the Carriel family since a tiny pup, when Howard Carriel had traded a toy watch for him, and had brought him home from school in his jacket pocket. Pup was his name to the last, when old age and pain made life miserable, and Fred Carriel sadly chloroformed the playmate who had loved him best.

For many years Professor Turner employed an amanuensis, first college students at intervals, later his granddaughter, Ella Carriel, and his grandson Arthur, for short periods. But the one amanuensis who, year in and year out, was the greatest treasure, who always came bright and happy, full of life and energy, ready for any conflict with Greek letters or Greek verbs, whose voice was sweet and gentle as any loving daughter's, and who read to him to the last day of his life, was Miss Georgia L. Osborne.

One cold, stormy night, when the air was full of sleet, in those days of bottomless mud before the streets were paved, Professor Turner had an engagement to speak at Strawn's Opera House. His wife tried to persuade him not to go. " It was dangerous for one of his age to attempt it; besides, there would be no one there to hear him." But he was not to be persuaded. When he had nearly reached home, at midnight, he slipped and fell, striking his forehead on the icy walk, so that he was stunned. It was several minutes before he could gather himself up and proceed. The next morning, to his surprise and delight, he found that the deafness that had been growing upon him, and that had caused him so much anxiety, had entirely disappeared; and it never returned.

A few years later, a neighbor, Mr. William Russel, while calling, referred regretfully to his terrible deafness. Professor Turner said: " I can give you an infallible remedy. Have some one take you by your heels and snap your head on the stone walk. It's a sure cure."

Several years after that, the neighbor came in and exclaimed:

" I have tried your remedy, and it is, as you said, a sure cure. As I was driving in my two-wheeled buggy last week, one wheel struck a hole in the street pavement, and I was thrown out backwards, landing on my head. I was picked up and carried into a doctor's office, but soon recovered consciousness, and ever since I can hear perfectly." Then the house rang with the laughter of the two old men.

When Professor Turner was eighty-nine years of age he lost his appetite, and became so weakened in health and strength that his family were very anxious about him. His family physician and lifelong friend, Dr. Hiram K. Jones, told his youngest son, Fred, that his father needed a tonic and he had better get him a case of beer. So this was bought and brought home; but, to Fred's surprise, his father positively refused to touch it, saying: " All my life I have struggled against the temptation to drink; and now, at this late day, I will not begin muddling my brain." The beer was returned, and he recovered without it.

One night in December, 1898, a loud call startled us at midnight. Running quickly down to my father's room, we found him quietly sleeping, but could not resist waking him to ask why he had called.

" Why? Did I call? What did it sound like? " he asked.

" As if you were hurrahing," we replied.

Then he laughed and gave the following explanation: " I dreamed a party of us had been to an old-fashioned barn-raising. After completing our work a wild-turkey shooting-match was on the program; and I dreamed that Governor Duncan made such a fine shot that I thought he deserved a cheer, so I was giving him one."

Only his friends knew his gentle, cordial, generous spirit, and his warm friendship, lasting through life—a friend once, a friend forever. They enjoyed his keen wit, quiet humor, and quick repartee, though often unable to keep pace or to sympathize with his advanced views. He was an athlete in physical and intellectual stature and strength, a most original genius, with the busiest of brains; a formidable foe in debate, giving no quarter and asking none, yet never descending to low personalities. The following letter illustrates the lasting quality of his friendships:

> BROOKLYN, NEW YORK
> November 26, 1891

Dear Brother:

I thank you for your book. I reciprocate your affectionate words to me " as an old friend of former years." We have always been sincere friends and never known the shadow of alienation.

We have not always thought alike, but have always respected each other's sincere convictions, and believed that we were acting under the law of supreme love to God and man. . . .

> Yours in Christ,
>
> EDWARD BEECHER

Professor Turner loved young people, and they loved him. Many a boy and girl, as well as grown young man and maiden, have left their play to talk with Grandpa. There was always something cheery, merry, or useful; something that was pleasant and good to remember; something that would return again and again in the days that were to come, with the gentle, loving look from those beautiful eyes, so expressive even in their blindness. All read to him; all told him their interests and claimed his advice. But the tenderest tie and sweetest intercourse was between Professor Turner and his son-in-law, Dr. Carriel. Congenial in habits and thoughts, the bond of sympathy strengthened with the years.

Soon after passing his ninety-third birthday, on the evening of January 10, 1899, while his daughter was giving him his supper, the call came. He turned his eyes with questioning surprise to Dr. Carriel's face; then quietly closed them, and soon fell asleep, fully dressed, in his library, never for one single day having been confined to his bed.

Appendix

Genealogy

The first of the Turner family to come to America was John Turner, who sailed from London, England, on the *Speedwell*, in May, 1635, when he was nineteen years old. The town of Roxbury, which was settled in 1630, but which is now a part of the city of Boston, finally became his home.

The old Turner home, at the corner of Center and Roxbury streets, was used for barracks during the Revolutionary War.

On July 22, 1761, in the second year of the reign of King George III, the town of Templeton, Massachusetts, was incorporated. Seven years later, in 1768, Edward Turner, the grandfather of Jonathan, bought land in this wilderness. He was a son of Joseph Turner of Walpole, and grandson of Ebenezer Turner of Medfield, near Boston, the line of descent being: first, John of Roxbury; second, John of Medfield, born in 1651; third, Ebenezer of Medfield; fourth, Joseph of Walpole; fifth, Edward of Walpole and Templeton; sixth, Asa of Templeton; seventh, Jonathan of Templeton, the subject of the present biography.

The land on which Templeton was founded was known as Narragansett Number Six, being a part of the land comprised within the seven townships granted by the Great and General Court of Massachusetts Bay to the soldiers of the Narragansett War. The inhabitants of Templeton were intensely patriotic during the War of the Revolution, and were among the first, previous to the outbreak of the war, to sustain the attitude of the colonies in their controversies with the mother country. The town voted not to use any goods subject to duty, and provided pay for its soldiers.

In the archives of the Commonwealth of Massachusetts' Revolutionary War Service (Vol. XII., page 63) we find the substance of the following record: the name of Edward Turner (the grandfather of Jonathan) appears, with the rank of sergeant, on the Lexington Alarm Roll, in Captain Joel Fletcher's company of Minute-men, Colonel Ephraim Doolittle's regiment, which marched from Templeton on the alarm of April 19, 1775, rendering service for a period of eight days. His name appears again with the same rank and under the same officers, August 1, 1775, he having enlisted April 27, 1775; time of service, three months and twelve days; residence, Templeton (Vol. XIV., page 86). His name appears again (Vol. LVI., page 156), with the rank of lieutenant on Continental pay account, in Colonel Putnam's regiment, for a service from January 1, 1777, to December 26, 1777, the date of his death (Vol. XVIII., page 256). By the same record index to the Revolutionary War Archive, on deposit in the office of the Secretary of the Commonwealth of Massachusetts, it will be seen that he was continued on the half-pay roll until December 26, 1784 (Vol. XIX., page 294).

The Baldwin family was one of wealth and influence. Richard Baldwin of Cholesbury, Buckinghamshire, England, had a great number of descendants, nearly three thousand of them being mentioned in the records. Most of the Baldwins of America are descendants from those in Buckingham, situated between Hertfordshire and Oxfordshire, and the name was to be met with before the Conqueror in the immediate vicinity of the Baldwins of Buckingham. The most prominent name connected with this family was that of Sir John Baldwin, who was Chief Justice of the Court of Common Pleas of England from 1536 until his death in 1545. Dundridge (parish Aston Clinton in Buckingham) and the "Braies" were granted to Sir John, and came to be owned by the branch of the family whose members emigrated to New England. Joseph, who was at the head of this branch, was the son of Richard Baldwin, and not twenty-one years of age when he came to America in 1630. He became one of the first settlers of Milford, Connecticut, and in 1639 his name appears among the free planters. Joseph the second, born in Milford, lived in Hadley, Massachusetts. Joseph the third, born in Malden,

Massachusetts, lived and died there. David, born in Malden, lived in Hingham, but moved to Spencer, Massachusetts, in 1740. Jonathan, who was born in Spencer, lived in Templeton, and became the grandfather of his namesake, Jonathan Baldwin Turner.

American Ancestry of the Turner Family

I. JOHN TURNER (of Roxbury, Massachusetts, afterward Medfield, Massachusetts, married Deborah) : Children: Elizabeth, Deborah, John, Isaac, Mary, Samuel, Sarah, Abigail, Hannah.

II. JOHN: Children: John, Stephen, Edward, EBENEZER.

III. EBENEZER (born at Medfield, Massachusetts, November 24, 1693) : Children: Ebenezer, Barzillia, JOSEPH, Edward, Abner, Elisha, Keturah, Esther, John, Seth.

IV. JOSEPH: Children (fourteen) : EDWARD, Joseph of Keene, New Hampshire, Ebenezer, of Quincy, Illinois; Reuben, of Farmington, Maine.

V. EDWARD (born November, 1744) ; died December 26, 1777; married Hannah Fisher) : Children: Adam, Lewis, ASA.

VI. ASA (born July 24, 1768; died August 20, 1856; married Abigail Baldwin) : Children: Sylvia (Mrs. Marshall Adden), Dulcina (Mrs. William Whitney), Avery, Asa, Nabby (Mrs. Benjamin Day), JONATHAN BALDWIN, Betsey (died in infancy), Hannah (Mrs. Luke Manning), and Edward.

VII. JONATHAN BALDWIN (born at Templeton, Massachusetts, December 7, 1805; died at Jacksonville, Illinois, January 10, 1899; married Rhodolphia S. Kibbe at Somers, Connecticut, October, 1835; she was born at Somers, September 13, 1810; died at Jacksonville, Illinois, January 6, 1879) .

Children—all born in Jacksonville, Illinois: Rhodolphus Kibbe, born September 11, 1836; died at Quincy, Illinois, December 18, 1880; married Ella Kibbe at Springfield, Massachusetts, August, 1863.

John B., born January 6, 1838; married Fannie B. Turner at Carlinville, Illinois, September 23, 1888.

William H., born June 30, 1839; died at Butler, Illinois, September 10, 1883; married Fannie B. Grobe at Hillsboro, Illinois, December 12, 1864.

Charles A., born April 11, 1844; died at Macon, Illinois, October 18, 1899; married Jane E. Retter at Jacksonville, Illinois,

December 31, 1868; and Mary P. Hatfield at Decatur, Illinois, February 14, 1889.

Mary L., born October 30, 1845; married Dr. Henry F. Carriel, at Jacksonville, Illinois, May 6, 1875.

Howard A., born June 25, 1850; died at Los Angeles, California, June 13, 1905; married Ada Davis, at Minneapolis, Minnesota, January 17, 1888.

Frederic C., born October 25, 1855; died at Jacksonville, Illinois, February 7, 1896; married Elizabeth Alexander at Alexander, Illinois, September 15, 1881.